Ethics in Mental Health Practice

Ethics in Mental Health Practice

Edited by

David K. Kentsmith, M.D.
Associate Clinical Professor of Psychiatry
College of Medicine
University of Nebraska Medical Center
School of Medicine
Creighton University
Omaha, Nebraska

Susan A. Salladay, R.N., Ph.D.
Associate Professor of Counseling
School of Education
CBN University
Virginia Beach, Virginia

Pamela A. Miya, R.N., M.S.N.
Assistant Professor
College of Nursing
University of Nebraska Medical Center
Omaha, Nebraska

Grune & Stratton, Inc.
Harcourt Brace Jovanovich, Publishers
Orlando   New York   San Diego   Boston   London
San Francisco   Tokyo   Sydney   Toronto

Library of Congress Cataloging-in-Publication Data
Main entry under title:

Ethics in mental health practice.

Includes index.
1. Psychiatric ethics -- Addresses, essays, lectures.
I. Kentsmith, David K. II. Salladay, Susan A.
III. Miya, Pamela A. [DNLM: 1. Ethics, Medical.
2. Mental Health Services. 3. Psychiatry. WM 62 E835]
RC455.2.E8E838   1986   174'.2   85-21878
ISBN 0-8089-1738-2

Grune & Stratton, Inc.
Orlando, Florida 32887

Distributed in the United Kingdom by
Grune & Stratton, Ltd.
24/28 Oval Road, London NW 1

Library of Congress Catalog Number 85-5477
International Standard Book Number 0-8089-1738-2
Printed in the United States of America
86 87 88 89   10 9 8 7 6 5 4 3 2 1

*To past, present, and future
decision-makers in
the health professions.*

Contents

Contributors

Jeffrey M. Brandsma, Ph.D. *Professor of Psychology, Department of Psychiatry and Health Behavior, Medical College of Georgia, Augusta, Georgia*

Spencer Eth, M.D. *Assistant Professor, Department of Psychiatry and the Behavioral Sciences, University of Southern California School of Medicine, LAC/USC Medical Center, Los Angeles, California*

David K. Kentsmith, M.D. *Associate Clinical Professor of Psychiatry, College of Medicine, University of Nebraska Medical Center, School of Medicine, Creighton University, Omaha, Nebraska*

James A. Knight, M.D., B.D., M.P.H. *Professor of Psychiatry, School of Medicine in New Orleans, Louisiana State University, Medical Center, New Orleans, Louisiana*

Pamela A. Miya, R.N., M.S.N. *Assistant Professor, College of Nursing, University of Nebraska Medical Center, Omaha, Nebraska*

Helen L. Morrison, M.D. *Director, The Evaluation Center, Chicago, Illinois*

James L. Muyskens, M. Div., Ph.D. *Professor of Philosophy and Associate Provost, Hunter College of the City University of New York, New York, New York*

E. Mansell Pattison, M.D. *Professor and Chairman, Department of Psychiatry and Health Behavior, Medical College of Georgia, Augusta, Georgia*

Domeena C. Renshaw, M.D., F.A.C.P. *Professor, Department of Psychiatry, Stritch School of Medicine, Loyola University, Maywood, Illinois*

J. Wesley Robb, Ph.D. *Professor of Religion, School of Religion, and Professor of Bioethics, Department of Psychiatry and Behavioral Sciences, School of Medicine, University of Southern California, University Park, Los Angeles, California*

Deborah A. Rosen, Ph.D. *Associate Professor of Philosophy, University of New Orleans, Slidell, Louisiana*

Mary Patricia Ryan, R.N., Ph.D. *Associate Professor of Nursing, Niehoff School of Nursing, Loyola University, Maywood, Illinois*

Susan A. Salladay, R.N., Ph.D. *Associate Professor of Counseling, School of Education, CBN University, Virginia Beach, Virginia*

Mark Sheldon, Ph.D. *Associate Professor, Department of History and Philosophy, Indiana University Northwest, Gary, Indiana*

Richard Sherlock, Ph.D. *Associate Professor of Philosopy, Department of Languages and Philosophy, Utah State University, Logan, Utah*

Margaret A. Somerville, A.U.A., LL.B., D.C.L. *Professor, Faculty of Law and Faculty of Medicine, McGill University, Montreal, Canada*

Preface

Many aspects of ethics are presently being examined in journals of all health professions. Ethics, within the context of health care, is a frequent subject for workshops, seminars, and professional meetings. With the scientific and technological advancements in health care there is an increased emphasis upon the protection of individual rights as well as concern about what it means to be engaged in a health profession.

The ethical issues presented in this book are related specifically to mental health practice, but these issues are certainly not unique to this one area of health care. Take, for example, the client's right to give an informed consent regarding psychotherapy. This vital ethical issue should be of importance and concern to all health professionals in clinical practice.

This book is by no means meant to be an exhaustive study of all issues related to ethics and mental health practice. The issues presented in the book are those that the editors and chapter authors thought to be among the most pressing. We hope that in their discussions students will consider these issues in other contexts of professional practice. It is through careful analysis that a student can further develop their ethical identity and begin to explore the place of ethics in professional practice.

Issues of ethics in health care often involve crucial decisions and are therefore ripe for emotional exploitation. It is important, however, that factual evidence be gathered about a particular ethical issue at hand and moral justification be set forth for that action. Reacting purely out of emotion to ethical issues will not serve students well in developing cognitive skills in ethical analysis. The ability to engage in objective ethical reflection and decision-making can greatly enhance personal and professional dimensions of interaction. The purpose of this book is to familiarize students with a variety of ethical issues in order that they begin to gain some degree of comfort with the process of ethical analysis.

Opportunities to discuss ethical issues with other professionals engaged in health care (whether that care involves physical or psychological care, social aspects, or spiritual support), should set the stage for teamwork. Rarely, if ever, does a health care professional work in complete isolation from other professionals. Ethical decisions regarding client care would best be made in concert with health team members directly involved in that client's care, as well as with the client.

This book is an example of professional teamwork. The editors and authors represent a variety of health care professions as well as the professions of law, philosophy, and theology. Communication among the editors and authors was of utmost importance in finalizing this textbook. The values and beliefs of the editors and authors are varied. Together we worked toward a common goal, saw it to completion, and look forward to further discussions regarding ethics in the health professions.

Each chapter in this book is preceded by a brief overview containing a short biographical sketch of the authors as well as a synopsis of the chapter. Discussion questions regarding aspects of ethics and professional teamwork conclude each chapter to encourage students to reflect upon a number of ethical concerns. It is important that students justify their answers to these questions with sound, rational arguments. In the Appendix students will find several codes of professional practice relevant to ethics in mental health practice and the American Hospital Association's "A Patient's Bill of Rights" to assist students in their discussions.

General objectives for the students and professionals using this book include the development of the following skills:

1.   recognize the ethical dimensions in mental health practice;
2.   recognize the role of their chosen profession in caring for a client facing an ethical decision regarding the client's own health and well-being;
3.   explain how roles and relationships between health team members and the client affect ethical decision-making;
4.   differentiate between rights-, duty-, and goal-based arguments;
5.   identify the major ethical theories of consequentialism and formalism and state their fundamental differences;
6.   begin to demonstrate clear, sound reasoning about ethical issues and problems;
7.   articulate and defend ethical beliefs and present congruent moral justifications in a nondefensive respectful manner;
8.   consider others' arguments and comments supporting ethical beliefs that are different from their own;
9.   begin to identify their own philosophy with respect to a variety of ethical issues confronting those involved in mental health practice;
10. develop an increasing ethical sensitivity through awareness of the ethical dimensions of health care practices.

The editors do not wish to endorse any particular view of any of the chapter authors. We hope the chapters, with their varying viewpoints, will stimulate many further moments of ethical reflection for students and health professionals.

Acknowledgments

Working together as co-editors has been an especially rewarding experience. Editing of this book has involved many hours of discussion, not only about the logistics of such a publication, but about ethics and its place within the context of health care, especially mental health practice. We have all been enriched through these discussions and through our individual reflections on the many aspects of ethics affecting the health professions.

Before declaring this project as complete we would like to thank the many individuals who have contributed to the culmination of this book. Thank you to our families, friends, and colleagues who have offered their support and encouragement. Their gentle words always helped us to maintain our sense of humor and an objective perspective.

David wishes to acknowledge Dr. W. Walter Menninger for his daily examples, as his mentor, of ethical conduct in psychiatric practice. He also wishes to thank Dr. Paul Pruyser, who introduced him to philosophy and helped him appreciate and identify personal values, beliefs, and morals, but especially to recognize what he had been taught by his own father.

Susan wishes to thank her parents and also to acknowledge the many special people -- friends, clients, and colleagues -- who reflect the love of Jesus in the quixotic world of the psychiatric hospital or clinic.

Pam extends a special thanks to Susan and David for their invitation to join them in the editing of this book. She is especially grateful to Dr. Ruth B. Purtilo for her stimulating instruction in ethics and for her continuing support and encouragement.

Last, but most certainly not least, we thank Dorothy Kersenbrock, who meticulously and patiently assisted us with the preparation of this text.

David K. Kentsmith
Susan A. Salladay
Pamela A. Miya

Ethics in
Mental Health
Practice

1

David K. Kentsmith
Pamela A. Miya
Susan A. Salladay

Decision-Making in Mental
Health Practice

David K. Kentsmith, M.D., a board certified psychiatrist and fellow of The American Psychiatric Association, is an associate clinical professor of psychiatry at Creighton Medical School and the University of Nebraska College of Medicine. He is the Chief of the Omaha Nebraska Veteran's Administration Hospital Mental Hygiene Clinic and has a private practice of psychiatry. He received his M.D. degree from the University of Nebraska College of Medicine and completed a psychiatric residency at the Menninger Foundation in Topeka, Kansas.

Pamela A. Miya, R.N., M.S.N., is an assistant professor in the College of Nursing, University of Nebraska Medical Center. She is a graduate of Purdue University and Indiana University. Presently completing her doctoral studies in education at the University of Nebraska-Lincoln, she is especially interested in ethical issues in higher education and the teaching of ethics in the health professions. She has attended a National Endowment for the Humanities Institute on the teaching of ethics in nursing and has authored articles on ethical issues in nursing.

Susan A. Salladay, R.N., Ph.D., is an associate professor in Counseling and Family Services at CBN University. She holds a doctorate in philosophy and has authored many articles in the field of ethics.

In this chapter the editors introduce methods of ethical analysis to improve decision-making in mental health practice. They acquaint the reader with philosophical and ethical terms and a decision-making model that might be used in ethical analysis.

ETHICS IN MENTAL HEALTH PRACTICE
ISBN 0-8089-1738-2

INTRODUCTION: USING ETHICS TO IMPROVE DECISION-MAKING

Mental health professionals must make tough ethical decisions and face conflicts every working day. They may not consider the ethical aspects of their daily professional activities even though they act ethically. Formally relating ethics to mental health practice involves the teaching, use, and application of reason and logic to facts. The hows and whys of human thought and action and the application of judgment, norms and values, roles, and responsibilities in the process of therapeutic intervention, is repeated many times each day in one's mental health practice. The mental health professional uses the scientific method, a logical and rational approach, to consider observable and reproducible factors that contribute to the processes that ultimately result in a behavior of the individual or in a group response.

Most practitioners, however, do not know how a study of ethics could be helpful because they are unfamiliar with philosophy and do not understand its effect on their own decision-making. Practitioners are taught to appreciate factors such as language in assessing the client. Data regarding what is perceived, what is done with perceptions as they are processed, and how one responds to perceptions are factors used in the evaluation and treatment of an emotionally disturbed person. Yet practitioners could make better decisions and be clearer in their assessments by applying ethical thinking to their practice.

This book will show how familiarity with ethics in mental health practice will help practitioners make better decisions. It will also illustrate how the mental health practitioner is affected not only by what his or her client says or does but by the evaluator's or practitioner's own mental processes, values, beliefs, attitudes, and morals. Figure 1-1 illustrates how one's decisions are affected often in a hierarchical manner from inception to final product. (See Fig. 1-1: beliefs, attitudes, values, morals, and ethics.)

(decisions)

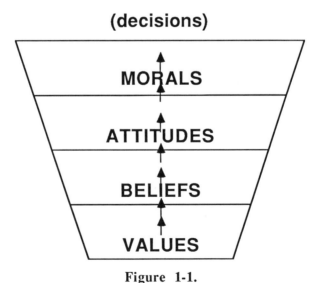

Figure 1-1.

Influences on decision-making.

The nature of a practitioner's involvement with the client is a significant factor in general medicine and mental health practice. Since the nature of the therapeutic relationship in psychiatry is private and subjective, it is particularly susceptible to the influence of individual values. If inappropriately developed by the practitioner, the relationship can adversely alter the outcome of the therapeutic encounter and result in injury to the client. This special relationship may produce injury if it is unequal or based on the assumed partial or complete lack of mental competence of the client.

The processes of transference and counter-transference have been well documented and studied from emotional, unconscious, and psychodynamic points of view.[1] Mental health training programs offer preceptor supervision to help new practitioners avoid distortions of the therapeutic relationship and learn their role with the client.

However, philosophy and techniques of philosophical reasoning such as ethical analysis to formally explore and understand basic assumptions, values, and the decision-making processes in mental health practice have not been commonly discussed or formally taught in the training process. Instead, one simply emulated the behavior of the supervisor (who was assumed to be rational and ethical). If one practiced the way the supervisor did (it was implied) one would be behaving toward clients in a rational, ethical manner.

Modern psychiatry is built on a foundation of Freudian psychology. Sigmund Freud developed his technique based on his clinical observations and studies. He was influenced by Greek and contemporary European philosophers such as Aristotle, Schopenhauer, and Nietzsche. Yet not until recently have the ethical assumptions of Freudian psychology been explored.[2]

The current interest in ethics in psychiatric practice may be sparked by questions raised by mental health practitioners working with clients who are survivors of traumas, wars, rape, holocausts, and other events of suffering and injustices. Today, many feel we are potential victims living under the constant threat of nuclear annihilation with rising levels of societal anxiety and despair. Being a victim of crime, a hostage on a hijacked airplane, or a survivor of a tornado or flood makes one acutely aware of one's own mortality, vulnerability, or fragility, and the inescapability of death. Survivors of traumatic events may be acutely aware of a feeling of randomness in being near death or witnessing someone's death. One may feel helpless or view the world as chaotic and unjust. One may attempt to change personal chaos into order by asking "why?"

Holocaust survivors, Vietnam combat veterans, victims of rape and assault may share in common a sense of shattered invulnerability to harm. The same may be true of cancer patients, schizophrenics, or accident victims. Therapy often involves questions about decisions and actions taken during the catastrophic event: (1) What happened?; (2) Why did it happen?; (3) Why did I act as I did then?; (4) Why did I act as I have since then?; and (5) What if it happens again?[3]

Therapy may help clients to understand that they are "normal" and did the "right thing." But each of these questions and judgments about "normal" and "right" involve philosophical presuppositions and ethical judgments. For example, the question "why did it happen?" may be understood both causally "the plane's engine failed, so the plane crashed," and teleologically "I had been bad, this was a punishment; it was my karma, etc." Mental health practitioners may be required to sort through the philosophical assumptions of such questions personally and with anxious clients. Problem solving involves insight and judgment skills. Judgment and insight are considered positive psychological assets and are valued by mental health professionals.

This book explores the formal processes of moral judgment in mental health practice, addresses various ethical problems and value conflicts that commonly occur in mental health practice, and addresses how clinicians in the field of mental health may resolve these dilemmas using tools of philosophical reasoning. The method by which a therapist or client makes decisions is often related to techniques of psychotherapy and psychological treatment. Use of philosophy, including study of the forms of human reasoning, can contribute significantly to improving the mental health practitioner's understanding of the methods he or she uses in assessing human behavior and will perhaps improve success in working with clients.

Understanding ethics by learning philosophical concepts helps mental health practitioners understand other viewpoints. But understanding alone has been shown to have little effect on changing one's own ethical makeup.[4] Training and education in ethics may produce an increased self-awareness. (Self-awareness is considered by some professionals to be a primary value in mental health practice.)

Clinical psychiatry and mental health practice desires a normal state of mental functioning, a state of "health." In addition to other capacities, mental health for an adult is a state of rationality, the ability to reason by abstraction and symbolic representation resulting in logical thought.[5] Rationality includes characteristic patterns of behavior guided by adherence to personal values and ethical ideals. Mental health, the full use of one's mind, means that one is able to perceive reality accurately, to consciously know external influences and internal needs that affect perceptions, and to have a disease free, efficient central nervous system that will integrate and process information accurately. Psychological health is the ability to perceive one's self both as subject and object and to use rational thinking and reasoning.

Mental health practice is based on processes of decision-making. Problem solving is done by following patterns and using rules of logical thinking to form conclusions. Decisions become ethical concerns when they involve moral choices about right actions.

PHILOSOPHICAL TERMS

In order to use philosophical thinking as a tool to improve the mental health practitioner's approach to the client, it is necessary to learn the language and understand the terms and concepts of philosophy. Forms of human reasoning (branches of philosophy) may be divided in a formal way into the following categories:

I. Metaphysics: a branch of philosophy concerned with the nature of the universe (cosmology), space, time, causality and freedom, the nature of existence, reality, and experience.

II. Epistemology: a branch of philosophy concerned with the origin, nature, methods, and limits of human knowledge and sources of truth, the basis for authority, and the nature of the knowing and learning process.

III. Logic: a branch of philosophy that investigates the principles governing correct reliable inferences; tools and techniques of clear and consistent reasoning.

IV. Ethics: a branch of philosophy that examines values and human conduct with respect to deciding between good and bad, good and evil, right and wrong, help and harm.

A. Axiology: the study of values and the greatest good (*summum bonum*).

B. Morality:

    1. Teleological theories are concerned with consequences, i.e., the greatest good for the greatest number. The comparative amount of good produced is at least as great a balance of good over evil as any available alternative.

       a. Ethical egoism

       b. Utilitarianism (John Stuart Mill)

    2. Deontological theories are concerned with the process rather than the outcome. Since we can never know the full outcome, the nature of the action or intent is what is important. Good is embodied in the act or intent.

       a. Categorical imperative (Immanuel Kant)

       b. Natural law

    3. Absolutist ethical theories determine the source of right or good to be God's law rather than human groups, societies, or individuals.

       a. Jewish ethics (The Ten Commandments)

       b. Christian ethics (The new covenant in Jesus Christ)

    4. Relativistic ethical theories determine that the source of right or good is relative to a particular person or group.

       a. Cultural relativistic ethics

       b. Power ethics ("might makes right")

COMMON ETHICAL TERMS

The critical ethical issues in mental health practice center around rights and duties. The term "rights" means properties or conditions to which an individual is entitled, for example: the right to autonomous choice or the right of self-determination.

Duties are referred to in various professional codes of ethics. Duties are moral obligations expected or entailed by professional roles and/or personal values. There are duties of nonmaleficence ("do no harm"), beneficence ("do the most good"), fidelity ("act faithfully"), and justice ("act fairly").

"Teleology" and "deontology" are two major normative ethical categories that determine the emphasis or structure of various ethical theories. Teleological ethical theories emphasize the importance of the consequences of moral choices and actions while deontological theories stress the importance of moral principles and actions over that of consequences.

The word "teleology" is derived from a Greek root "teleos," which means "end," "goal," or "consequence" (that which is "aimed at"), and the suffix "logy," which means "to study." In teleological theory, moral good is determined by the consequence or the end result.

One of the most common teleological approaches in medicine is utilitarianism, a consequentialist theory. The utilitarian justifies a particular action by appealing to overall "utility value," that which promotes the most good over evil for the greatest number of people. A utilitarian's primary moral justification is found in the consequences of a particular act. A "good" act is one in which the consequence maximizes or promotes a greater amount of good results for more people.[6]

Deontology holds that moral justification for a particular action is duty or right principles. The Greek prefix "deontos" means duty or obligation. A deontological ethical theory, such as "formalism," places more value on how one acts in carrying out certain duties based on ideal principles such as nonmaleficence, beneficence, fidelity, or justice, rather than on the end results or consequences a particular action may produce. For example, in deciding what information to give a client, a deontologist might follow the moral principle "always tell the truth" while the teleologist might try to first determine how the client would react to certain information. On these differing bases a deontologist may be less likely to withhold certain "upsetting" information from a client than a teleologist would.

WHAT IS ETHICS?

Ethics is a branch of philosophy that examines right and wrong, what should or should not be done, and the moral justifications for action. Ethics have both professional and personal aspects. Examples of publicly stated professional ethics are contained in a variety of professional codes that are developed by professional societies. Morals are those principles and values to which people are actually committed and follow in daily life.[7] Values are the constants or points of reference for measuring worth in our lives. In problem solving, one considers information and forms conclusions based on what one believes and values. Although all people have values and beliefs, they may act very irrationally. An understanding and use of ethics may allow one to more carefully define ethical dilemmas and clarify choices.

An ethical dilemma is any controversy that involves conflicting moral principles in which one experiences different moral "pulls."[8] In such a situation, one makes moral choices based on values, attitudes, personal beliefs, duties, and obligations. Human reasoning and logic are employed in the process of making the choice. If a person understands ethical theory, this information may assist decision-making. A sense of tension, due to the inherent nature of conflicts, is a part of all moral decision-making. For example, a person may refuse a particular medical treatment the treating physician knows will save the person's life. The physician's personal value that the person has a right to make an autonomous choice about the treatment conflicts with a sense that, as a health care professional, he or she also has a duty or "moral obligation" to do good and to preserve life. Is it better to respect the client's right to refuse treatment or to make a paternalistic (parent-like) decision by instituting the treatment against the person's wishes? An added complication of this dilemma involves psychiatric clients whose reasoning processes and volition may be affected.

What is illustrated in this example is a common conflict most health care professionals, in particular mental health care professionals, experience many times each day when they function in their professional capacity. One feels like the "jam in a sandwich," that is "caught in the middle." One recognizes that either choice of action can be morally justified as being "right" but the courses of action are inconsistent with one another. Ethical dilemmas, of the sort just described, are seen to beconflicts between duties, between rights, and between duties and rights.

PRINCIPLES OF ETHICS IN MENTAL HEALTH PRACTICE

Ethical codes of conduct regulate mental health practice. But how does one learn these principles and how are they applied? The usual method for learning how one ought to practice ethical mental health care relies on a preceptor. A preceptor is a model, an ego ideal, who through his or her behavior demonstrates how one ought to behave. Most people who provide mental health care today probably have not read or studied their own disciplines' ethical codes. Most, however, would probably regard the tenants as common sense and useful methods to use to practice good mental health care. If asked why the code of ethical behavior makes sense, is useful, or seems the right thing to do, people often repeat what a preceptor has demonstrated, but they have difficulty explaining why the action is right. Formalized systems and codes of ethics for the practice of psychiatry, psychology, nursing, and social work are included in the Appendix to this book. These codes cover a number of key issues:

1. A responsibility to the client.
2. An obligation to act ethically.
3. A respect for the client and other professionals.
4. A commitment to the client's good.
5. An obligation to tell the truth.
6. A respect for the law.
7. An institutional commitment.
8. A commitment to improving the community.
9. A commitment to develop and share knowledge.
10. An obligation to extend or limit professional responsibilities.

ETHICAL DECISION-MAKING

Analysis of ethical dilemmas will be enhanced by the use of systematic problem solving tools. Logic in the exploration of ethical situations can assist in overcoming emotional overtones that may distort issues and cause decisions to be based on emotions alone without regard to facts or ethical principles. Decisions or discussions in ethics will be facilitated by a systematic procedure or decision-making model.[7-10] The following is an example of a decision-making model:

Determine the facts. Logical thinking is based on an accurate determination of the facts. Stereotyping, emotional reactions, or assumptions could distort perception. If one is selective in data gathering, admitting only certain information for consideration, one is distorting. How does one determine the facts? One can ask "what additional information about the situation does one need to have before making a decision?" "What facts about the case or about the problem are unclear?" A list of unanswered questions about an ethical problem allows a person to proceed systematically to gather the answers from a variety of sources. How or who decides what is a source of data will affect the facts available for consideration. For one mental health professional the client may be the most appropriate source -- for another the least appropriate.

Analyze the ethical aspects. Information gathered must be analyzed for its ethical aspects. Does the problem involve ethics? What are the ethical issues involved? Does the dilemma involve specific conflicting duties or rights? Summarize the ethical aspects of the case in one or two brief sentences.

Outline the options. The various options for action must be considered. Discussing the options with other health team members or listing the options on paper with corresponding possible consequences or outcome(s) may be helpful. Each option should be evaluated with considerations about its effects on the client, the health care team, the institution, and society. What moral justification can one offer for each option? As options are narrowed, look at the moral justification that is offered to determine if principles and values are consistent.

Make a decision. Deciding on a morally justified course of action involves asking several questions. "Has the problem been perceived accurately?" "Has the problem been analyzed sufficiently?" "Have alternatives and consequences of alternatives been considered carefully?" The decision should reflect the nature of the good or the end result that is desired as well as the nature of the method or the means that will be used to accomplish this good goal. Moral rules and principles may be held up to the desired ends and means for comparison or contrast.

Take action. Act in a responsible and accountable manner on the decision you have made. Your action should reflect the values and principles that you considered in the above steps.

Evaluate the decision. To evaluate a decision, one may ask: "Did I proceed in the decision-making process without obtaining all the relevant facts?" "How well did I analyze the ethical aspects?" "Did I identify all the options?" "Did I accurately foresee the consequences of the chosen action?" "Could I justify the action? (Were the means and ends morally acceptable in accord with an ethical ideal?)" "Was the action indeed best in light of the present circumstances?" Askng such retrospective questions helps one reflect upon the ethical situation and the effectiveness of the decision-making process. This reflection can serve to enhance future ethical decision-making and analysis.

FACTORS AFFECTING AUTONOMY

One of the mental health professional's tasks in psychotherapy may be to help the client develop options for decision-making. Ideally, exercising choice assumes the client is functioning at some optimal level, free of hindrance, able to make a decision and arrive at it autonomously. Probably only rarely, if at all, does anyone make clear, unencumbered choices. Some clients seek therapy because they make choices inconsistent with what they value and are in conflict over their actions or are unable to act. Therapy may be directed toward illuminating encumbrances and helping clients recognize alternative choices or accept responsibility for actions. A person who is experiencing pain and suffering is not entirely free to make a decision. A person whose mental processes are clouded because of physical disease or mental illness is not completely free to decide. Individuals may be "free" (have the will) but lack the capacity. There are, besides physical and mental factors, others that affect one's autonomy. These factors include duties and obligations, legal considerations, and undue influence, coercion or duress by others. One's emotional state may affect one's capacity for objectivity, strongly influencing one's decisions and judgments resulting in actions contrary to logic and reason. Situational constraints also affect autonomy. For example, a Nazi holocaust victim, a rape victim, or a disaster victim under influence of the emotion of intense fear may make choices he or she could never make at any other time. But the choices could be very logical and appropriate to the circumstances and duress. Finally, intellectual ability can affect one's choices. If, for example, one is mentally retarded, one simply may not be able to mentally develop a full range of alternatives from which to choose.

Autonomy includes the freedom to make an irrational, harmful, or even stupid decision. The option to make a stupid or irrational decision indicates one understands the nature of the alternatives and the consequences. To one person suicide may seem highly irrational and yet to the person committing suicide it may seem an appropriate choice. (One could raise the question can a person really know the consequences of dying if one has never been dead? Or can a person ever really know the consequences of marrying or parenting or going to medical school? However, this line of thinking obscures the real issue of the moral rightness or goodness of any act. The consequences of any act may be more or less unfamiliar but what makes them right or wrong? Is it just the degree of familiarity?) Irrational choices involve ethical considerations.

Suicidal clients, senile clients, or psychotic clients by their own actions may require another person to make decisions for them. These decisions may not be what that client would choose for himself or herself. Is this a violation of a client's autonomy and dignity or a compassionate response on the part of concerned others? What response is ethically justifiable and why?

In the health professions, the question of when a person is no longer able to exercise autonomy or when that ability is restored is one of the most difficult dilemmas to resolve. Is autonomy a right or entitlement by virtue of one's basic humanity that cannot be given or taken away? How autonomous is a person who is sick? Until his or her state of health is restored, can he or she truly be free to decide? One then must consider levels of competence. Is there an ideal state of health in which one is able to be completely autonomous? Are there degrees of autonomy dependent on multiple factors?

Perhaps these questions provoke additional questions regarding how mental health care professionals value autonomy. Is the appropriate role of the mental health care provider to facilitate the client's capacity to be autonomous? How can this be done?

One may work toward enhancing the client's capacity to be autonomous by accepting two beliefs: (1) that autonomy is a right everyone is entitled to by virtue of one's basic humanity (not a privilege one is granted), and (2) that the client's need for autonomy is good.

The capacity to be autonomous, legally referred to as competency, is affected by three factors: capacity, knowledge, and voluntariness. One's mental ability to make a choice, capacity, can be improved. For example, a physical disease like uncontrolled diabetes mellitus effects brain tissue metabolism. Persons with this disease can experience coma. Medical treatment with insulin can significantly improve brain tissue metabolism and as a consequence affect mental functioning.

Educating the client so he or she understands what the choices are also enhances the client's competency. This is the basis of informed consent. Finally, one attempts to eliminate outside coercive influence on the client to promote voluntariness.

CONCLUSION

Ethical decisions and conflicts are a part of everyday mental health practice. Although one may behave ethically, one may not know how ethics can be helpful in making better decisions. To provide initial familiarity with ethical thinking, terms used in ethics were defined. Professional codes of ethics and the value of autonomy and one's capacity to express it were discussed. In the following chapters ethical processes, logical thinking, and specific ethical problems will be further elaborated upon as the various authors discuss clinical application of ethics in mental health practice.

REFERENCES

1. Ellenberger HF (1970). *The Discovery of the Unconscious: The History and Evolution of Dynamic Psychiatry*. New York:Basic Books, Inc.
2. Grunbaum A (1984). *The Foundation of Psychoanalysis: A Philosophical Critique*. Berkeley, California:University of California Press
3. Green BL, Wilson JP, & Lindy JD (1985). Conceptualizing post traumatic stress disorders: a psychosocial model. In C Figley (Ed): *Trauma and Its Wake*. New York:Brunner/Mazel, pp 53-69
4. Cabot R (1926). *Adventures on the Borderlands of Ethics*. New York: Harper Buetherg
5. Wahl CW (1984). The architectonics of human happiness. *Neuropsychiatric Bulletin, 8:4*, 3
6. Frankena WK (1973). *Ethics* (2nd ed.). New Jersey:Prentice-Hall, pp 15-16
7. Jameton A (1984). *Nursing Practice: The Ethical Issues*. New Jersey: Prentice-Hall, p 5
8. Purtilo RB & Cassel CK (1981). *Ethical Dimensions in the Health Professions*. Philadelphia:W.B. Saunders, p 7
9. Miya PA (1984). An ethical dilemma in nursing research: duties and rights. *Image: The Journal of Nursing Scholarship, 16:4*, 105-108
10. Miya PA (1984). Do not resuscitate: when nurses' duties conflict with patients' rights. *Dimensions of Critical Care Nursing, 3:5*, 293-298

DISCUSSION QUESTIONS

1.   Mental health practice assumes a normal state of mental functioning. Discuss how one decides what is good or normal mental health.

2.   List and prioritize values used in mental health practice, i.e., autonomy, logic, rationality.

3.   Discuss how the private and subjective nature of the therapeutic relationship in mental health is particularly susceptable to the individual mental health practitioner's values and ethics. What effect does this have on the client? How do the client's values and ethics affect the practitioner?

4.   Within the last ten years professional organizations and schools have begun to formally examine their codes of ethics. Discuss why there now seems to be concern for examining values and codes of ethics.

5.   How are personal values and ethics developed? What changes one's ethical make-up? Can a person, group, or culture influence another person's ethics and values? If so, how?

6.   Discuss the common principles contained in the codes of ethics of psychiatry, nursing, social work, and psychology. What are the differences?

7.   Using the decision-making model described on pages 7-8, choose an ethical dilemma you have confronted recently to see if the resolution of the dilemma is facilitated by use of the model. Are there problems with the model? How would you design another model?

8.   What is autonomy? How does one aquire it?

9.   How does a formal understanding of ethics improve the mental health practitioner's ability to make good decisions?

10.   How does a client learn about the mental health practitioner's values and ethics? Discuss why it might be important to know the mental health practitioner's values and ethics before beginning treatment.

2

Susan A. Salladay

Ethical Responsibility in Mental Health Practice

Susan A. Salladay, R.N., Ph.D., joined the faculty of CBN University in 1984 after five years at the University of Nebraska College of Medicine on the faculty of the Department of Psychiatry. At CBN University Dr. Salladay is an associate professor of counseling. She received her Ph.D. in philosophy specializing in ethics and philosophical psychology from Boston College. Dr. Salladay is a registered nurse working in mental health and hospice care. She is on the editorial review boards of the *Journal of Christian Nursing* and the *American Journal of Hospice Care.*

In her chapter Dr. Salladay examines the theoretical foundations of ethical decision-making as they involve both personal values and professional responsibilities for mental health practitioners. She considers differing presuppositions and expectations underlying absolutist and relativist ethics, showing contrasts among four ethical positions popularly held by mental health practitioners and consumers.

Take any person, administer one full dose of professional education, apply license or credentials and professional attire or uniform, and insert in any psychiatric hospital or clinic anywhere. What happens? Little bursts of real person keep popping out from behind the professional role: personality, idiosyncrasies, likes and dislikes, and many other sorts of surprises.

ETHICS IN MENTAL HEALTH PRACTICE
ISBN 0-8089-1738-2

Star Trek's Mr. Spock might say disdainfully, "Of course, this is why human beings are such an unpredictable species." The endless variety is what keeps us fascinated with ourselves, you and me. This is what creates ethics, too, because fascination can change to confusion and even conflict when people must cope with personal and professional differences.

ETHICS: PERSONAL AND PROFESSIONAL

Ethically speaking, it is impossible to separate real person from professional role. The consequences of this inability to separate are profoundly significant: as a mental health professional you cannot tuck your professional ethics into a drawer or locker marked RIGHTS AND WRONGS -- 3 TO 11 SHIFT at the end of a working day. *You* keep interrupting. *You* keep breaking in upon professional codes of ethics, patients' bills of rights, or hospital policy manuals. It is *you* who live ethical decisions.

The lived decision is actually a major part of any human being's life task. Consider that all we do between birth and death is fill (or kill) time. Living, more than merely existing, means searching for quality time, for what is meaningful or satisfying, for happiness. If human beings had no hope of finding these, suicide would not even be an ethical issue. But reproduction might be the greatest immorality.

Searching for the good life, for what is worth living for, is ethics. This is an ethical life task because evaluating, judging, and choosing are involved. Whenever a determination of what is best or of greatest value is at issue, then ethics are activated.

Ethics not only involve deciding about what is good or best but also doing something about the decisions. In this sense ethics always involve links between choices and responsibilities. Nobody has ever come into existence with "operating instructions" tucked inside the "packing carton." We are not programmed; we are not living on auto-pilot; we simply ARE. This means that every day human beings live on the brink of their own personal freedom with all the risks of the unknown. Each event and relationship in life is new. Human ethical actions and moral behaviors are generated by what is valued as quality. Ethical choices connect the determination of quality with personal responsibility for obtaining or implementing it, providing motivation.

Moral problems, ethical decisions, doubt, and guilt cause intense personal suffering, sometimes creating acute and chronic confusion or division among patients, staff, and institutions. Every day in hospitals and clinics people are injured through unintentional harm done to them in the midst of the very good health care providers struggle to produce. "Harm" here does not mean the specific result of negligence or malpractice. Rather, it is the damage we manage to inflict on each other as persons at the level of the dignity of the human spirit when anyone (patient or professional) leaves the health care system a nonperson, brutalized by numbers, forms, red tape, rules, financial burdens, unanswered questions, and hopelessness but pronounced "well."

Anxiety, depression, suspicion, and fear are the most common products of confusions about moral rights and responsibilities. Questions that typically emerge out of such confusion often reflect great personal stress: "What should I do when I think my patient is being used as a guinea pig?" "What should I do when I think a

procedure is wrong but my supervisor says to do it anyway?" "Is doing the right thing ultimately just a matter of guesswork?" "Does my being here make any positive difference?"

A MATTER OF JUSTICE

It seems that despite the most sincere efforts of mental health practitioners, there remains an inexplicable intertwining of noble intentions and iatrogenic suffering. Every advance in the mental health professions seems to bring along with it some new legal nightmare. Is our mental health system now so sophisticated that a certain rising amount of suffering is tolerated as the price we must be prepared to pay to maintain a very high level of success? Must the few, the losers, the poor, hurt to benefit the recoveries of the many, the socially credible, and the well-heeled? What kind of a moral system is this? Some will say that this is a sad but expected outcome and, in reality, is a small price to pay. But others reflect in their faces, voices, and choices the anguish of such a deadly compromise.

It is because of this dilemma that we have seen a rising interest in health care ethics with the hope that there is a way out and that justice might prevail somehow. Whenever we are talking about suffering, we are implicitly talking about justice; suffering provokes a moral sensitivity, a cry for fairness and justice, for who is it who "deserves" to suffer and why? At the very heart of the relationship between health and illness is the problem of justice. It is this that propels us into ethics.

The central issue that is uncovered in addressing problems of wellness, illness, suffering, and justice in this way is much older and deeper than its representation in the mental health professions. The same ethical tension exists in all spheres of human interaction. Why does any conflict occur, with violence, anxiety, guilt, and despair? The primary ethical problem that has just been touched like an open wound is the problem of moral authority. Is life responsive to, hostile to, or indifferent to the cry for justice? Who has the right to say? The crucial ethical task necessary to answering the questions is discernment and acknowledgment of legitimate versus illegitimate moral authority.

Since conscience is internal (a private voice of judgment), my conscience speaks only to me and yours to you. What happens when our consciences disagree? When other people disagree with our moral judgments, we may keep up a good face of moral tolerance by saying, "Of course, it is your right to disagree and whatever you think is right, is right for you." This approach to moral authority is called moral relativism. Behind it lurks the unspoken assumption: "Just don't involve me or infringe on my rights with your crazy ideas." But moral relativism is really just a polite cover-up job. It quickly gives way to a power ethic: "If you do attempt to involve me, my way will have to prevail as right."

Patterns of action makes this dynamic abundantly clear as people jockey for position and power with each other, protect turf, or watch out for number one. Does each person have an ultimate moral obligation to watch out for number one? Is it important for you to survive no matter what the cost?

To avoid a constant bloody struggle for power, human beings enact laws or policies and use tradition or professional group (peer) pressure to pronounce certain things acceptable and maintain a general functioning level of agreement. This is the grand "conspiracy" of the social ethic, which most human beings have been trained from birth to play along with and pass on to others. When it functions without a hitch, we rarely even see it for it is as natural as breathing. For example, the ingestion of food is considered by most cultures to be an enjoyable and public function. The elimination of food is considered a private and personal function. Imagine if these two value judgments were reversed: if you gave a dinner party, you would have to set up little toilets around the living room. But you would have to go to the rest room whenever you wanted to snack on a cookie or candy bar. How would this reversal of moral norms alter our understandings of "acceptable" and "unacceptable" behavior? One small example: "dine" might become a "four-letter word."

Many ethical problems occur in situations in which no norms are transgressed and no laws are broken yet people get hurt. Consider the situation of "the woman who died in a box."[1] Rebecca Smith, age 61, was found on the street one morning in January dead in a cardboard box. The box had been her "home." She died of hypothermia. Her situation had not gone unnoticed by others. A social worker had reported Rebecca's living conditions to the police. A psychiatrist visited her and found out that she had been released from a psychiatric hospital. Instead of going to live with her sister, Rebecca Smith struck out on her own. Why did she die? Was someone at fault here? What laws were broken? Could more or better laws have solved the problem? How was justice served or abused?

An even larger moral problem, incomprehensible most of the time, is this: consider that if we had spent one million dollars every day since the birth of Jesus, we would have spent only one half of what the United States plans to spend on the military budget in the next five years -- one and one half trillion dollars. What if such an amount of money were available instead for food, clothing, housing, and health care? SHOULD IT BE? Moral insight involves seeing connections between this problem and the death of Rebecca Smith.

Ethics confront familiar and fundamental notions of love, justice, mercy, goodness, equality, and causation. The basic issue of moral authority challenges people to ask: "Who is in charge?" "Who is responsible?" "Who should decide what is right?"

ETHICAL THINKING AND MENTAL HEALTH PRACTICE

In many areas of life we depend on warning signs to alert us to dangers. "Caution: children crossing." "Warning: high voltage wires." "Attention, the National Weather Service has just issued a tornado alert." "Do you know the seven warning signs of cancer?" These are just a few of many examples. We have yet to invent the announcement: "Caution -- ethical dilemma in progress; proceed at your own risk."

What are the warning signs of an ethical dilemma beginning to build? They are most commonly: stress and tension intrapersonally or interpersonally; ineffective communication patterns such as avoidance, nagging, or silence; heightened emotional sensitivity with the feeling of self-doubt and the awareness of being trapped.

When any of these becomes a chronic condition in a work setting, it is easily mistaken for normal. This confusion may cause professionals working in mental health settings where such conditions are chronic to become desensitized to moral dilemmas.

Ethics are concerned with analyzing and resolving moral dilemmas. But moral dilemmas can be overlooked or ignored until they reach crisis proportions; this usually means that an issue has been submitted to the courts and resolution may be impossible without massive compromise. Yet moral dilemmas are usually not difficult to diagnose and can often be treated preventively.

What can health care professionals reasonably expect from ethics?

1. It is reasonable to expect ethical theory to provide effective skills for clarifying moral problems. Personal agendas, passive decisions, and other "fallibility factors" often complicate the resolution of a moral dilemma. Tools such as values clarification can help overcome this.
2. Ethics provide standards for evaluation and problem solving in situations of interpersonal conflict. Understanding key differences regarding assumptions and presuppositions in various ethical positions will help accomplish this.
3. Health professionals should not expect easy or simplistic solutions to complex ethical dilemmas. The easiest solutions -- denial and avoidance -- are usually the least effective.
4. Health professionals should not assume that because there are no easy answers, no meaningful resolution is possible. The assumption that there are no right answers to ethical problems leads to moral fatalism and the belief that whatever is done or decided will make no real difference.
5. Mental health practitioners should not expect responsibility trade-offs from ethics. Many people do tend to view ethics as a way of finding someone else to take responsibility for telling them what is right and wrong. This is often why hospital and clinics hire ethics experts. Responsibility trade-offs disguise rather than address the issue of personal moral responsibility.

The study of ethical thinking involves examinations of both morality and axiology. Morality is that area of human behavior in which people are held accountable and responsible for their actions based on distinctions between right and wrong. Morality is also a complex system of rules, laws, and moral norms that regulate human behaviors and interactions. Axiology is the study of goods and values that motivate moral behavior and choices. Axiology endeavors to determine life's greatest good (*summum bonum*), the highest standard by which all other good things are evaluated and arranged in order of importance in the understanding into a value hierarchy. All human beings have values, either consciously or unconsciously held, which motivate and direct moral behavior. Values are strong positive or negative investments of psychological energy in persons, places, things, ideas, goals, or causes. Because many key values are established early in life, often prelinguistically, people may remain unaware of their deepest values or may continue through life with values adopted unconsciously from others (parents, teachers, or peers), which are inconsistent with other, more significant values they hold. Such value conflicts can cause intrapsychic stress and initiate moral dilemmas insofar as it becomes difficult for people to understand the connections between their desires and their patterns of behavior. They have difficulty explaining why they act as they do. The technique of values clarification is one tool that mental health professionals find useful in bringing unconscious values to consciousness and connecting them with behaviors.[2]

The nature of morality also causes confusion in the evaluation of behavior. The word "moral" has three opposites: immoral, amoral, and nonmoral. To act immorally means to act contrary to moral norms. Immoral behavior is defined as behavior that is done with a conscious knowledge of moral requirements. Thus, someone who acts immorally understands right and wrong but acts wrongly. Such a person is held morally responsible for wrongdoing.

Sometimes people do wrong with no clear comprehension of the differences between right and wrong. This was the situation of Peter F. who poisoned his wife and 5-year-old daughter. In court Mr. F. was not clearly aware of the proceedings. At times he asked where his wife was. But he also stated that he had made sure his wife and daughter would always be safe (in death) and that he would be joining them soon.

Mr. F. was declared not guilty by reason of insanity. His lawyer presented expert testimony from mental health professionals to prove that Mr. F. had acted amorally, not immorally, although he had acted illegally. When people act immorally, they are held morally accountable. This accountability requires a balancing of the moral account books, punishment may be imposed to right the wrong. But justice does not exact punishment from people who cannot understand why they are being punished. It is not easy, however, to determine what an individual actually knows or intends in acting.

Nonmoral actions are those that have no moral implications; instead, they often involve personal taste or preference as a motivation to action. For example, a person would not be held morally responsible for choosing to have pie rather than cake for lunch. Yet the distinction between moral and nonmoral choices is not always clear. For example, is the choice to smoke one of moral rights or personal preference? Does the nonsmoker have moral rights? The person with emphysema who is seated next to a foursome of smokers in a restaurant might have a legitimate reason for asking them to stop. Do the smokers have a moral obligation to extinguish their cigarettes? Suppose the customer does not have emphysema but just dislikes the smell of smoke? Do the smokers have a moral right to continue?

To resolve moral dilemmas ethical theorists examine what is meant by concepts such as "right" and "obligation." In many moral dilemmas rights conflict with obligations in some way. The circumstances (like having emphysema or disliking the smell of smoke), the time factors (being in the middle of a meal, not ready to leave), and the personalities of those involved all set the stage for an ethical dilemma. Of course economic factors are involved, too. Few of us can say, "I will give you a hundred bucks to put that cigarette out."

In any moral dilemma the following considerations usually have an impact on the problem and must be assessed: circumstances, setting, time factors, economic factors, personalities, roles, rules, and values.

In examining value systems and morality ethical theorists use a dual approach, a combination of "descriptive" and "prescriptive" methods.[3] The descriptive function of ethics involves observing and documenting individual and group moral behaviors and values. Ethics share this function with psychology, sociology, and anthropology. Mental health professionals routinely participate in this function in documenting their patients' needs and problems. For example, this information was charted on one new patient: Ms. L. states, "When I was growing up, my parents used to fight all the time. They sometimes hit me and locked me in my room." Or the record might read: the patient's parents have refused to attend family therapy sessions. The descriptive function of ethics is to describe and record moral behavior but not to evaluate it.

It is the prescriptive function of ethics that evaluates moral behavior. Necessarily we need to know how people do behave and interact morally. But ethics also examine how people should interact morally. We must responsibly decide how people (ourselves and sometimes others) should uphold rights and carry out obligations.

When moving from "do" to "should," we move from the descriptive to the prescriptive function of ethics: responsibly judging moral behaviors and values. Psychology, sociology, and anthropology do not contain prescriptive functions.

INHERENTLY MORAL ENDEAVORS

All health care professions are inherently moral endeavors because they contain prescriptive functions. Each care-related act rests on a professional judgment about what is right and best for a patient. Professional decisions and actions involve relationships of responsibility with patients. But when expectations surrounding these relationships are unclear, moral problems emerge. These conflicts most often involve ethical issues of autonomy or paternalism. "Autonomy" refers to individual freedom -- a patient's or professional's right to meaningful and effective self-determination. "Paternalism" refers to the ethical obligation to decide and to act on behalf of another. Ethical dilemmas often occur in mental health settings when an individual's autonomy is partially impaired by illness or circumstances. Thus, moral dilemmas often involve rightly prescribing the degree of professional responsibility morally due a patient whose autonomy is limited but not completely absent.

Many ethical decisions are made each day in mental health settings in the course of professional practice. But *how* are these decisions made? Each decision may be more or less competent. Sometimes the decision process is nothing more than a mental drawing straws.

Some advocate that ethical decisions be made quantitatively by weighing the amount of good to be produced relative to the amount of expected discomfort as each may affect the number of people involved. This approach, the utilitarian position, aims at measuring or calculating consequences of ethical decisions relative to the number of people beneficially or adversely affected. Utilitarianism is an approach to ethical decision-making that takes as its ideal goal, or *summum bonum*, the greatest good for the greatest number. A risk-benefit analysis is done to determine the variables in the decision that can be manipulated to produce this ideal of good.[4]

Another popular approach to ethical decision-making is the pragmatic approach. This position favors choosing the most workable alternative. However, what equates "practical," "workable," and "right" may not be clearly specified. If, for example, workability is equated with convenience for the doer of the act, the result becomes a very self-serving morality. Professional judgments performed on this basis may become rationalizations -- pseudo-reasons to justify actions that are nothing more than personally convenient.

How are moral decisions made responsibly in the health care settings in which we practice today? How can mental health professionals avoid rationalization in moral decision-making?

How do you usually decide what is right? Do you remember a specific point in your life when you felt responsible to make a choice about right and wrong that would affect your future and others'? You may remember two types of situations: either you had an idea of what was really right but found it difficult to do or you really did not know for sure what was right. Perhaps you considered what you could do based on the alternatives as you saw them. You may have speculated on what might happen, considering various consequences to yourself and to others.

You have thought about what others were expecting you to do and weighed their view of you against your own self-image. But how was the decision actually made?

ETHICAL RESPONSIBILITY INVOLVES HUMAN RESPONSE-ABILITY

All ethical values and actions are the result of what is believed about human nature and the human capacity to respond to needs and problems. Whatever forms a person's desires and shapes a sense of good will determine ethical responsibility. Ethical responsibility is ethical response-ability, ultimately to that which is believed to hold the greatest happiness or satisfaction.

Ethical values, choices, and actions flow from human response-ability to a *summum bonum*. Most people remain unaware of their *summum bonum*. Ethics offer the opportunity to clarify the *summum bonum* and to coordinate actions and decisions in relation to that which is considered to be most worthy of response.

Relativistic ethical positions, including self-realization, hedonism, stoicism, utilitarianism, and pragmatism, locate the *summum bonum* and the source of happiness in the individual decision-maker. Thus, right and good become relative attributes of particular situations, times, places, and circumstances.

An absolutist ethic, such as the Christian ethic, locates the source of right, good, and happiness outside the individual decision-maker, group, or society. In an absolutist ethic good is not created by particular moral choices in particular circumstances. Rather, it is evaluated by comparing particular moral choices against an unchanging standard of good, God. As Lutzer notes in describing an absolutist ethic:

> When God gave us His revelation concerning morality, His precepts were not arbitrary; they were not selected at random. The moral law is a reflection of God's own character.[5]

Throughout history people have examined the issue of ethical responsibility, trying to determine what goals held the greatest worth in shaping lifestyles. Although many attempts have been made, four ethical positions characterize human history's most pervasive and popular answers. These four ethical positions are as popular today as when they were first presented several thousand years ago. Each springs from a different *summum bonum* and offers a different understanding of what is worth living for and responding to ethically. Three are: relativist in nature (self-actualization, hedonism, and stoicism) and one is absolutist (the Christian ethic). However, in each a person's choice will reflect certain values. Choices are the mirrors of values. When a person makes an ethical decision, it is as if she or he declares at that moment, "See, here is the value I will be working to express in action by my choice". People do not often see their ethical choices (especially the routine daily choices) as such concrete statements.

Despite our human ethical myopia, ethical choices do accumulate to create lifestyles. And throughout history four ethical lifestyles or positions emerge, although there are many variations and many other positions as well. Each of the four ethical positions creates a particular lifestyle through which an individual expresses values and seeks quality or happiness.

I. The Ethical Position of Self-Realization

For many people today the drive for personal achievement, the drive to excel, is paramount. The key value in their lifestyle is self-realization. Choices and actions are directed towards gaining the satisfaction of fulfilling highest personal potential or seeing this reflected in achievements of family.

In this ethical system "be all that you can be" is much more than a recruiting slogan. It is a lifestyle and a *summum bonum*. This view is a popular one today and is held by many from the "type A" executive to the quiet young student. The executive just wants to be company president and the student just wants to marry successfully, buy a good house, and be respected in the community. In each case the individual is seeking what she or he believes will bring maximum personal fulfillment.

For most people good health (especially good mental health) is viewed as a crucial supporting value necessary to achieving one's full potential. Many popular psychologies, such as that of Abraham Maslow, prioritize physical and mental health as essential to the desired end of self-realization: "this final craving to become all that one is capable of becoming and to feel that one is doing what is right for him or her."[6]

In this ethical position the primary advantage of living in a democratic society is the opportunity such an environment offers one to self-actualize. Indeed, self-actualization is the primary ethical obligation and whoever shirks this duty (by dropping out of school, going on welfare, or becoming mentally "ill," for example) is considered to be acting immorally. Thus, health professionals who promote this ethical position could be critical of patients who smoke or drink too much, who are noncompliant with medications, or who do not seem to care about staying healthy.

Since this ethical position is such a popular one today, it surprises many people to learn that it is one of the oldest in existence. The self-realization ethic traces its roots to the Greek philosopher Aristotle (384-322 B.C.). As Aristotle sought to define the good life that ought to shape human response-ability, he came to believe that it was something to be achieved by realizing an individual's highest potential. He based his ethical position on observations of the process of human development. Today many people find evidence for this ethical position in theories of evolution as well.

Aristotle observed the insufficiency, helplessness, and "frustration" of newborns and concluded that the infant is not yet a person but is a potential person. Growing up is the process that holds the potential for achieving personhood, ideally to the fullest possible potential.

> An individual who fails to do this will suffer discontent as a result of his or her thwarted goals and this frustration will show itself in the form of illness or unhappiness.[7]

Aristotle's ethical system permits both abortion and infanticide. Slavery was morally justifiable because slaves were, by definition, nonpersons; they had no personal potential to fulfill but were thought of as living machines, existing to fulfill the personal potentials of others.

One ethical issue that this position proposes is the question: is self-actualization ever really possible? Is anyone ever fully human or fully satisfied? If so, what does one do next? If not, is it right to promote an ethical ideal that no one can achieve? And can a person be held morally responsible for not reaching her or his full potential if this is ultimately unreachable?

   This ethical system is a very private one. Who can say what self-actualization should include for any individual? Only the individual herself or himself. And self-actualization is something that no one can accomplish for anyone else. Thus, in the ethical position of self-realization, the primary ethical focus of each person will be the individual self. Achieving an individual potential is each person's unique responsibility, a responsibility to oneself.

2. The Ethical Position of the Pleasure Principle

   "Go for the gusto." "It can't be wrong if it feels so right." These are popular slogans today. For some people a lifestyle of pleasure, enjoyment, security, and entertainment is all that really matters. They will do anything (including spending thousands of dollars for particular euphoria-inducing chemical substances) to avoid pain and maximize pleasure.

   Each moment, say the advocates of this ethical position, should be devoted to the highest quality of pleasure: working out, gourmet food, luxurious clothing, vibrant sex, peak volume stereo music, a beautiful home, etc. Good health is, of course, a necessary prerequisite to appreciating pleasure. No one can really enjoy the good life if she or he is sickly or anxious. And the American advertising industry certainly does its part to promote the desirability of this ethical position as an obligation that every citizen should be committed to pursuing. The men and women "created" by advertising display vigorous good health and an enthusiastic sensuality.

   This ethical position creates an obligation to a lifestyle in which new highs and constant variety are sought. Although the quest for true pleasure seems a contemporary phenomenon, this ethic is also one of the oldest in existence. It can be traced to several Greek philosophers including Epicurus (342-270 B.C.). Epicurus taught hedonism, a system of ethics in which one's highest moral good (*summum bonum*) and duty is to achieve pleasure and avoid pain, making this a lifestyle.

   Some Greek hedonists (like the Cyrenaic school of philosophers) urged followers to "eat, drink, and be merry for tomorrow we die." Only immediate physical and emotional pleasures were of any value since one could never be sure of the future.

   However, other hedonists like Epicurus believed that the real task of living was to discriminate among the "higher" pleasures and to select lasting over transient pleasures.

   What are the ethical consequences of hedonism? Many assert that it is this ethical position that presents life's greatest challenge: learning how to balance the pleasure of life against its pain. Others have gone on to wonder if indeed pain is and must be a necessary component in life. Is it only by comparison with pain that we are capable of appreciating pleasure? And other ethical thinkers have wondered what right any individual has to the enjoyment of pleasures if that enjoyment entails the exclusion of others' suffering from one's awareness.

   These questions raise ethical concerns about the true nature of pleasure. How, for example, are the pleasures of parenting to be weighed against its pains including the physical pain of childbirth and the mental stress of a lifelong commitment to guiding a child into maturity?

   Perhaps this is an ethical position that can be appreciated only by the very, very rich. How then do we account for the wealthy who commit suicide because their lives are empty?

Mental health professionals speculate on another aspect of this ethical position of hedonism when they address social deprivation theories of mental illness. In 1958 the World Health Organization defined health as "a state of complete physical, mental, and social well-being and not merely the absence of disease or infirmity."[8] This famous definition has created much controversy. The definition reflects the World Health Organization's belief that world health is intimately bound to world peace. It also reflects belief in the abilities of medical science, particularly psychiatry, to achieve world health.

> The world is sick and the ills are due to the perversion of man...superstition, ignorance, religious intolerance, misery, poverty -- these psychological evils must be understood in order that a remedy might be prescribed.[9]

Like hedonism, the World Health Organization claims evil in the world is the same as sickness and suffering. But medical ethicist Daniel Callahan notes that:

> There seems to be no historical correlation whatever between health and peace, and that is true even if one includes mental health.How are human beings to achieve happiness (if) infinite human desires are constantly thwarted by the limitations of reality?[10]

The difficulties in delineating pleasure in its ultimate forms and correlating these with such goods as peace and health cause this ethical position to be intriguing and elusive.

3.   The Ethical Position of Self-Control

While it may not be humanly possible to so perfectly control all the circumstances of one's life so as to produce the maximum happiness of sustained pleasure and freedom from pain, many people do believe that the greatest good in life (the *summum bonum*) is control -- control of one's own destiny. The ethical position of self-control values being in control of oneself in any situation, despite circumstances that may create pain. Control of one's responses to any circumstances and control of one's attitudes are the keys to happiness.

This position, known as Stoicism, asserts that both body and mind can be brought under the control of the will in order to produce health and tranquility. Illness, it would follow, is simply ignorance -- being unaware that such powers of health and peace lie within the self. A person may be healed or cured when she or he becomes fully aware of such powers and uses them rightly, since (because illness is destructive of body and mind) wellness is a moral obligation of the enlightened individual.

So even in the midst of pain and poverty, disappointment will not disrupt the inner tranquility and health of the one who rightly understands self-control. Peace and serenity are possible through a proper mental effort of transcendence over any difficulty. The "power of positive thinking" or "mind control" is an attractive and profound value for many in today's complex and chaotic world. Clearly mental health is essential to this ethical position.

This position, like the others presented, is both ancient and contemporary. Its roots are found in the writings of Epictetus, a Greek Stoic philosopher (50-120 A.D.) who taught that "there is nothing worth becoming disturbed about; peace of mind is of superlative value."[7] Self-control, the mastery of one's own mind and desires, is the *summum bonum* of life, the highest ethical good, and the supreme duty.

Evidences of the Stoic approach to morality can be found as presuppositions underlying a variety of diverse fields today: biofeedback, wellness movements, Christian Science, Scientology, EST, Silva Mind Control, Transcendental Meditation, visual imagery therapies, etc. All emphasize the controlling powers of the human mind in creating one's own good: physical and mental health, inner peace, enlightenment, truth, happiness.

Likewise, when someone is physically or mentally ill, it is possible to conclude that she or he consciously or unconsciously desires to be sick or is willing to be sick, in which case the sick person may be held ethically responsible for the condition or for failing to recover. Psychiatrist Thomas Szasz remarks that:

> Mental illness -- as a deformity of personality -- is often regarded as the cause of human disharmony. The concept of illness...implies deviation from a norm and when one speaks of mental illness, the norm from which deviation is measured is a psychosocial and ethical one.[11]

4. The Ethical Position of Divine Covenant

The ethical position known as the Christian ethic is similar to the others presented in that it, too, is both ancient and contemporary. Unlike the others, it is an absolutist ethic since the source of good (*summum bonum*) is found outside the self (it is found in God), rather than within the self (as the potential to self-realize, the capacity to pursue pleasure, or the ability to control the self).

The Christian ethic centers in a loving, faithful, and just God who is the source and standard of all good. A basic premise of this ethical position is that if "self" remains the center of attention, gratification, and control, then we will never be truly happy. Self-satisfaction is impossible because human desires are for infinite happiness but the self is finite, limited, and changeable. This position asserts that if the center of good and moral authority is within the self (either individually or collectively in society), we have become our own "gods," creating idols of the ego or systems of "salvation:" medicine, law, religions, economics, politics.

In this secular worship, whatever way we turn, suffering, anxiety, and hopelessness find a way in among our highest ethical ideals and we remain bound to serve the gods of our isolated, frustrated selves and limited imaginations.

In the Bible God is shown creatively intervening in human history to change that limited focus. At the heart of the Christian ethic is a covenant relationship between God and the people He created. A covenant, like a contract, is a legally binding agreement entered into by two or more parties in good faith. The covenant described throughout the Bible is God's expression of His commitment to the well-being and good of human beings individually and collectively. Yet people reject the offer of covenant from God and choose instead to go their own way, attempting to secure their own good and well-being. It is this human rejection, not any shortcoming on God's part, which leads to all the effects of a broken covenant between God and human beings: injustice and suffering among people, a feeling that God is remote or even "dead," anxiety, despair, guilt.

Many people who desire to find their greatest good in God assume that it is their own human longing to do good deeds, right wrongs, make correct moral decisions, and win God's approval that will restore the broken covenant. The "bad news" of the Christian ethic is that it is impossible to restore the relationship between God and His creatures by human effort. The "good news" of the Christian ethic is that God has restored the broken covenant Himself, through His Son Jesus.

The ethical basis of Christianity is found in a personal relationship with Jesus as Lord and Savior since the *summmum bonum* of this ethic is Jesus Himself rather than a theology, creed, or church system. It is an individual, a living Person, not a theory or ideal who is the greatest good of the Christian ethic. The Christian ethic is much more than an ethical ideal demonstrated in the life of Jesus.

It is the claim of this ethical position that Jesus' death for our sins and His resurrection are historical facts capable of changing human beings' moral and spiritual status before God. Jesus claimed to create a new covenant between God and human beings in His own body and blood so that anyone who believes in Him receives a new relationship with God.[12] Thus, the Christian ethic begins with the requirement for a change of status, a change of heart within the doer before the deeds can become good. The change involves the whole person -- body, mind, and spirit -- since the healing of bodily and mental illness is also part of Jesus' restorative work. The change necessary for realizing goodness and happiness cannot be accomplished by self-effort but only by trust in Jesus.

The Christian ethic is a response to God's initiative. This ethical position insists on the uncompromisable dignity of each human being because God loved each person so greatly as to willingly die for that person in order to bring him or her back into covenant, into happiness. Thus, no human system of rules, institutions, or governments can rightfully threaten or compromise the value God has placed on each human life.

THE TASK OF ETHICAL DECISION-MAKING

Searching for what is truly meaningful and satisfying, for how to live best, is the beginning of ethics. This is an ethical life task. Evaluating, judging, and choosing are involved. Professionals in mental health find themselves responsible to these tasks as they enter into therapeutic relationships.

Ethical decision-making begins when people identify moral problems and injustices that require change. Problem solving involves three steps: determining a need for action, developing alternatives from which a choice will be made, and evaluating the alternatives. These three steps lead to making the choice to solve the problem.

As decision-makers, most people believe that they make good moral choices because they see the problem clearly, are aware of all available alternatives, and choose the fairest possible outcome.

Psychological research and everyday experiences show that people are not quite so omniscient in their decision-making, however much this may be an ethical ideal. Human beings have a limited capacity for comprehending the inherent complexity of moral problems. Fallibility factors, including the five listed here, are present in all moral decisions. If these fallibility factors are ignored or denied, the resolution of ethical dilemmas will be obstructed.

Bounded rationality. Human reason and judgment are finite in the capacity for comprehending and weighing all aspects of any problem. Instead of making a decision based on knowledge of all possible courses of action and their consequences, each person constructs a mental model or selective representation of the problem. "Primary effect," one psychological phenomenon involved in forming the mental construct, causes decision-makers to give greater value and higher priority to information gathered first in the course of problem solving.

> Complexity is reduced to the level at which a human being can make a decision within the limits imposed by his or her own thinking capabilities and knowledge. The values and personality of the decision-maker strongly influence these mental abstractions.[13]

Projection. In moral decision-making both professionals and patients tend to assume that others share their same values, motives, and expectations. This can obscure meaningful communication with the assumption that people are saying the same things in different words.

Mixed motives. Instead of basing an ethical choice on one moral principle, ethical ideal, or stated ethical position, human motives tend to be mixed. Several different goals and needs may shape decisions about a course of action. Often some of the needs and desires that motivate our actions remain at the unconscious level, forming a "hidden agenda" in problem solving. Conflict often occurs because hidden agendas take priority over declared ethical ideas in arriving at a decision.

Passive decision-making. When a conflict is especially threatening or the risks of the unknown make change very difficult, professionals and/or patients may opt out of the decision-making process by an implicit choice not to choose, instead of confronting the need for a moral decision directly. The desire for a passive decision and the shifting of moral responsibility to another decision-maker may be expressed verbally ("What would you do if you were in my shoes?" "Just tell me what to do, Doc, and I'll sign the consent.") or nonverbally through silence, withdrawal, or apparent indifference.

Settling for the easy way out (early alternative selection). People tend to be uncomfortable with ambiguity. The process of making a moral decision, before a resolution is actually reached, may be a tense and anxious time. In order to reduce the stress of decision-making, the fear of the unknown, and the threat of real or imaginary deadlines, people often settle for the first available option, the safe choice, or the majority opinion. In avoiding risks they may also reject or subtly punish those they see as procrastinating in the decision process.

ONGOING QUESTIONS

Ethical decisions are those decisions that evaluate issues of life's quality, the rightness of human interactions, and the response-ability of professionals in service to their patients. Mental health professionals *must* make decisions of a moral nature in the course of their work because the mental health professions are inherently moral endeavors and the role of the trained professional involves judgments about the use of expertise towards the best interests of others.

Mental health professionals *may* make good, adequate, poor, or even cruel decisions. But all decisions are made relative to personal and professional values that are prioritized by the individual. Guiding the prioritizing of values is the individual's *summum bonum* or greatest good. Various ethical positions advocate ferent highest values, each of which is believed to hold the possibility of happiness.

Value hierarchies and ethical choices "accumulate" into the personal/professional expression of a lifestyle or way of being and choosing consistently, expressing a world view.

Ethical problems and moral dilemmas result when world views and lifestyles conflict. Conflicts also involve differing ideas about the nature of moral authority (whether it is relativistic or absolutistic). Additional problems in decision-making result if real differences in individuals' values, expectations, and ethical positions are ignored or denied.

Ethical dilemmas are more likely to be resolved and fair decisions reached when differences in values, expectations, and ethical positions are scrutinized and fallibility factors accounted for.

This chapter has been largely descriptive in nature, examining ethical theory and its relationship to mental health professions. But deeper questions remain. They are prescriptive in nature: "How *should* ethical decisions be made by mental health professionals?" "Which ethical position and which values are *best* in mental health settings?" "Are people morally responsible for how they choose to live, even if they are mentally ill or impaired?"

Some people (let's call them Group X) claim that there is no one true right way to live. Instead, each person must decide for herself or himself which ethical position is to be personally preferred.

There can be no moral truth. The ultimate reason for this is that moral concepts are based on emotions and the contents of an emotion fall entirely outside the category of truth.[14]

Others disagree (let's call them Group Y). They state that there is a true right way to live and they assert that human beings are "responsible" to choose the right way and live accordingly. If they refuse this way, unhappiness and unhealthiness result.

We are created by God to live in relationship with Him. God has plans for us whom He created.Therefore, we as creatures are not free to define our own values, goals, and limits, but must discover those designed for us by our Creator.[15]

At this point the reader, rather than the author, must complete the chapter. Completion of the chapter means being able and willing to locate *yourself* in either Group X or Group Y. Are you?

As you continue to work in the field of mental health, you will find that each new day involves you in an exploration of this ongoing question about the nature of morality. All ethical problems will bring you face to face with conflicting views about human rights and responsibilities. As you reflect on this situation, you may wish to consider the following questions in depth, in private, and in conversation with other mental health professionals:

1. What is the single greatest reason for burnout among mental health professionals?
2. Are you now experiencing a sense of satisfaction and joy in your profession?
   A year from today, where would you like to be and what will you be doing? Do you look forward to this future with enthusiasm (please explain)?
3. As a mental health professional what values are most important to you in your everyday activities with patients and staff? If your children were to enter your profession, would you want them to share the same values? Why or why not?
4. What is the greatest evil in the world today: poverty, ignorance, selfishness, or apathy?[2] Explain your choice.

The challenges in ethical analysis and action represent perhaps the most exciting and frustrating area of investigation confronting mental health professionals today. And the challenges are impossible to ignore or avoid because this is an area of investigation which requires each individual mental health practitioner to make her or his unique contribution.

REFERENCES

1. Hopper K & Kittrie S (1982). The woman who died in a box. *The Hastings Center Report, 12(3)*, 18
2. Simon SB, Howe LK, & Kirschenbaum H (1972). *Values Clarification -- A Handbook of Practical Strategies for Teachers and Students*. New York: Hart
3. Thiroux JP (1980). *Ethics Theory and Practice*. Encino:Glencoe, p 3
4. Johnson OA (1974). *Ethics Selections from Classical and Contemporary Writers*. New York:Holt, Rinehart and Winston, p 258
5. Lutzer E(1981). *The Necessity of Ethical Absolutes*. Grand Rapids:Zondervan, p 82
6. Baily JT & Claus KE (1975). *Decision Making in Nursing Tools for Change*. Saint Louis:CV Mosby, p 30
7. Sahakian WS & Sahakian ML (1966). *Ideas of the Great Philosophers*. New York:Barnes and Noble, pp 33-36
8. World Health Organization (1981). Preamble to the Constitution of the World Health Organization. In TA Mappes, JS Zembaty (Eds):*Biomedical Ethics*. New York:McGraw-Hill, p 203
9. Chisolm B (1981).Technical Prepatory Committee Minutes, World Health Organization Meeting 1946. In TA Mappes, JS Zembaty (Eds): *Biomedical Ethics*. New York:McGraw-Hill, p 205
10. Callahan D (1981). The WHO Definition of Health. In TA Mappes, JS Zembaty (Eds): *Biomedical Ethics*. New York:McGraw-Hill, pp 203-211
11. Szasz TS (1981). The Myth of Mental Illness. In TA Mappes & JS Zembaty (Eds): *Biomedical Ethics*. New York:McGraw-Hill, pp 222-228
12. Luke 22:20 (1973). *New International Version of The Holy Bible*. East Brunswick:International Bible Society, p 967
13. Robbins SP (1980). *The Administrative Process*. Englewood Cliffs:Prentice-Hall, p 104
14. Westermark EA (1981). The Relativity of Ethics. In AK Berman & JA Gould (Eds): *Philosophy for a New Generation*. New York:Macmillan, p 38
15. Fish S & Shelly JA (1978). *Spiritual Care: The Nurses Role*. Downers Grove:InterVarsity, p 29

DISCUSSION QUESTIONS

1.   After answering questions 1-4 at the end of this chapter, discuss your answers together with those of other mental health professionals. How do your answers reflect personal values and specific demands of your professional role?

Are your answers harmonious with your lifestyle? For example, how are you already coping with whatever you believe to be the main cause of professional burnout? How does this reflect what you believe about quality of life? What is your *summum bonum*? Would you support other mental health professionals in acting as you do; why or why not?

2. Ethical issues often generate intense conflict before they can be resolved. Discuss the differences between functional and dysfunctional conflict. What specific techniques should be used to promote functional rather than dysfunctional conflict among mental health team members as they work to resolve ethical dilemmas?

3. What is double bind? How do double binds obscure and obstruct the resolution of moral problems? Examine various cases presented in other chapters as examples of moral dilemmas to determine the psychological and ethical effects of double binds.

4. Franklin B. is a 33-year-old unemployed construction worker. He has come to the mental health center because he feels despondent. His father died eight months ago. Before he died, he told Franklin that his last wish was for Franklin to finish high school, go to college, and "really make something out of your life." Franklin explains, "I don't want to let my old man down but I ain't never gonna be nothin' more than just plain Franklin. School's no fun. Ain't life for havin' fun? What am I gonna do?" How should the mental health team approach planning and intervention for Franklin? Consider what values Franklin expresses. What do you think is his ethical position and *summum bonum*?

5. Margaret C. is a 40-year-old bank president who has just been told she is a diabetic. She is now refusing to give herself insulin by injection, claiming, "This is just the doctor's way of trying to convince me I'm sick or something. But I simply refuse to admit sickness into my life. Nothing has ever happened that I can't handle through correct thinking." A liaison psychiatrist and a social worker have each been called to consult with Margaret. The psychiatrist holds a self-actualization ethic while the social worker is a hedonist. How do you think these three will interact? What potential conflicts might arise in planning and intervention in this case and how can they be most successfully resolved?

6. Joan G. is a clinical nurse specialist at a Local Psychiatric Institute. She has been working with Sally Ann R., age 19, who has paranoid schizophrenia. Sally Ann is 3 months pregnant; the father of the baby is unknown. Sally Ann's father (her mother is deceased) insists that Sally Ann have an abortion "the sooner the the better. She's already had three kids and all of them are in foster homes somewhere. I'm not taking care of this kid, believe me. I got a right to my own life and Sally Ann is enough problem for me, sick like she is." Sally Ann is terrified of her father, the police, and anyone "who wants to take my babies away." Joan is a Christian who believes that abortion is morally wrong because taking the life of an unborn child is a violation of God's love and will. As a Christian she is also aware of her responsibility to love Sally Ann and her father with the love of Jesus Christ. What is Joan's responsibility in this situation and to whom? What ethical dilemmas are present here? What rights and professional obligations are involved in assessing and planning treatment? If you were a member of the mental health team at Local, what would your recommendations be and why?

3

James A. Knight
Deborah A. Rosen

Ethical and Value Issues Encountered in Liaison Psychiatry

James A. Knight, M.D., B.D., M.P.H., is a professor of psychiatry at Louisiana State University, School of Medicine in New Orleans. Major teaching experience includes teaching in general psychiatry and in medical ethics. He serves on several editorial boards and has authored numerous articles dealing with the subjects of psychiatry, ethics, and religion. Dr. Knight is the author of many books, the more recent being, *Medical Student: Doctor in the Making* and *Doctor-To-Be: Coping with the Trials and Triumphs of Medical School*. Dr. Knight served as President for the Society of Health and Human Values (1983-1984) and has served as a United States Navy chaplain.

Deborah A. Rosen, Ph.D., holds appointments as an associate professor of philosophy at the University of New Orleans, and as a clinical associate professor of medical ethics in the Department of Psychiatry, Louisiana State University. She has presented numerous papers and has authored a variety of articles in philosophy.

Drs. Knight and Rosen explore liaison psychiatry within today's medical context. They discuss this role in relation to the other members of the health care team and emphasize a collaborative approach towards client care. Ethical issues and questions arising out of this role are cited and examined in several case studies.

ETHICS IN MENTAL HEALTH PRACTICE
ISBN 0-8089-1738-2

In perhaps no previous time in the history of medicine has there been such a pronounced need for health care professionals to be trained in ethical and value issues. Medicine is emerging as an increasingly effective science in a highly technological age. Consequently, the growth and future prospects of medicine will be enormously challenged to preserve the physician's personal role in patient care or to provide an equivalent substitute using a cooperative team of health care professionals. Having a conceptual grasp on the value dimensions of medical care, particularly in light of recent and foreseeable changes in health care, will be an enormous challenge for the physician. As Lewis Thomas sees it, medicine is becoming less the laying on of hands and more the reading of complex signals from machines. Thomas writes that if he were a beginning medical student or intern, he would be most concerned about this aspect:

> I would be apprehensive that my real job, care for sick people, might soon be taken away, leaving me with a quite different occupation of looking after machines. I would be trying to figure out ways of keeping this from happening.[1]

Liaison psychiatry can and does play an important role in preserving that ancient expectation that the caregiver be intimately concerned with the patient as a person. Liaison psychiatry is also in many ways uniquely placed to perceive and articulate broadly the patients' medical concerns in a perspective that will be helpful to the patient, the patient's family, and to the network of medical persons responsible for the patient's care. Also, as is often emphasized, liaison psychiatry transmits a framework or viewpoint for integrating psychological, social, biological, and ethical dimensions in the care of patients. In today's complex medical environment, unless this integration takes place, there will be no humanistic care.

THE ROLE OF LIAISON PSYCHIATRY

Liaison psychiatry is a rapidly growing branch of medicine and psychiatry that has emerged from the need to employ the psychiatrist's specialized training and skills in all areas of patient care, in the training of medical personnel to understand the psychological stresses of illnesss and hospitalization on patient and staff, and in the building of effective networks of communication among health care personnnel, administration, and patients. The liaison psychiatrist is particularly well-suited to understand the reactions of patients and their families to medical and surgical illness. The reactions that people have to illness and to the hospital or clinical environment may vary from the mundane to the unusual. Whether "normal" or "abnormal," these reactions often require interpretation or treatment. Optimal patient care requires comprehensive and humanistic treatment of all the patient's needs, social and personal as well as biological, and an understanding of these parameters by all the patient's caregivers.[2]

Ethical and value concerns occur sharply in medical contexts, and these can be given focus by the comprehensive approach of the liaison psychiatrist. The liaison psychiatrist must have a close working alliance with that branch of philosophy known as medical ethics, as well as the opportunity for interaction and consultation with academic medical ethicists. These ethicists, trained in the newest branch of philosophy, are ready and eager to learn from and consult with liaison psychiatrists on the ethical dimensions of optimal patient care and medical education. Moreover, the burgeoning philosophical literature in medical ethics will help in providing a conceptual framework for systematic understanding and application of value concerns.

The collaborative work of the liaison psychiatrist may involve a wide range of persons, all involved in the treatment and care of the patient. There are, for example, colleagues of the psychiatrist, usually untrained in psychiatry, who might wish to take advantage of the liaison psychiatrist's special knowledge and skill in understanding the patient's emotional and behavioral responses to the stresses of illness. The liaison psychiatrist thus is specially situated to extend his or her skills, not only to the patient, but to this larger network of health care personnel, including the administrative staff, who might wish to understand better and more comprehensively the patient's efforts to get well, or indeed not to get well, and generally to cope with illness in an unfamiliar setting. The liaison psychiatrist might well be involved in consultation with others, regarding the following: (1) the patient's efforts and those of the patient's family to cope with the concepts and reality of illness, debilitation, and fatigue; (2) the threat to the patient from loss of income, loss of control over one's body, loss of one's life patterns, separation from loved ones, and inability to take care of one's obligations; (3) the fear of death and dismemberment, and at times, fear of loss of love and approval; (4) guilt, often over being ill; (5) intimidation by medical authorities and by other persons who may be strangers but who control the therapeutic program and the environment; (6) new and complicated technology; and other factors that the patient and the patient's family often find mysterious, threatening, or enervating.[2] The liaison psychiatrist can help the therapeutic team, the patient, and the patient's family to understand the patient's illness, the hospital milieu, and other factors that affect the patient's understanding and progress. The liaison psychiatrist works not just with the patient and the patient's family but is often a mediator between them and the therapeutic team and, where helpful, the hospital administration as well. In much of this activity, ethical and value issues are at the forefront.

Liaison psychiatry also helps in building valuable alliances among the caregivers. Such alliances are of great value. In bringing together, in an effective fashion, those who furnish direct or indirect care to patients, and by enlisting their support, the liaison psychiatrist can often bring out postitive changes in patient care. The liaison psychiatrist's work also can create a hospital milieu that better reflects a responsiveness to the broad range of patient needs and concerns: psychological, social, biological, and ethical. Where ethical problems and questions surface, or ought to surface, the trained and sensitive liaison psychiatrist is well-situated to address effectively these value concerns as well as biopsychosocial concerns. The liaison psychiatrist can help the caretakers not to depersonalize, or disassociate from, the patient or the patient's illness beyond that necessary for the optimal performance of one's duties in bringing about the patient's recovery and relief from suffering. Even where the patient cannot be cured or where suffering can only partly be mitigated, the caretaker can always provide a comforting and reassuring milieu that keeps the patient at the epicenter of concern.

The viewpoint of liaison psychiatry, as one would expect, is holistic. It accepts a model of health that is broadly comprehensive: a biopsychosocial model. The acceptance of this model of patient care is part of the mission of liaision psychiatry. With the growing acceptance of this model in the hospital, the focus of concern is shifting from the disease to the person. As a natural consequence, the health professional's work becomes person-oriented and not disease or illness-oriented.

In the milieu in which the liaison psychiatrist works and indeed helps to create, ethical questions and issues tend to get sharp and frequent exposure. Value concerns are often the focus of discussion with the patient, the patient's family, the health care personnnel, and the hospital policy-makers. When an ethical issue exists in the context of the clinical situation, it deserves swift and accurate recognition. A trained resource person can help in the recognition and resolution. Because of psychiatry's long involvement in ethical and value issues related to patient care, the liaison psychiatrist is frequently the one who will be consulted on these issues.[3] The liaison psychiatrist often finds it helpful to bring to the clinical situation, for dialogue, a philosopher who specializes in medical ethics or a hospital chaplain trained in biomedical ethics to aid as a resource person.

A preliminary example of the kind of ethical issue that might arise in the hospital setting will underscore the usefulness of having at hand a trained and skillful resource person. Informed consent can be a complicated matter, involving medical, legal, and ethical dimensions. One has to give information and options in a language the patient will understand. One might well ask the advice of the liaison psychiatrist as to whether less is more in terms of the benefits to a particular patient and whether and how the patient and family may already be subjected to information overload. In such a situation, the liaison psychiatrist can help to satisfy the ethical imperative, as enunciated recently by the President's Commission for the Study of Ethical Problems in Medicine, to give the capable patient all the information relevant by "doctors of broadly humane sympathies who are both committed to and skilled in communication with patients."[4] The chairperson of the President's Commission, a lawyer, is himself a leukemia patient. Thus, under chairman Morris Abrams' direction, the Commission helped to crystalize the nation's concern for providing patient care unequaled in excellency at a cost that is not excessive and with a sensitivity to the value issues in the vital relationship of the patient and the practitioner.[5]

CASE STUDIES

In teaching hospitals such as Charity of New Orleans, a large city-state facility with services in all the specialties, liaison psychiatry is organized in such a way that it is readily available for consultation and interaction. Ethical and value-related problems, as well as psychiatric matters of a more routine nature, become the daily work of the liaison psychiatrist. Often the ethical and value-oriented problems furnish the greatest challenge for the liaison psychiatrist and offer opportunities for in-depth interaction with colleagues and patients in the resolution of these problems and in finding solutions that protect the largest number of defensible values.

To illustrate the variety of clinical situations encountered and to give a broad sample of the kind of ethical issues that might arise, several case vignettes will be given. The cases show some of the value questions that need to be raised in order to find a solution that will satisfy. It is impressive how many ethical problems in hospital cases relate to autonomy versus paternalism, competence, informed consent, control, treatment refusal, dignity, "bad" versus "good" patients, withholding treatment from the terminally ill, and disclosing unwelcome information.

Case Study 1: 55-year-old Refusing a Potentially Life-saving Operation

The patient came to the hospital because of a growth in his mouth. He was found to have a malignant tumor of the soft palate and tonsillar area of the mouth and throat. Surgeons informed him of the nature of the tumor, their recommendation of a surgical procedure involving a radical neck dissection and probably radiation therapy after the surgical procedure. The patient was told that his condition was serious but not without hope. It was possible to bring the tumor under complete control, but if that did not turn out to be true, then the time he had left would be made more comfortable by the treatment prescribed. If he received no treatment the physicians predicted continued growth of the tumor, and, in time, marked interference with the patient's respiration, food and fluid intake, swallowing, and speech.

The patient listened attentively to the treatment plan, was given an opportunity to ask questions, and was checked to see if he understood what would be done and the expected consequences, both with and without surgical intervention. The patient refused the treatment plan in totality and said that he understood what was recommended but that he preferred to take his chances and receive no treatment. The picturing of a grim and dismal prognosis did not change the patient's mind.

The surgical staff requested that the liaison psychiatrist evaluate the patient and the situation. They felt that the patient had to be emotionally disturbed, and, in fact, implied that the patient had to be "crazy" to refuse treatment when he was clearly informed of the consequences.

In the evaluation of the patient and situation, a critical question related to the patient's psychological competence. A careful examination showed that the patient's decision-making competency was intact. He was oriented in all spheres, had good recent and remote recall, and evidenced no confusion in any area of his life. The quality of the patient-professional relationship was explored, and the patient gave all indication of being on excellent terms with doctors and nurses. Also, the patient expressed no dissatisfaction with the hospital and its overall care of him.

It was difficult for the surgeons to accept the liaison psychiatrist's evaluation that the patient was psychologically competent. They felt that the patient's decision to refuse treatment was an unreasonable, irrational act. The life-and-death situation, they contended, imposed enough stress on him to interfere profoundly with the requisite mental and emotional stability to make an informed choice. They went on to say that in refusing treatment and leaving the hospital, the patient would be back soon with far advanced cancer, and they would be the ones to take care of the patient with massive feeding and breathing problems. The patient held firmly to his decision in spite of efforts to listen, guide, and persuade.

The patient's autonomy, his right to make decisions about himself, had to be respected. He had a right to refuse treatment, a right grounded in sound ethical principles, as well as rooted in both constitutional and common-law principles. Kant, for example, argued that a rational person should be autonomously self-regulating. He expressed his view of the centrality of autonomy when he stated that freedom is autonomy meaning "the property of the will to be a law in itself."[6]

Of course, the loophole in the right to refuse treatment is that the patient must be competent: capable of making an informed decision. Questions may surface about competency, and disagreements may arise. In this case, the surgeons doubted the patient's competence and found it difficult to accept the liaison psychiatrist's clinical judgment that the patient was psychologically competent. The courts at times wrestle with the same issue. For example, in 1966, in a case in Washington, D.C., the court put forth a competency test: "Can the patient understand the situation, the risks, and the alternatives? It does not matter whether the patient's choice is rational or not, as long as the patient is able to make a decision."[7]

Of course, such a court decision raises questions about the nature of competency and rationality. An important point, however, is that in ascertaining whether or not a patient is competent one must remember that it does not matter whether the patient chooses as *we* would choose in a particular situation, or whether the patient would choose as we would like the patient to choose. Whether we consider the patient's choice to be a rational one in the circumstances is not the issue, but it still philosophically may be requisite that the patient's decision from the *patient's* own framework be rational in order to be competent.

To take the matter of rationality a step further, one should remember that "rational" and "irrational" are terms used as attributes of the decisions made by patients. An irrational decision is one based on an irrational *belief*, such as a patient not believing he or she has cancer in spite of overwhelming evidence or on an irrational *desire*, such as a patient preferring to die rather than have a gangrenous foot amputated, but can give no reason for that choice. Irrational desires may include the desire to die, to suffer pain, to be disabled, or to be deprived of freedom. The crux of the matter is that it is not always irrational to desire these things, but it is irrational to desire them *without* some adequate reason.

Further discussion about competency is indicated at this point. In many situations it is difficult to determine whether the patient is competent or incompetent, in a general or specific sense. Ethical or legal issues impinge on each such determination. Some guidelines include four areas that need exploration: (1) Does the patient understand the condition for which the treatment is proposed? (2) Does the patient understand the nature and purpose of the treatment? (3) Does the patient understand the risks and benefits involved in undergoing the treatment, including the effects? (4) Does the patient understand the consequences (risks and benefits) of alternative forms of treatment or of *not* undergoing any treatment at all?[8] Other guidelines are similar, but often contain some additions. For example, Gutheil and Appelbaum urge a careful examination of the patient's use of rational processes for arriving at a decision. This would include the basic components of the mental status examination -- orientation, memory, intellectual functioning, judgment, impairments of rationality (delusional thinking, hallucinations), and mood alterations.[9] Further, they emphasize that spurious indicators of possible incompetency must not be overlooked such as the psychodynamic factors involving deep fears that invoke emotional defenses, for example, when a patient faces a serious operation involving cancer or situational factors such as conflicts and misunderstandings between the patient and doctor. No stone was left unturned in evaluating this particular patient. At the same time, while it was the liaison psychiatrist's clinical judgment that the patient was competent, not all the members of the health care team, especially the surgeons, shared that judgment. Of course, there is a strong societal and health professional bias in favor of treating treatable patients, and such biases can easily influence one's clinical judgment about competence. Treatment refusal in patients such as the case under discussion here can easily become tantamount with incompetency.

Respecting the patient's right to refuse treatment may demonstrate a sensitivity toward personal interest in bodily integrity and self-determination. The patient's refusal may not be a callousness toward life, as is often assumed. Yet, the question continues to emerge: "Do a patient's rights include a right intentionally to allow oneself to die?" Some have compared such a course of action to a form of suicide.

Another question relates to the equity of those other than the patient, the protection of innocent third parties, for example, children. It is rare that a person exists alone; but rather, as a human being one exists in mutual relationships of responsibility and in an arena of care and concern. This particular patient had no immediate family, and he felt that he was a free agent in deciding his course of action. In fact, the great libertarian John Stuart Mill believed that coercion was justified only on the grounds of preventing harm to others: "[The person's] own good, either physical or moral, is not a sufficient warrant."[10]

While this patient's refusal to accept life-saving therapy was not interfered with, many on the hospital staff felt that this should have been otherwise. Their arguments centered on one or another of these points. Some regarded a refusal of life-saving treatment as clearly unreasonable, even if competently decided. Further, they argued that the state has a "compelling interest" in preventing this patient's death. Others took a strong paternalistic position: the competent adult person's liberty of choice should be limited for his or her own good in order to prevent harm from befalling the person.[11] The argument that most of the patient's physicians put forth challenged the patient's refusal on the grounds that a patient in a life-or-death situation, by that very fact, does not possess the requisite mental or emotional stability to make an informed choice. To put the issue another way, they were taking the view that the patient's autonomy was impaired by his illness and his reactions to the illness. As Ackerman would express it, the issue in a more general sense relates to the components in a patient's illness that can involve serious constraints to his autonomous behavior.[12]

The question remains: why did this patient refuse treatment? What reasons did he give for refusing treatment? He saw the operation as mutilation, as causing considerable disfigurement of his face and neck. He abhorred the thought of that. At some level, he seemed to think that the doctors were wrong in their diagnosis and that "the thing" that was happening to him would pass away of its own accord. He never articulated this openly but implied it. Thus, one has to raise the question of how denial was operating in this patient, and how much of a factor it was in the patient's refusal of treatment.

There is another important problem raised by the patient's view of the proposed operation as a mutilation. He saw this mutilation of his body as so disfiguring that he would have us believe that he chose to die rather than to submit. Some saw the patient's professed choice as sufficient grounds in itself to doubt the patient's competency to reason clearly and rationally about his situation. Who would want to die rather than lose part of his neck? Is it not possible that the patient saw his dignity, among other things, to be at stake?

The question of dignity is an important one in the medical context. Whether and to what extent the patient's dignity is involved in a situation would have to be determined on a case by case basis. In this case, we would want to rule out on empirical grounds the possibility that the patient was depressed or suicidal and did not mean what he said at that time. Here the choice of death to the disfiguring operation remained the patient's stated choice on what appeared to be full reflection while fully informed, absent for the sake of clarification the question of denial. The liaison psychiatrist might use the concept of dignity as part of the analysis of the situation.

The question of the patient's dignity can be approached in many different ways, and can be expected to affect people differently. The patient's sense of dignity can also be expected to be closely involved with the patient's sense of self-respect and self-esteem, and also with the patient's self-concept. It is helpful to see the patient as having a sense of dignity as a person and also a sense of dignity as a particular sort of person.

A person's self-concept and self-respect could include, as an essential part, physical characteristics and bodily continuity. In the breast mastectomy patient, for example, the loss of bodily integrity and of perceived sexual attractiveness may be an enormously important assault on the patient's self-concept. In dermatology, one sees patients whose concern with dignity lies much deeper than the notion of cosmetic improvement would suggest. Some women patients who present with nodular port-wine hemangiomas on the facial areas, and sometimes with unilateral hypertrophic scarring of the lips, wear large hats and heavy pancake make-up, avoid socialization, and are immensely threatened by ordinary social interaction. Recognizing the difficulties that such patients have may be helpful in the case study under discussion. One's neck is close to one's face, ordinarily immediately visible to others, and one's initial front to the world. Furthermore, the neck is connected to one of our most human of functions: speech. It is the sounding instrument with which we express some aspects of our deepest human nature. In counseling the patient contemplating radical neck surgery one must be aware of the patient's spoken and unspoken concerns.

A patient also has dignity as a *particular* sort of person. Many patients have a modesty or sense of privacy that is assailed when they are inappropriately draped or undraped. Some patients are finding it increasingly difficult to address their physician as Dr. So-and-So when the physician addresses them on a first name basis. Self-concept in terms of one's profession or role may be involved in one's sense of dignity. An operation likely to affect one's ability to perform competitively would be enormously threatening to the athlete whose self-identity is tied to sports performance. A premenopausal childless woman facing a hysterectomy has to contend with the loss of her identity as a future mother. A young male facing an operation that might affect his future sexual performance or potency could well feel immensely threatened as a father and as a sexual partner. Perhaps in this case study the 55-year-old man so consistently ruled out radical neck dissection because he saw it as a mutilation of his self-concept as much as of his body. The physician should proceed with the utmost caution here. One would never expect consent for such radical surgery to be easy. And where life itself is at stake, one would expect in the normal circumstance that the person would eventually choose life, although painfully and reluctantly.

To act with dignity is not merely to act sedately. It is more than behaving with formality, bravado, or calm reassurance. Each patient is fully human and individually demarcated from all others. Beneath the posturing there lies the intricate individualized self-concept. The liaison psychiatrist will quite often and for many reasons wish to explore the patient's self-concept and sense of dignity. The patient will want throughout to be treated by others respectfully and with taste and sensitivity. The role of the physician as the healer has been treated with the greatest dignity throughout history. The patient, sentient and wounded, deserves to be treated with equal dignity and respect.

To treat a patient with dignity is not a matter of sentimentality or reciprocity. It is one way of bridging the distance between oneself and another human being. It is a way of acknowledging the patient's status as a person entitled to respect and courtesy. Further, it is a way of saying that the patient is not merely "a case." Whatever distance may be necessary in an individual case to allow the health personnel to operate effectively and professionally, the right distance is always the one that preserves, to the maximum extent possible, the patient's inherent dignity.

Case Study 2: Throwing a "Bad" Patient Out of the Hospital

A 30-year-old white male was admitted to the oral surgery service with a broken jaw that had become infected. Several days before admission the patient had been in a fight and sustained an injury to the jaw. He neglected getting treatment until he began to have a fever and to feel ill. At that point he checked into the hospital.

The staff of oral surgery stabilized the patient's broken jaw with a formidable array of steel pins and braces and began intravenous antibiotic therapy. The patient was put in a somewhat isolated ward in that it was at the end of a hall where only a few other patients were housed. At night no nurse remained continuously at the nurse's station but came to the ward in answer to a patient's call.

One night the patient pushed the call button for a nurse, and fairly quickly a nurse appeared at his bedside. Without saying a word he reached over, grabbed her, and lifted her into bed with him while managing to strip off part of her clothes. The nurse was surprised by the patient's actions and took a few moments to realize that she was being sexually assaulted. After realizing what was happening, she wrenched herself from his clutches and ran from the ward. She reported the incident to the nursing service. The nursing service decided that its nurses would not care for this patient and requested the hospital administration to discharge the patient (actually dismiss him). Otherwise, the nurses would not set foot on the ward where the patient was located.

The oral surgeons were distraught by the nursing service's request to the hospital administration and the administration's willingness to have the patient discharged. They were afraid the patient would not survive if he were thrown out of the hospital because of the patient's serious infection and continued need for intravenous antibiotic therapy. Although they could understand the nursing staff's position, they felt that there were other options better than the course of action decided upon by the nursing staff and hospital administration. They asked for a consultation from liaison psychiatry to have the patient evaluated psychologically and to explore the ethical and psychosocial issues related to the patient's care.

At the time of the psychiatric evaluation, the mental status examination revealed some instability in the patient in that he was subject to confusional states probably related in part to his elevated temperature and some metabolic derangements. Particularly at night he was likely to become confused. On the night of his aggressive sexual behavior toward the nurse, he had witnessed a young woman dressed in white (whom he thought was a nurse) visit a male patient on the other side of the ward. Because the curtains were only partially drawn around the bed, the patient saw them embracing and fondling one another. He did not know this woman in white was the man's wife. He thought she was a nurse and expressed later the recollection that he had been pleased to see "a nurse" involved in this kind of activity in the hospital. He then pushed the call button for a nurse and when she appeared he made his move.

In seeking an acceptable course of action to take with the patient, many ethical and value questions were raised. The privacy and safety of the nurse had been violated as well as her rights as a person. She wondered, however, if she were abandoning the patient in her decision not to go back on the ward and care for that patient as well as the other patients there. Questions were raised about whether a patient should ever be put out of a hospital for disruptive behavior before every means of controlling that behavior are tried, especially if the patient's survival would be put at risk. At the same time, does not a hospital have an obligation to maintain a safe and respectable environment for the staff? Whose rights take priority in a hospital: those of the patient or those of the staff? Should not the patient be first? The doctors tending this patient could not see ethically any course of action but to treat, protect, and care for the patient. Thus, they wanted the patient retained on the oral surgery service and the hospital order for the patient's discharge cancelled or disregarded.

The liaison psychiatrist was confronted with the task of leading the health professionals involved to accept a solution that protected the largest number of defensible values. The patient on evaluation was found to be marginally competent psychologically. His toxic state, probably caused by his fever and electrolyte imbalance, was most likely a major contributing factor to his behavior. A review of his personal and medical history and long-term functioning identified characteristics compatible with the diagnosis of borderline personality disorder. A patient with such a diagnosis often exhibits sociopathic behavior and is much more likely to be a management problem than the usual hospital patient.

The patient was told about the possibility of his discharge and efforts to find other alternatives. He was confronted strongly with what was expected of him and the consequences if he did not comply. Three proposals had been made: (1) transfer the patient from the oral surgery service to the psychiatry service, with the oral surgeons caring for him while he was on the psychiatry service; (2) place the patient in restraints and keep him on the ward of the oral surgery service; (3) give the patient tranquilizer medication in sufficient quantity to keep him under physical control. The patient had no objection to any of these proposals and said he would accept them voluntarily at any time the staff felt they were indicated. A verbal contract or covenant was entered into by all parties concerned with the patient that none of the options would be carried out now. The patient would remain in his present location in the hospital. The nurses would continue to care for the patient, and the hospital would withdraw the order to discharge. If adverse changes took place in the patient's behavior or reality testing, then one or more of the plans would be carried out immediately. The patient remained a model patient and recovered. He fulfilled the duties of a patient as emphasized by Talcott Parsons. He maintained a strong desire to get well and he cooperated with the prescribed treatment regimen.[13]

At one stage in his treatment, after he attacked the nurse, he was threatened and coerced in response to his hospital behavior and to some extent dehumanized. The rights and responsibilities of the patient, the hospital, and the health professionals were in conflict. The resolution of these conflicts may have required some compromise, but in the long run the patient's health was protected. In a general sense, one can say that a utilitarian view was taken where defensible competing values were added up and attempts were made to optimize the maximum number of those principles that can be satisfied in this situation.

Case Study 3: The 9-year-old
Asserting His Autonomy

This young person had a malignancy and was being treated in the hospital with a drug that he received every two weeks intramuscularly. However, he announced that he did not want any more "shots" or any other kind of treatment. The physicians and nurses were not successful in discovering what the young man considered wrong with his treatment, but they did notice that he was depressed and seemed to want to give up. They submitted a request to the consultation-liaison service for help in evaluating the situation and preventing the therapy of this young man from being derailed. They wanted the patient's cooperation and consent although the parents had given consent and wanted treatment to continue.

The liaison psychiatrist spent some time with the patient and found him open, psychologically clear, and remarkably articulate for his age. He stated his situation openly. After receiving an injection he felt nauseated for several days. Then for a few days he felt well and could play and enjoy himself. Then he was due the next injection with its accompanying nausea. In thinking about his situation, he decided it was not worthwhile to have only a few good days every two weeks, so why not stop the medication and take his chances? That much he expressed openly, but other concerns were half-hidden and emerged slowly.

He was afraid he was going to die and wondered if he was being punished for something he had done or failed to do. Also, he was angry because he was being cheated out of many of the good things in which children his age are involved -- play, peers, planning for the future. He had doubts about the effectiveness of the "shots" and wondered if they would make a difference in how long he lived. Thus, why put up with the extra suffering? Further, he expressed indirectly the feeling that his doctors were displeased with him because he was not getting well and responding better to the treatment. He expressed his fear of losing control by asking if he would become sicker, soil the bed, and be mentally confused.[14]

When a patient does not respond to a prescribed treatment regimen that is expected to work, doctors often feel deskilled and impotent. Overt or covert hostility may be shown the patient, and problems develop in the doctor-patient relationship. This was happening to some extent with this patient and became a contributing factor in the patient's refusal of treatment. Another factor was the patient's inability to control the malignancy and maintain a sense of autonomy and self-determination in his life. Although he could not control the cancer, he could control the doctors. Thus, the treatment refusal brought an increased sense of competency and control.

A few sessions with the patient and the staff clarified some issues and expedited the treatment process. Although a minor, this patient deserved to be treated as a person and not a thing. Despite his age, he was made a partner in decision-making. Effective treatment would require his participation, commitment, and search for health. Thus, it was necessary to blend the patient's autonomy with the doctor's obligation to act on behalf of the patient.

The patient agreed to continue with the treatment because "his mother wanted him to continue." Important to him was the fact that his mother did not want to give up. The persistence for treatment on the part of doctors, nurses, and parents may have provided a constancy of care and neutralized any fear of abandonment. He was helped with his fear of losing control by utilizing a way of giving control back to him. Rather than being told what doctor wants or mother wants he was asked "What do you, the patient, want -- when, from whom, and in what circumstances?"

One cannot help raising the question that if the patient had continued to refuse therapy, would his refusal have been overridden? Probably yes, because of his age and the nature of his malignancy. Some of the hospital staff, early in the crisis of the patient's refusal, had reservations about letting a 9-year-old be a partner in deciding what was in his best interest. Moreover, they suggested that probably the patient's illness prevented him from being capable of acting autonomously, with due consideration of his age.

The issue of autonomy versus paternalism arises in many varied but common situations. It is helpful to review the issues involved. To be paternalistic involves interfering with another person's liberty of action, but not because it may bring harm to others. Strictly speaking, being paternalistic is to act coercively for the agent's own good; that is, for reasons referring exclusively to the agent's own well-being. It is an ethical dilemma quite simply because it involves interference with another's freedom by coercion if necessary. It is defended on grounds that the agent's own good is the goal of action.[15] This was, for example, the reason given for original legislation requiring motorcyclists to wear safety helmets, for laws making suicide a criminal offense, for forbidding dueling, for regulating sexual conduct, and for compulsory schooling.[15] It is the reason most people give for demanding of their children that they wear seat belts and not smoke. It is for their own good and not the good of others that we act paternalistically for another, and, even there, we would do so with the least possible restriction to their liberty and autonomy that still would accomplish the desired goal.[*,15]

On the other hand, to be autonomous is to act as one chooses regardless of what others want or demand. It is, as the Greek derivation suggests and as Kant has made clear, to rule oneself. It is to act as one believes best from one's own frame of reference, to be independent, and, as Gerald Dworkin puts it, to do one's own thing.[16] In acting paternalistically, one does deprive the other person of his or her autonomy. Thus, the two moral principles of autonomy and paternalism come into natural conflict.

It is reasonable to suppose that health is so widely recognized as a good that a rational person would want always to pursue it; but the pursuit of health is often neither easy nor simple. The case study of the apparently thoughtful 9-year-old refusing medication shows that a patient will not always agree to promote what is in the best interest of health, as some other person construes it, even if the other person is one's physician. Further, there are competing goods. Especially and most vividly in the health care context, someone might choose some other value over health and indeed over life itself. A Jehovah's Witness might well refuse a life-sustaining blood transfusion. Of course, the liaison psychiatrist or other caregiver will want to be sure the patient does indeed know and appreciate the risks involved and is competent to assess the situation. Part of the reason for informed consent and truth-telling in medicine is to set down the conditions that made possible the maximum yielding to the patient's autonomy in the normal circumstance.

While the health context should optimize patient autonomy, certainly questions of paternalism will remain. There will be cases where the physician will arguably have to intervene: where the patient cannot act rationally, where the patient is comatose or drugged, or where the patient cannot satisfactorily understand his or her medical condition. If one wishes fully to respect the patient's autonomy, the most helpful guideline is to ask the question: what would the patient have preferred had he or she been rational, conscious, and competently informed? The question, if one leans toward paternalism, is: what is in the best interests of this patient whether or not the patient agrees with the assessment? The liaison psychiatrist may be called in to decide for individual cases what would be the best way to maximize the desirable values in the circumstance.

Two final comments about paternalistic action are in order. Briefly, the first is this: intervention always overrides someone's autonomous decision (the patient's own decision or perhaps the decision of the patient's family where the patient is a

---

*Dworkin calls this the principle of the least restrictive alternative: accomplishing the desired end with the least restriction of liberty.

damaged neonate, for example). At the same time, intervention may also preserve other rights or values (the patient's alleged right to life, for example, or the patient's alleged right to a minimal standard of health care). The second comment is this: whenever we intervene, if always for another's good and not our own, we explicitly acknowledge the importance of that person and the importance of our relationship to that person. Our willingness to act in and on another's behalf can and should be an act of love. It is quite natural and loving to act vigorously in behalf of another human being. One of the great problems of pacifism is that pacifists cannot consistently intervene or act to defend innocent loved ones.[17] Yet, to the extent that a patient's autonomy is the value to be preserved, the physician's paternalistic interest in the patient must be held in check or balanced by other considerations.

Case Study 4: The 14-year-old
with a Bicornuate Uterus

A 14-year-old girl was hospitalized on the obstetrics-gynecology service for problems related to menstrual pain and a palpable mass in the uterus. She usually suffered with severe pain during menstrual periods. Her mother reported that she believed her daughter to be sexually active and was afraid that she would become pregnant. The situation was further complicated by the fact that the daughter was severely retarded. She seldom spoke a complete sentence, only words and phrases. She played with simple toys and seemed happy most of the time. She could, however, easily cry or laugh and alternated quickly from one mood to the other. She related poorly and showed little understanding of anything. Physically she was well-developed, attractive, and appeared her stated age.

On examination, she was found to have a bicornuate uterus. In the horns, or bifurcations of the uterus, menstrual blood was being trapped. Emptying was interfered with because of the anatomical abnormality. The physicians caring for her had some grave concerns. Her symptoms of pain would recur on each menstrual period because of the deformed structure of the uterus. If she became pregnant, the uterus or that part of it that contained the fetus could rupture readily and perhaps early in the pregnancy. With her limited ways of communicating, such a rupture could result in her death if not addressed surgically right away. Further, it was obvious to her physicians that she could not care for and could abuse a baby, if only by neglect. The physicians caring for her felt that a reasonable solution to her problems would be a hysterectomy -- removal of the deformed uterus. They were aware that she was only 14-years-old and severely retarded. Yet, any other course of action would not solve fully the patient's medical problems.

The patient's mother had some reservations about the hysterectomy. Her daughter was young, and one so young should not lose organs of the body, if it could be helped. Also, the mother hoped that her daughter's mind would improve and then she would be better able to cope with herself and possibly be able to take care of a baby. Her wish, of course, was not realistic and at some level of her thinking she realized that her daughter's mental status would change little over the years.

Many value issues emerge in this case. The patient is psychologically incompetent or mentally incapacitated because of severe mental retardation. Also, she is a minor and sexually active. How can she be protected from sexual exploitation? Since the hysterectomy is medically indicated and possibly could be life-saving, should not that be the primary concern of all? Should a less restrictive option be used with this patient, an option such as sterilization or a birth control device such as an IUD? Will a hysterectomy cause a change in body image or be viewed by the patient as mutilation in later life? Further, will the chosen procedure protect and serve this mentally retarded minor rather than society, the parents, or the caregivers? A number of issues were at stake in the mother's reluctance to consent to her daughter's hysterectomy. The mother wanted to do what was right for her daughter and properly exercise her obligations as a parent. She was aware of the aspirations of a parent for a child to have a future family. She recognized the difficulty of being objective when her own child was involved.

The mother consented to her daughter's hysterectomy when she was shown that it was probably the best option for protecting the health and well-being of her daughter. The physicians recognized in this patient two sets of questions: one concerned technical issues and the other concerned the value dimensions. The liaison psychiatrist was able to open a number of these issues to discussion. Although no option could protect all the values at stake, the final decision did seem to offer the most ethical and practical alternative.

Case Study 5: A Prospective Kidney Donor with a History of Mental Illness

A 40-year-old woman volunteered to give her 38-year-old brother a kidney for transplantation. The brother was in renal failure and a good candidate for a transplant. He wanted a kidney transplant from a living donor such as his sister and could not bear the thought of a donation from an unknown source such as an accident victim. His sister was a good match and willing and available to donate the kidney. In fact she was the only one in the family who was histocompatible with the patient.

Fifteen years earlier the sister had had a mental breakdown and was placed in a state psychiatric hospital. After a few months there she recovered and was discharged. Since then she had done well with no subsequent breakdowns. The physicians were worried, however, about taking a kidney from a former mental patient. They asked if such a person could give valid and informed consent and whether the stress of the operation could or would precipitate another mental breakdown.

The psychiatric evaluation of this prospective donor did not reveal any present mental illness. There was no clinical evidence of any residual illness from her breakdown 15 years ago. Further, a study of her hospital record did not give a clear picture of whether she had had a schizophrenic disorder or an affective disorder, but the clinical evidence in the record pointed more to an affective disorder. This point of diagnosis was important because affective disorders carry a better prognosis than does schizophrenia. The fact that she had gone 15 years without a recurrence of the illness was another point in favor of the affective disorder diagnosis.

She genuinely wanted to give her brother a kidney, was clear in her motivation, and fully informed about all that was involved in taking and transferring the kidney. She insisted that she had a right to give the kidney and wanted her right honored.

The physicians on the transplant team found it necessary to give serious consideration to a general rule in transplant surgery. A previous history of significant mental or emotional instability is generally viewed as a contraindication to donating a kidney. Such a rule relates to whether a previous mental patient is now a free agent in decision-making. Can she give consent that is free, informed, and competent? Further, would such a patient be more vulnerable to pressure from the prospective recipient or family members to give the kidney? Under the best of circumstances, what kind of freedom does a family member have to refuse to give the kidney if she is the only available and eligible match in the family, as was the position of this person?

In the sessions held with the prospective donor, every effort was made to arrive at informed consent in the finest meaning of the term. No pressure to donate the kidney was identified from any person or from internal forces such as shame, guilt, or unrealistic feelings of indebtedness to her brother. Two physical risks were mentioned: the risk of the surgical procedure and the risk arising from the fact that the volunteer is sacrificing "a spare part" that one day may be needed. (Both risks are small.) As for psychological risks, one had to mention that the stress of the donation could be more burdensome to her because of her earlier mental problems. Other factors that were mentioned included the possibility of a reactive depression over "the loss" of a kidney, a possible change in body image or change in her relationship with the recipient. The possibility of rejection of the kidney by the recipient was discussed as a form of anticipatory guidance. At the same time, she was informed that the expectation of success was good and that all factors pointed toward success.

The easy solution in donation may be to reject all present or former mental patients. Would not this be ethically and morally wrong, for present and former mental patients have rights, and one of them may be to donate a kidney to a family member? This former mental patient did donate a kidney to her brother without any detectable ill effects, physically or psychologically. Also, as time passed after the donation, she gave the impression that her act of altruism was having far-reaching constructive effects on her life.

Case Study 6: The 18-year-old Paraplegic, 5 Months Pregnant

This patient, 5 months pregnant, recently sustained a gunshot wound to the spine that left her a paraplegic. She had two previous pregnancies that ended in spontaneous abortions because of an incompetent cervix. Her physicians believed that the fetus, because of its size, would soon give her respiratory difficulties because the patient was relying heavily upon her diaphragm to aid in breathing. Since there was a likelihood that she would not carry this pregnancy to term, why not abort the fetus now? On the other hand, suppose she did carry this pregnancy to term and deliver a viable baby? This could possibly be the only baby she would have, especially in light of her incompetent cervix and paraplegia. Further, should she not have a hysterectomy, for it would include the abortion and also protect against future pregnancies that medically are contraindicated for her?

The patient was a Roman Catholic and morally opposed to abortion unless her health or life were at stake. Discussion centered on both technical and value issues related to abortion or hysterectomy versus no surgical intervention. Some of the questions raised were: Whose rights have priority -- those of the mother or those of the fetus? Does the defenseless fetus need a champion or advocate in this case? Although the patient was not married, should the father of the fetus have any part in the patient's decision? Is a woman's alleged or arguable right to control her body the only right at stake?

This young woman was at a critical juncture in her life and decisions had to be made. She needed to understand all the options and to share in the decision-making. She was sick and under great stress. Could she understand the options open to her and consent to or refuse any or all of them? Was her psychological competence compromised or interfered with by the severe stresses impinging on her? The consultation request to liaison psychiatry from the obstetricians asked if "the patient is together psychologically, emotionally, and spiritually to the extent that she knows what problems exist and the choices in resolving these problems?" A thorough psychiatric evaluation indicated that she was "essentially together" and should be considered capable of giving informed consent and participating in decisions about herself.

In her circumstances, she considered herself in serious physical jeopardy and therefore would accept an abortion but not a hysterectomy. The course of action then decided on was to perform an abortion. Before any intervention took place, however, the patient developed a fever with a temperature elevation of 105° F, and aborted spontaneously.

Although the ethical questions were raised and discussed, there were no objections to the abortion and no strong insistence that the hysterectomy would serve better both the short- and long-term interests of the patient. All seemed relieved, however, that nature offered its own solution promptly and unceremoniously.

Several landmark philosophy papers have been helpful in setting up a conceptual framework in which to understand both the ethical issues involved in abortion and their seeming intractability. Judith Jarvis Thompson makes the point against the conservative position, as it is often framed, that it is not sufficient merely to point out that the fetus is a person and that to abort the fetus is to kill it, since not all killing even of persons is wrong.[†,18] So the personhood argument simply shifts the debate to whether killing a particular fetus would in that case be unjustifiable. Further, as Jane English argues against the liberal position as it is often stated, it is not sufficient to say a woman may do what she pleases with her body. Of course, you cannot do what you please with your body if it affects adversely other people's rights and interests. To take a simple case, I cannot stick my hand in your soup simply because it is alleged that I can do with my body what I like.

Moreover, it will not do for the liberal position simply to contend that the fetus is not a person, because you cannot do whatever you like to nonpersons.[19] As Peter Singer, among others, has made clear, even nonhuman animals have rights interests, needs, or a life of their own that entitles them to our moral concern.[§,20,21] The problem of abortion is an extraordinarily difficult one and the philosophical, moral, and human dilemmas complex. The liaison psychiatrist can expect to be called on to aid the patient and caretakers in making the best long-term decision in light of present laws and the multiple values both of society and the patient.

---

†Thompson is talking of the *moral* position on abortion. The *legal* position, in light of *Roe vs. Wade*, would arguably be altered if the fetus was held to be a person with all the rights given to persons under the Fourteenth Amendment.

§A good review of recent theories about who (and what) counts morally is given by Johnson E (1983). Treating the dirt: environmental ethics and moral theory. In Regan T (Ed): *Earthbound.* New York:Random House, pp 336-364

Case Study 7: The Elderly Patient and
Decisions about Resuscitation

Whether or not to resuscitate elderly, senescent patients and whether orders not to resuscitate should be written or should never be written are among the questions emerging almost daily in the large general hospital. A clinical case study described in *The Hastings Center Report* [22] and commented on by Carson and Seigler raises the ever-recurring issues in the care of elderly patients. Bringing into harmony what the family wants and what the patient probably would want may create for the mental health professional ethical dilemmas not easily resolved.

The patient was a retired 90-year-old senescent male who was admitted to the hospital with bronchial pneumonia, advanced pulmonary edema, urinary tract infection, and anemia. As his condition worsened, his wife asked the attending physician to do "everything possible." On the fourteenth day a nurse entered the patient's room and found him not breathing and with all vital signs absent. The doctor who was summoned decided not to attempt to resuscitate. The cause of death was recorded as ventricular fibrillation. The patient's physician had left instructions that a Code Blue not be called. A Code Blue call would have summoned staff members with portable defibrillators and other equipment to the bedside.

When questioned about the incident, the physician argued that "doing everything" for the patient did not, in his mind, include cardiopulmonary resuscitation. The physician also remarked that the patient was deliberately not sent to intensive care. The physician gave two reasons for this decision. One was that there was a shortage of beds there. The second reason was that the patient, in the opinion of the physician, did not seem to belong there since it was the physician's view that he was not acutely ill.

The patient's wife disagreed with this assessment and emphasized that the decision was against her express wishes. "Doing everything," she says, "is the difference between life and death. The doctor was playing God...."

A liaison psychiatrist should expect to be called in to help with the various ethical aspects of a case like this one. The liaison psychiatrist might function not only with the patient, family, and health-care staff but on the hospital ethics committee or review board to decide the hospital's policy on the conditions under which life-prolonging technologies should be routinely used. The particular problem of the right use of ordinary and "extraordinary" measures to prolong life will probably continue to be a sharp problem in the years ahead as medical technology and skills of physicians improve and proliferate. The public is already taking an active interest. There are states with "death with dignity" statutes. Also, there are many individuals preparing written documents, such as living wills, expressing their own wishes to be used, if necessary, to aid physicians and family with the intricate legal and moral matters involving the issue of when to allow the patient to die and how to make the death as "natural" as possible.

Many issues are involved here. One is whether the patient, to the extent that the patient's wishes can be determined, would have in the circumstances welcomed death. There are those who put the greatest amount of ethical weight on the principle that one should follow the patient's informed wishes when these are available. When they are not available, then to the extent that it can be determined what the patient would have wanted had he been capable of expressing his wishes is what should determine what is done. In *The Hastings Center Report* case study, the wife's opinion is that her husband would have wanted to live. While that opinion should be taken seriously and would ordinarily be the final arbiter, in the circumstance the physician might also have sought the opinions of other family members and possibly one or more close friends of the patient. With information from one's family and friends, the physician is in a better position to ascertain whether the patient had said or done things on former occasions that would be relevant to determining the patient's own view in the extremist circumstances.

A second issue, especially for family in the Roman Catholic tradition, is whether *extraordinary* aid is needed for the extremely elderly patient or for the patient who is terminally ill and irremediably and extensively brain damaged. Here many individuals draw the line on those measures that they consider extraordinary. Generally, antibiotics and intravenous fluids are not considered extraordinary. These would now typically be considered routine and normal procedures where indicated. Procedures like the following would generally not be done: placing a tube within the trachea for artificial respiration, electrocardiac shock, emergency placement of a pacemaker, etc. Some consider cardiopulmonary resuscitation to be more like an invasive procedure and less like the so-called ordinary procedure. For a family who wishes that extraordinary treatment not be given, it might be helpful to ascertain roughly where the line is for the Do Not Resuscitate (DNR) order. Where there is time and the case is confusing or complex, it is likely that the liaison psychiatrist will be called on for a consultation on the DNR order. At the least, the liaison psychiatrist can expect to consult closely with the primary physician on such matters.

It perhaps should be mentioned that there is no reason to believe that the physician in *The Hastings Center Report* case was acting in any way inconsistent with his belief as to what was in the best interest of the patient. The patient was in the sunset years of life. There was the possibility of irreversible brain damage. Also, there is the general question whether a patient at such an advanced age is less worthy of the resources of advanced health care, especially or perhaps only where those resources are scarce or prohibitively expensive. This problem will soon be particularly acute. Our population demographics indicate that there will be an enormous increase in the number of older people in the next few decades, and correspondingly the costs of maintaining life and the quality of life at advanced age may be extraordinarily high. The ethical dimension tends to be most evident where the hardest choices have to be made.

In this case study the physician acted against express wishes of an informed adult whom one would typically expect, as the significant other, to be able to speak on behalf of the patient. While this consideration has enormous weight, it will be important to be able to balance the weight of the patient's presumed preference with the medical-scientific reality of what could realistically be achieved for the patient and at what economic cost to the patient's family and to society. This will be a difficult balancing act. One would hope always to be able to yield to the patient's expressed or implied preferences. However, it is quite possible that realities will force harder and harder choices, and health professionals and hospitals will have to decide, in view of their actual resources, what they can and cannot do to maximize their health programs. The liaison psychiatrist can work with the hospital in helping establish ethical priorities and, among other things, determine the policy on CPR and other complicated or invasive procedures in cases where the person is of advanced age, has a poor prognosis, and is suffering acutely, or is severely and irreversibly brain damaged. Policies and procedures should probably be spelled out in detail and reviewed often.

Another issue involved in not resuscitating the severely ill, senescent patient deserves mention. The general public has probably a romanticized notion of so-called "natural death." The recent "right-to-die" and "death with dignity" movements have been particularly successful in educating the lay community that there are some extraordinarily hopeless medical conditions where efforts to prolong life may actually be inhumane and where the physician should be allowed legally and morally to let the patient die. This is known as passive euthanasia, and it is generally thought to be protected legally and morally by the competent patient's right to refuse medical treatment. Incompetent patients may have their wishes and interests expressed by proxy action of family members or guardians under court decisions like Quinlan and Saikewicz.[23,24] Some states have passed legislation to protect the physician's option to withhold treatment if the patient has executed an explicit directive when previously competent.

In these matters, the focus of discussion has generally been on ascertaining what the patient's own wishes would be in the face of irreversible terminal illness, the ethical responsibilities of the caregivers, and the legal protections of the physician and other caregivers. There is another side to this issue, however, that is hinted at by the etymology of the word euthanasia: a good or easy death. There is a general belief by the public that in letting a patient die "naturally," and in letting the patient forego artificial life-extension therapies, the patient's death will *ipso facto* be an easy, peaceful one where the patient slips from life to death with dignity. As Battin has recently underscored, most people have a stereotyped notion of the natural death as being pain-free and dignified.[25] The case of the 90-year-old who was not resuscitated does not bring out this ethical aspect sharply enough. This patient had a cardiac arrest and was not resuscitated. He was unconscious, without pain, and died within seconds. Other untreated deaths may not be so dignified. With untreated infections, there may be delirium, light-headedness, and interference with organ function. With kidney failure, there may be nausea, vomiting, gastrointestinal hemorrhage, neuromuscular twitching, and finally convulsions. Dying may take weeks. When patients or their proxies are considering the option of withholding artificial life-sustaining therapies, in order that their consent be competently and fully informed, they should be given a realistic picture of the kind of death to be expected. The patient or the patient's family could well be hoping for a quick and easy death when the only legally protected strategy, refusal of treatment, may not be an effective means to the desired end.

Liaison psychiatrists can thus expect ethical discussions to sharpen around the legally unprotected area of active euthanasia where the patient's life is indisputedly intolerable and hopeless and where the patient's consent is implicit or explicit. Here a key question is whether and under what circumstances it is ever morally right for the caretakers actively to bring about the patient's death. Would a lethal overdose of an appropriate drug in a particular case be morally and humanely permissible, even ethically mandatory? What would be the decent thing to do? Many ethicists find the matter of "making die" radically different from "letting die." The former is unquestionably a deliberate killing, and if wrongful, then it could be considered murder. Its justification, if there is one, must address that issue squarely. Two philosophers and ethicists, James Rachels and Philippa Foot, are among those who have addressed the issues related to active and passive euthanasia. Much controversy has been spawned by their antithetical positions.

In this now classic paper, published in the *New England Journal of Medicine* in 1975, James Rachels argues that the distinction between active and passive euthanasia is not in itself morally relevant. He notes that withholding extraordinary means to prolong life, or other forms of passive euthanasia, is defended on the grounds that it is wrong to let a person suffer needlessly. Rachels makes the obvious point that a given patient may suffer more if treatment is withheld and suffer less if direct action is taken, perhaps immediately, to hasten the end. Rachels states his position boldly: killing may not be in itself morally worse than letting die. Of course, both may be wrong. The question for Rachels is whether there is a moral versus emotional difference in preferring one to the other. He seeks to sharpen our ethical intuitions with this imaginary test case: Is one who lets a child drown in a bathtub morally less culpable than one who directly drowns the child?

Rachels thus pointedly raises an agonizing problem of whether killing is always less defensible than letting die. Rachels is aware that most people seldom think about killings except where they are clearly terrible, as in the case of murders reported in newspapers. Thus, there is a natural tendency to recoil from discussing the matter at all.

Liaison psychiatrists are frequently called on to provide guidance to patients, health professionals, and ethics committees about euthanasia. The matter of active euthanasia is emerging as an important issue on that agenda. The ethical dilemmas surrounding euthanasia are growing in complexity for the public as well as the health care community Many individuals will no doubt still be comforted the most by the idea that their physician should simply make the best choice for them. At the same time, many physicians as well as many others will no doubt find it helpful to have a stated and careful policy, or set of guidelines, for this area of decision-making.

One point deserving discussion is the notion that in letting die, cancer or some disease process is said to cause the patient's death; whereas the doctor who would give the lethal injection would be the cause of the patient's death. On this point Rachels points out that the doctor who lets die still has done something: namely not performed actions that could have been performed. And that action of letting die is just as much subject to moral appraisal as any other -- wise or unwise, right or wrong, compassionate or sadistic, reflective or hasty. Rachels believes that the moral praise or blame appropriate would be the same whether the doctor actively or passively brings about the patient's death. Either action can be right, either action can be wrong; and the dimensions of assessment from the moral point of view are, he believes, exactly the same.[26]

What Rachels' discussion brings out is the question of the right or just thing, that we are to determine what our moral and legal obligations are. There is also the question of what is the decent or gracious thing to do. To put the matter in religious terminology, what is the supererogatory or virtuous thing to do in the circumstance? Philippa Foot has done work in this area and comes out with some interesting conclusions. She believes that Rachels' discussion leaves out entirely the important notion of charity and focuses too narrowly on the virtue of justice. To leave a child to drown, she contends, may not be contrary to justice but it glaringly demonstrates a lack of charity. Foot's intuition here is interesting even if the charity-justice distinction is not quite the proper way to put it. She states that it may not be obligatory from the point of view of what justice requires of us to give money to help starving children in a far-away land, but such an inaction certainly would show a lack of charity and decency. Moreover, Foot disagrees with the conclusion Rachels draws from his principle. Foot is willing to concede that it may sometimes be more humane to kill than to let die but it does not follow, she says, that the distinction between active and passive euthanasia is morally irrelevant. There may be moral objections that arise because other rights might be infringed: alleged rights to life for example; or rights to certain services needed to maintain one's life; or the rights to what the patient can reasonably expect.[27] As Foot's observations make clear, the liaison psychiatrist might well find the ethical issues in euthanasia to involve a complicated discussion of matters of justice and rights, of what is the decent and charitable thing to do, and a determination of the expectations of the patient in the matter of terminating versus letting die.

Case Study 8: Full Disclosure, Partial Disclosure, or Lying to the Patient

Sharing information with a patient, particularly bad news, is seldom an easy task for the health professional. How, when, where, and what to tell are all facets of truth-telling. Sometimes considerations other than what is best for the patient may enter the picture. These considerations may involve the patient's family, economic factors, the hospital, the doctor, or even public policy. Some consideration may actually operate unconsciously or at least with little conscious awareness in the decision-making of the primary physician.

Sissela Bok, in a book on lying, describes the case of a 46-year-old man who came to a clinic for a routine physical examination needed for insurance purposes. He was diagnosed as having a form of cancer from which he was likely to die within six months. No known cure existed. Chemotherapy might have prolonged his life by a few months but would have had serious side effects. The physician believed additionally that chemotherapy should be reserved for those patients with a chance of recovery or remission. The patient had no symptoms giving him any reason to believe he was not perfectly healthy. In fact, he expected to take a short vacation in a week. The physician thought through his choices. He chose to inform the patient of the diagnosis immediately but chose not to mention the possibility of chemotherapy. A medical student working with the doctor and several nurses disagreed; they thought the patient should be informed of the possibility. They were unsuccessful, however, in persuading the physician that this was the patient's right. When persuasion failed, the medical student elected to disobey the doctor and inform the patient of the alternative of chemotherapy. After consulting with his family the patient asked for the treatment.[#,28]

For most non-Kantian ethicists, it is sometimes permissible to lie. The utilitarian, for example, asks that the justified lie promote the greatest balance of good for all the people involved. The greatest good in this case would be that the man live, but chemotherapy does not guarantee this nor appreciably raise the probabilities. The utilitarian would seek that solution that would maximize as many consequential values as possible. Would this particular man at this particular time be needlessly confused about the alternative treatment? Clearly not. Would the man be caused unnecessary pain or discomfort? Only if the man dies in spite of the chemotherapy. Would mentioning chemotherapy raise a false hope? Perhaps. In what way is unwarranted optimism bad if it eases the patient's pain and perhaps improves the patient's psychological condition and attitude? Perhaps not at all. Would an established medical policy known by the public of not lying to patients reassure other potential patients that they will be made fully aware of their condition, its prognosis, alternatives, and risks? Surely such a policy is comforting to most of the potential patient population.

One reason why this case is difficult is that it is not obvious that lying to the patient harms him in terms of his health and well-being. Thus, we have here a question of whether it is permissible in the exceptional case to depart from the general policy of telling the truth. The question is: does the competent patient

---

[#]This discussion of lying owes much to Professor Bok's arguments in her book.

always have the right to know? We expect lawyers, politicians, and journalists always to tell the truth or enough of it not to deceive. Physicians, on the other hand, who are generally believed to be best able to act in the patient's interest and who are privy to knowledge that may be complicated and threatening to the patient are sometimes held to be the one person who can withhold the truth or lie to the patient in the exceptional case.[28] There are rules, however, in these matters. Such deception must always be for the patient's good or where the patient may be a neonate, terminally and painfully ill, or irrevocably comatose, then for the good of the patient's family or as the patient would have wanted it. These were perhaps the ethical deliberations behind what the physician did in the case of the 46-year-old when he attempted to do what he thought was right. The medical student was arguably wrong since only the primary physician had the right to make that decision; but the problem of deception is deeper.

In general, patients want to be told the truth. Sissela Bok has reviewed studies to see if patients themselves desire to know the truth. She found that a large majority say they would like to be told. In most of the studies, in fact, over 80 percent asked to be told the truth.[28] And, of course, incompetent patients can have a guardian or family member review the correct information for them and in their behalf. Of course, it can be difficult to tell the truth not merely because it is often bad news but because it is hard work. Certainly, also, it is time-consuming to make complicated matters understandable and to communicate in language the patient readily understands.

Suppose the physician believed, and in Bok's case study he apparently did, that telling the truth would harm the patient, that is, on balance would bring more harm than benefit to this particular patient. The doctor ruled out chemotherapy as indicated in the case both because he deemed it ineffective and because he saw the side effects unnecessarily detrimental. Sissela Bok argues that such a position is untenable, since by lying to the patient, the patient cannot participate in a choice that concerns his own health and life. Obviously, persons who are knowingly near the end of life normally choose to make plans: to be near their family, to arrange for the funeral, and to put their affairs in order.[28] This patient actually had been looking forward to a vacation. Would he now take it?

Some doctors, however, are afraid that a patient upon hearing bad news might be radically injured by it: commit suicide, have a heart attack, cease to struggle. Bok, however, believes that, as a matter of fact, in the general case the benefits of being informed are substantially greater than the potential damages. Informed patients usually tolerate pain better, cooperate with therapy, and are not corroded with worry about what they do not know but vaguely suspect. Bok does not rule out the possibility that an individual case might be an exception to the rule, but her studies and those of others give us a clear idea of what the majority of patients prefer. And physicians should be cautious to watch out for the rare and exceptional patient who shows signs of continuing distress at learning the truth. The information itself might actually result in a serious deterioration of the patient's condition.[28] There was no good reason in the 46-year-old man's case to believe he would be more harmed than benefitted by the news of chemotherapy as an alternative therapy with low probability of success. It was thus incumbent on the physician to have given the patient this information. The burden of proof, a helpful rule of thumb always, was on the physician to show that concealing the alternative was better for this patient.[28] In light of the disagreement of the medical student and nurses, the physician could well have approached the family. Further, where the primary caregivers reached different conclusions, the liaison psychiatrist could have been consulted to help adjudicate the different principles and perspectives involved.

Physicians should also realize the general value of the belief among the patient population that physicians will disclose all the relevant information. Every time a patient is deceived, whether needlessly or not, and that fact enters the public domain, patients' trust in their physicians is correspondingly reduced. In the case of the terminally ill, the best effort should go not into concealing but, as Bok suggests, into leaving some hope of recovery, however small, or some note of reassurance that the patient who needs help will not be abandoned.[28]

It is difficult for people who are not themselves directly involved in a health care setting to appreciate fully the complexities of truth-telling in patient care. There are children too young to fully understand their situations and yet too mature not to form a part of the decision-making process. Also, there are patients who are extraordinarily sensitive to bad or disruptive news, and truth-telling by indirection may be the only way open. Further, there are patients who sometimes ask or obliquely suggest that they do not want to know all of their diagnosis. Moreover, the caretaker's time is not unlimited; and his or her powers of explanation, while perhaps good, are not perfect.

Thus, it may be impossible to do what would seem to be ethical: to disclose unwelcome information to the patient. Hippocratic wisdom enjoins the physician to do no harm. Yet a contemporary ethical position such as Professor Bok's enjoins the physician to keep the patient fully informed of any matter significantly affecting the health history. In light of these apparently conflicting principles, how does the physician enhance the patient's possibility for recovery, ease the patient's suffering, and keep the public's faith in the credibility of the physician?

The linch-pin for resolving many intractable individual cases is arguably this: what decision would the patient come to welcome? The notion of future-oriented consent, or what the patient would come to welcome, may be the single most important concept in the process of deciding whether and how to disclose unwelcome information. What is meant by "what the patient would come to welcome?" Simply this: what at some later date the patient, fully informed and rational, would agree to. Consideration to paternalistic action on behalf of others must always make reference to what the competent patient would take to be in his or her best interest. It is not merely on behalf of the patient but for the patient's behalf. Thus, if and when it is ever right to withhold the truth, even temporarily, from a patient, three conditions at least must be met. First, it must always be for the patient's own overall long-term good and not merely, for example, to save the patient from temporary grief or the doctor from the problem of confronting the patient with a difficult piece of information. Secondly, it must be demonstrable or highly likely that more harm would result from telling the truth than from withholding it. Thirdly, not only must a patient be told as much relevant information as is possible in a way that can be understood, but any undisclosed information ought to be made available to a competent family member.

Some of the problematic features and value issues in truth-telling are illustrated by a doctor's handling of the following case.¶ The doctor was asked to see an 80-year-old woman in very poor health. The family feared she had cancer but would be unable to handle the news. The adult daughter and chief caretaker of the patient, on behalf of the family, called the doctor and explicitly asked that the patient not be told if it were cancer. The doctor explored with the daughter all of the reasons for fearing that the patient's condition would seriously deteriorate if she were told the truth. The doctor was careful and sympathetic, and the daughter seemed comfortable when the doctor told her that the doctor's general policy was

¶Elizabeth I. McBurney, M.D., dermatologist and laser specialist, September 6, 1983. Personal communication.

that the patient deserved a fair and honest assessment of her condition so that she could make necessary plans, have realistic expectations, and not be worried that information was being withheld. The doctor promised to reevaluate her policy when she examined the patient and determined her condition. Also, the doctor promised to make a medical assessment as to whether a stroke would be imminent upon hearing sensitive news, because the family was afraid this could happen to the patient.

The doctor saw the patient and, after numerous examinations and tests, determined that the patient had end-stage mycosis fungoides. The doctor and patient by this time had a good and cordial relationship; and it was the doctor's decision to tell the patient the diagnosis and prognosis, with the daughter present. In this way, the family both knew what the situation was and could help re-communicate the information to the patient in the event she could not remember all that was said. Since the doctor ran a special university clinic treating patients with these severe and terminal forms of cancer, she was experienced in counseling the patient and giving the patient the benefit of experiences of others facing a similar foreshortened future. The patient seemed reassured and grateful. In conversation later with the daughter, the physician was graciously thanked for her decision to tell the patient and for her guidance, counseling, and therapy for the patient and for the family.

Case Study 9: Prolonging Life When the Quality of Life is Intolerable

David Hellerstein, M.D., reports the case of an elderly alcoholic who was brought into an emergency room nearly dead.[**][29] His bloated belly was rigid. His body had all the signs of end-stage alcoholism: beef-red palms, dilated webs of veins across the stomach, spidery broken vessels on his face and chest. None of the emergency room personnel hesitated. Intravenous lines were started, blood drawn, and catheters inserted. The patient was wheeled to the operating room, shaved, and prepped. The surgeon made an incision along the line of the ribs. The patient's insides were a jumble of scars and adhesions. All knew there was a high incidence of uncontrollable bleeding in end-stage cirrhosis of the liver. Indeed, each time the surgeon cut, new blood bubbled up. The electric bovie and its cauterizing jolt only brought forth new oozing. The patient's blood pressure dropped. Intravenous lines were opened wide and the blood bank quickly supplied precious bags of blood. Dozens of bags were squeezed until hands went limp and others took over. More than thirty units traveled through the patient's leaky system when finally the chief surgeon said "Stop." Everyone stood still in the stainless steel and tile operating room, gowned and gloved, as the pressure fell and the patient died.

The patient's son, upon being told, expressed no surprise. Really, he said, it was for the best; the family had been expecting it for years. In the monthly morbidity conference, someone mentioned the high incidence of uncontrollable bleeding in such cases. The surgeon commented that as soon as he made the first incision, he knew he wouldn't be able to stop the bleeding, but once he'd started, what choice did he have?

One member of the medical team, Dr. Hellerstein himself, reported that the whole episode seemed bullheaded and pointless, a display of technique for its own sake. His concern was that in so many areas of medicine, we are aggressively

---

[**]The discussion here is based on the important issues raised by Dr. Hellerstein.

treating where there is virtually no hope of survival. Hellerstein in writing of this case says that we don't seem to know how *not* to cut, how to stand back and let nature have its way. "To decide not to treat pneumococcal pneumonia in a dying patient seems like negligence -- even if it may be mercy. To leave a cancer drug on the shelf seems like a crime."[29]

This kind of case is growing in familiarity, and is becoming an important part of the work of the liaison psychiatrist in consulting with other members of the health care team. It raises issues beyond those raised in the case discussed earlier of not resuscitating the terminally ill elderly patient. There was no question by the medical team in the case of this alcoholic patient that the slightest hope of recovery existed. This fact weighed more sharply than the patient's age. There was no question that the emergency room personnel acted properly in initiating care immediately and then letting the surgical team, upon closer inspection, make the final decision. A new intern or resident, seeing that kind of case for the first time, would learn much about dealing with the failure of multiple systems. There may have been thoughts of a lurking malpractice attorney or the family outraged at less than everything. And aggressive, high technology treatment certainly looks reassuringly like one is doing both something and everything.

The question that lingers here is whether medical teams and medical education are overly enamored with highly specialized, state-of-the-art technology that results in overtesting and overtreating. What really are our overall goals if it is not possible, and sometimes not desirable, to do everything for everybody? If the central purpose of medicine, as affirmed through the years by the profession, is to heal the sick and relieve suffering, why then would we swamp with expensive technology a patient with virtually no chance of being cured rather than working to relieve his or her terminal pain?

Hellerstein reports that during his internship an old man dying of stomach cancer was brought to his floor.[29] He was in a terminal state, but an enormous workup was done including CAT scans, x-rays, and fluid collections. The patient waited days for tests, sure of a cure, and reassured by the efforts on his behalf. He was given a second regimen of anticancer drugs and then a third. He suffered not only from the pain of his disease but also from the chemotherapy, and the tests, and the waits for the tests. He would cry. In the last day or so, the patient himself realized the medication was having no effect and began screaming that the doctors were killing him. There was no way to console him.

Hellerstein points out that, while the medical treatment was not what was killing the patient, it was not doing the patient any favor either. In fact, the treatment added to the patient's expense and suffering and misled him. Perhaps the patient should have been informed sooner of his condition and of how woefully inadequate technology would be in curing it. Then, he could have begun the work of acceptance of his death, the final stage of life.

With all the effectiveness and promise of medical technology and highly specialized skills, there is also the corollary that doing everything is usually expensive, often wasteful, and infrequently inhumane. It has a tendency to draw the medical student's attention away from basic values and strategies: treating minor problems; taking a good history; using basic instruments correctly, such as a stethoscope; improving diagnostic judgement; listening to patients; discerning which tests are unnecessary and which are helpful; and questioning at what point, if any, treatment should be abandoned. With artificial hearts and kidneys, and some day many other organs, we may soon face a day, Hellerstein writes, "when all our hospitals will be filled with very ill people whose physical existence can be prolonged almost indefinitely but whose quality of life will be intolerable."[29]

The liaison psychiatrist can be very helpful here, both in patient care, on hospital review committees, and in medical education. Hellerstein suggests a team approach, a group of medical professionals who would go on regular hospital rounds and evaluate the use of technology in patient care. The technology evaluation team could consist of an internist, an intensive-care specialist, a psychiatrist, a nurse, and a few patient advocates.[29] The setting up of such a team and leadership on it would likely fall to the liaison psychiatrist in many hospitals. The team would help decide on reasonable treatment goals and the best use of technology. Such teams will be of great help for physicians who have been trained to never give up, and who may feel it strange to contemplate standing aside. We can no longer avoid an issue at the heart of medicine's future: whether doing everything one can will always be the best course for the patient and the most reasonable course for the total patient population, given scarce and expensive resources.

CONCLUSION

As mentioned at the beginning of this chapter, it is important to note how many ethical and value issues in clinical stituations relate to autonomy versus paternalism, competence, informed consent, control, treatment refusal, dignity, "bad" versus "good" patients, withholding treatment to the terminally ill, and disclosing unwelcome information. Because liaision psychiatry explicitly encompasses a biopsychosocial understanding of human nature, its humanistic and psychodynamic emphases address ethical concerns that are clinically meaningful and relevant. [30]

By joining colleagues in identifying and clarifying the ethical and value issues in difficult clinical cases, the liaision psychiatrist is not assuming the role of moral guide or judge, nor are his or her associates classifying moral choices as pychiatric problems.[31] Because many, indeed most questions of clinical ethics have complex psychiatric dimensions, the liaison psychiatrist is drawn legitimately and appropriately into the medical team. He or she thus has an unusual opportunity to promote recognition of the complexities of ethical questions and to foster the humanistic elements of patient care.

REFERENCES

1. Thomas L (1983). *The Youngest Science*. New York:Viking Press, pp 58-60
2. Strain JJ & Grossman J (1975). *Psychological Care of the Medically Ill: A Primer in Liaison Psychiatry*. New York:Appleton-Century-Crofts, pp 1-10
3. Krakowski AJ (1979). Liaison psychiatry: a service for averting dehumanization of medicine. *Psychotherapy and Psychosomatics, 32,* 164-169
4. Lasagna L (1983). The professional-patient dialogue. *The Hastings Center Report, 13,* 9-11

5. Abrams MB (1983, June 5). Ethics and the new machine. *New York Times*, pp 68-100
6. Kant I (1938). *Fundamental Principles of the Metaphysics of Ethics* (Otto Manthey-Zorn, trans.). New York:D. Appleton-Century, p 65
7. Backer B, Hannon N, & Russell NA (1982). *Death and Dying -- Individuals and Institutions.* New York:John Wiley and Sons, pp 180-182
8. Cahn CH (1980). Consent in psychiatry. *Canadian Journal of Psychiatry, 25*, 78-85
9. Gutheil TG & Appelbaum PS (1982). *Clinical Handbook of Psychiatry and the Law.* New York:McGraw-Hill, pp 210-252
10. Mill JS (1962). *Utilitarianism, Liberty and Republican Government.* AD Lindsay (Ed), London:JM Dent and Sons, p 73
11. McCormick RA (1981). *How Brave a New World? Dilemmas in Bioethics.* Garden City, New York:Doubleday
12. Ackerman TF (1982). Why doctors should intervene. *The Hastings Center Report, 12*, 14-17
13. Parsons T (1951). *The Social System.* Glencoe, Illinois:Free Press
14. Nannis ED, Susman EJ, Strope BE, *et al.* (1982). Correlates of control in pediatric cancer patients and their families. *Journal of Pediatric Psychology, 7*, 75-84
15. Dworkin G (1972). Paternalism. *Monist, 56*, 64-84
16. Dworkin G (1976). Autonomy and behavior control. *The Hastings Center Report, 6*, 23-28
17. Ryan CC (1983). Self-defense, pacifism, and the possibility of killing. *Ethics, 93*, 508-524
18. Thompson JJ (1971). A defense of abortion. *Philosophy and Public Affairs, 1*, 47-66
19. English J (1975). Abortion and the concept of a person. *Canadian Journal of Philosophy, 5*, 233-243
20. Singer P (1975). *Animal Liberation.* New York:Avon Books
21. Regan T & Singer P (Eds) (1976). *Animal Rights and Human Obligations.* Englewood Cliffs:Prentice-Hall
22. Carson RA & Siegler M (1982). Case studies -- does "doing everything" include CPR? *The Hastings Center Report, 12*, 27-29
23. *In re Quinlan* 335 A 2d 547, NJ 1976
24. *Superintendent of Belchertown v. Saikewicz* 370 N.E. 2d 417, MA 1977
25. Battin MP (1983). The least worst death. *The Hastings Center Report, 13*, 13-16
26. Rachels J (1975). Active and passive euthanasia. *New England Journal of Medicine, 292*, 78-80
27. Foot P (1977). Euthanasia. *Philosophy and Public Affairs, 6*, 85-112
28. Bok S (1978). *Lying: Moral Choice in Public and Private Life.* New York:Pantheon Books
29. Hellerstein D (1983). Overdosing on medical technology. *Technology Review, 86*, 13-17
30. Sider RC & Clements C (1982). Psychiatry's contribution to medical ethics education. *American Journal of Psychiatry, 139*, 498-501
31. Perl M & Shelp EE (1982). Psychiatric consultation masking moral dilemmas in medicine. *The New England Journal of Medicine, 307*, 618-621

DISCUSSION QUESTIONS

1.   Often times individuals are consulted on a case to help resolve a particular ethical issue. They themselves are not directly involved in the client's care. Should they be allowed access to the client's chart? Consider the issues of confidentiality and privacy.

2.   In the second case cited in this chapter, what do you believe about nursing services' decision not to let nurses return to the ward? Do nurses have the right not to care for a particular client(s) or is it always a duty to care for clients?

3.   In the second case the client was presented with three options. Do you feel that the client was competent to make such a decision about his care?

4.   What criteria would you use in considering whether or not a child is capable of making an informed decision about his or her care?

5.   As a student you know that a client's diagnostic tests are indicative of a poor prognosis. You are caring for this client during this clinical rotation. It is apparent that the client has no idea about the outcomes of the tests. When the client asks you what the tests revealed, what would you do? Would your actions be different if you knew that the client's family was aware of the results and had asked that the results not be revealed? To formulate your answer, use the decision-making tool included in Chapter 1.

6.   Should a client's permission be sought before a liaison psychiatrist joins the health care team as a consultant?

7.   In your clinical facility are liaison psychiatrists consulted? What do you see as their role within your clinical facility?

8.   What criteria would you use in determining whether or not a liaison psychiatrist should be consulted for a particular case?

9.   Who should pay for the services of a liaison psychiatrist?

10.   What is a "model patient"? Is it fair to clients that such a concept exists? How does this model influence client care?

4

Margaret A. Somerville

Legal and Ethical Aspects of Decision-Making by and for Aged Persons in the Context of Psychiatric Care

Margaret A. Somerville, A.U.A., LL.B., D.C.L., is a professor on the faculties of Law and Medicine of McGill University, Montreal, Canada. Her teaching duties include a course in comparative medical law and instruction in medical ethics and jurisprudence. Dr. Somerville has presented numerous papers and has published many articles dealing with medical, legal, and ethical issues.

In this chapter the author examines aspects of decision-making as it relates to aged persons and in relation to mental health practice. Competence, involuntary hospitalization, involuntary de-hospitalization, informed consent, and the psychiatrist's role in decision-making are among the issues that Dr. Somerville addresses. Ethical and legal principles and implications are examined. Legal aspects are discussed in light of both United States and Canadian law.

Decision-making is both a process and an event. When decision-making is looked at as a process, the focus is more on the circumstances and events leading up to and surrounding the delivery of a decision. Emphasis is on decision-making as an event when a decision outcome is the focus; that is, emphasis on the

ETHICS IN MENTAL HEALTH PRACTICE
ISBN 0-8089-1738-2

point in time at which, for instance, the aged psychiatric patient is called upon to articulate his or her choice or another person makes a decision for the patient. Both the decision-making process and event have legal and ethical elements and implications. For instance, the setting in which decision-making takes place can affect the legal validity of the resulting decision via such factors as "duress," "coercion," or "undue influence." These are legal concepts that, when they apply, indicate that a person's decision, although given while competent and under-standing what he or she was doing, was subject to unacceptable pressures, such that the decision cannot be regarded as a free expression of that person's will and, hence, is legally invalid. Further, such factors have not only legal ramifications, but also ethical ones. It may also be that coercion, for instance, of an aged person, which would be of insufficient degree to have a legally invalidating effect on a decision taken by the aged person, could be ethically reprehensible. Certain decision outcomes can also be invalidated by the law through another mechanism, under the general and discretionary rubric of their being contrary to "public policy" in common law systems,[1] or "public order and good morals" in civilian juris-dictions.[2] For instance, a person's decision to have his or her leg amputated, for no therapeutic reason, would not only be unethical, but also illegal, if he or she sought to implement it. In other words, the law does not allow all decision outcomes to be legally validated provided a proper decision-making process is followed, nor does following such a process automatically render them ethical. Some decision outcomes are held, in themselves, to be contrary to "public policy" or "public order and good morals" and cannot be validated. Which outcomes these are, is often decided by a court in the exercise of its discretion, because a wide range of variables can affect that determination.

However, legal and ethical aspects of decision-making are sometimes "second order" issues, in the sense that issues such as how to encourage persons to enter a decision-making setting, or how not to inhibit them from doing so, can be regard-ed as primary. For instance, before considering legal and ethical rights of access to medical care, we may need to consider whether there are practical factors that affect a patient's decision whether or not to seek care. In this respect, one can compare making psychiatric care available in an out-patient clinic attached to a general hospital where the clinic is not overtly identified as offering mental health care, with such care being offered within a specialized, identified, and exclusively mental health care institute. Some persons, including the aged, may be reluctant to attend the latter type of establishment because of the stigma they, or others who influence them or whose opinion they value, attach to mental illness, whereas this reaction may not be generated in relation to the former type of facility. Conse-quently, these persons' access to care is limited, not because of lack of facilities, but due to the effect of labelling and the inhibition this causes. Similarly, some people may not seek care, if they fear that it could result in their being institu-tionalized. In such cases creating legal rights to medical care would not solve any problem of inadequate access to psychiatric care, as this would not address the cause of the problem and, hence, would not augment the real opportunity to have such access.

There is also another wide perspective from which decision-making processes and events can be viewed. Decisions of an individual patient, in order to be imple-mented, can only involve realistically available choices or alternatives, and deci-sions are also involved in establishing this range of choices or alternatives. This is, probably, a more obvious fact in a fully socialized health care system, such as in Canada, but it is true, to some greater or lesser degree, of all health care systems. Consequently, in Canada, for example, limitations on this range depend, first, on the allocation of resources to medicine as compared with other governmental activities, for instance, other social services or defence spending. Secondly, such limitations depend on the allocation of resources within medicine; for instance, if it is considered a priority to build peri-natal intensive care units, rather than mental health care facilities for aged persons, whether because this is the most harm-avoiding course of conduct, or because of valid aims of beneficence, or for political or "for profit" reasons, the fact remains that, no matter what the basis for the decision, some old persons may be deprived of care, as a result of such a decision being taken. Decisions are and must be made with respect to both these allocations, and they do not just occur spontaneously as one is sometimes inclined to think when the decision-making process involved is not highly publicized or public, which is often the case. In short, there may sometimes be a need to look to decision-making behind decision-making, in order to fully and adequately assess a given decision-making situation.

How should the range of health care choices available to any individual person be established? Who should make these decisions and according to what procedural or substantive rules or guidelines? Regulating health care decision-making is one of the most complicated tasks that a society can face. It has been suggested that it involves choosing between, on the one hand, unfair and unfortunate outcomes, which cannot be allowed, and, on the other hand, unfortunate, but not unfair, results, with which one may have to learn to live.[3] Should allocation be simply on the basis of need? How is that need to be judged when there are competing claims and not all can be met? Is there to be equal allocation to all age groups, in which case aged persons will be worse off than young ones, because aged persons use proportionately more of the total medical resources than the young? Such an approach would offend the laws of the many jurisdictions that prohibit discrimination on the basis of age.[4,5] What is the effect of the ability of individuals to pay for treatment and should this alter allocation decisions? Can principles of triage be applied, that is, people divided into those who cannot be helped, those who, possibly, can be helped but where it would be very expensive to do so or the attempt may not be successful, and those who can be helped and where it would be most useful and least expensive to do so? What substantive and procedural principles of decision-making are, or should be, used, ranging from applying rules of distributive justice, to deciding through "veils of ignorance,"[6] to the extreme of a lottery system? Does it make a difference, in terms of the principles that should be applied, at what level of decision-making one is operating, namely, whether a government, an institution, or an individual is making a decision that affects, for instance, a person's access to health care?[7] And does it make a difference whether one is developing rules governing decision-making between strangers, when justice and fairness may predominate, or for governing decision-making in the context of intimate relationships, such as parent and child, when principles of equity in the sense of reasonableness, responsiveness, and discretion, may need to be given priority?[8,9] These are all very complex questions, which will not be addressed directly in this chapter; however, in order to put the discussion in its broader and proper perspective, it is necessary to be aware that health care decision-making by or for an individual takes place within the context of this wider range of modern dilemmas, conflicts, and unanswered questions.

This discussion of legal and ethical aspects of decision-making by and for aged persons in the context of psychiatric care, starts from a "competent adult in the general health care context" model. The modifications needed in principles, rules, laws, or approaches when the person whom the decision concerns or the situation involved varies in some relevant respect from this model are then examined. Two such variations are when the person is aged and the health care is psychiatric. The reasons for adopting such an approach have been explored elsewhere.[10] Essentially, this is done because many issues relevant to decision-making relating to psychiatric care are also relevant to and, often, have been more fully investigated in relation to health care in general. Moreover, one avoids the dangers of surreptitiously making less favorable rules for old or mentally ill persons, by looking, first, at the rules that apply in general. The discussion will be centered around issues arising in the following areas: (1) competence; (2) involuntary hospitalization; (3) involuntary de-hospitalization; (4) decisions relating to medical treatment of aged persons; and (5) the role of psychiatrists in decision-making relating to medical treatment.

COMPETENCE

There are two concepts of competence relevant to the law: legal competence and factual competence. Within this section, examples taken from Canadian law will, in general, be used, but, a range of possible approaches will be considered. The reader should compare these, with that taken in the relevant respect, in his or her own jurisdiction.

Legal Competence

A classic example of legal incompetence related to age, is that of minors. In general, persons under the age of majority, which today is usually 18,[11] are legally incompetent. There are exceptions, in various statutory laws, to the legal incompetence of minors, including, for instance, the ability of a minor child to consent to his or her own health care at 14 years of age in the Province of Quebec,[12] or the common law exception that a "mature minor" may likewise consent.[13] At the other end of the lifespan spectrum, old persons may be legally incompetent, because the normal presumption of legal competence of all adult persons has been rebutted by a court order of interdiction or commitment.* The effect of such an order, which is still given in Quebec, for example, on the medieval grounds of "an habitual state of imbecility, insanity or madness," is, as in most jurisdictions, to make the person subject to it legally incompetent with respect to decisions conerning both himself or herself and his or her property.[14] Such decisions must then be taken by a curator or guardian appointed by the court to act on behalf of the interdicted or committed person.

---

*The term used to describe a court order of legal incompetence is interdiction in the civil law province of Quebec, and commitment in the United Sates of America and common law provinces of Canada.

Under the law in most jurisdictions, and certainly under traditional approaches, interdiction or commitment has a global effect, that is, it makes the person legally incompetent for all purposes. In comparison, a more modern approach is displayed in the Alberta *Dependent Adults Act*.[15] This Act has been applied in practice as requiring assessment of the person's ability to perform the functions in relation to which competence is being determined, for example, to give consent to health care, or to live by himself or herself, although this approach is impliedly, rather than expressly, required by the Act.[16,17] What is called a "plenary guardianship order" (which is equivalent to interdiction) is only given after the court has satisfied itself that the person concerned is incompetent in all the relevant respects listed in the Act.[18,19] If this is not the case, and the person is only incompetent with regard to some area or areas of his functioning, "partial guardianship," which takes away legal competence only in those areas in which the person is incompetent, will be ordered.[20] This is to respect a person and his or her freedom to the maximum degree possible, which are important values for the law to uphold and affirm. Moreover, it is even more important that the law is not seen as detracting, and does not detract, from these values, except where this is unavoidable and to the most limited extent that is essential. Adopting a concept of "partial guardianship" implements such an approach.

Interdiction or commitment is a necessary institution in the law and should be protective of the persons to whom it is applied. However, we must never forget the effects of such orders on persons subject to them including effects on their own perceptions of themselves and the perceptions that others have of them. A commitment order is stigmatizing and, to the extent that the person concerned is aware of its significance, it could be the source of severe psychological trauma. In this respect, it is worth noting that legal incompetence persists whether or not the person subject to it has intervals of factual competence, what is sometimes referred to in the law as "lucid intervals." Hence, it is possible that a person could be fully aware of the significance of the order and of the effect it has on him or her, as well as others' attitudes towards him or her. Consequently, to the extent that some less drastic mechanism could achieve the desired protection of the person, it should be used, or, if such alternative mechanisms do not currently exist in the law, we should give thought to what is needed. That is, we should devise and adopt the least restrictive, least invasive alternatives reasonably available.

Factual Competence

In contrast to legal competence, factual competence, as the term denotes, requires assessment of whether a person is in fact competent at the time at which it is relevant to make the assessment. This is the type of competence we are more frequently involved with and concerned about assessing in health care situations. There is debate as to what constitutes factual competence and there has been a great deal of literature generated in discussion of this topic. One series of tests displays a possible range of criteria for assessing competence, which are of increasing stringency. This starts with a proposition that a person is competent if he or she can evidence a decision, to requiring rational reasons underlying the decision, to requiring a rational outcome of the decision, to a concept that the person should apparently understand the information on which his or her decision is based, to the most demanding level, which requires that the person must subjectively, that is, actually, understand this information in order to be adjudged competent.[21] Other views emphasize that competence involves assessment of a dynamic situation and not a static state, and that legal theories relating to competence may not make adequate provision for this reality. Criteria that have been suggested for use in a more dynamic assessment of competence are:

> (1) psychodynamic elements of the patient's personality; (2) the accuracy of the historical information conveyed by the patient; (3) the accuracy and completeness of the information disclosed to the patient; (4) the stability of the patient's mental status over time; [and] (5) the effect of the setting in which consent is obtained.[22]

It has been shown that the more the patient's decision varies from what the health care professional thinks he or she would have decided in the same circumstances, and the more serious the outcome of the patient's decision, for example, a refusal of treatment necessary to preserve life or health, the more likely it is that the patient will be labelled incompetent.[21] In terms of the current discussion of decision-making by and for aged persons in the context of psychiatric care, we should be aware that there may be a greater tendency to label the aged, in comparison with younger persons, factually incompetent. This can occur because noncompliance with treatment regimes or refusal of treatment by aged persons is taken as a sign of incompetence. It is interesting that we regard the emergence in a young child of the ability to say no, as a sign of development and maturation and yet we may ascribe the opposite significance to this characteristic in aged persons. Perhaps, in this respect, we should keep in mind the maxim, "*Nego ergo sum*" (I am because I deny).[†] It should never be forgotten that a finding of incompetence is a detraction both from the recognition of that person's rights as an individual, in terms of autonomy and self-determination and, equally as importantly, from his or her dignity, in his or her own eyes, and that of others.

The functional approach to assessment of competence (for instance, that taken in Alberta under the *Dependent Adults Act* in order to determine whether to appoint a partial or plenary guardian, that is, whether to declare partial or plenary legal incompetence) has already been mentioned (see p 63).Under a functional approach the purpose for which competence is being assessed must be determined and the ability of the person to function in relation to that purpose must then be assessed. If the person can perform the functions necessary to achieve the particular purpose, he or she is competent. For example, the most usual situation in which we seek to establish factual competence in the health care situation, is to determine the patient's ability to give informed consent. Consequently, the competence assessor needs to ask what does the patient have to do in order to give informed consent? The answer is that the patient must understand the nature of the treatment being proposed, the alternatives, and the consequences of having or foregoing any of these treatments and of having no treatment. If the patient can understand these matters he or she is competent to give informed consent, even though the patient may not be competent in other respects. A functional approach to assessment of factual competence has even been enshrined in legislation. One example can be found in *The Mental Health Act* of Ontario. This defines a "mentally competent" person as "having the ability to understand the subject matter in respect of which consent is requested and able to appreciate the consequences of giving or withholding consent."[23]

[†]I am indebted for this idea to Dr. Stanley Cath, M.D., of Tufts University, Massachusetts, and his lecture delivered at the Symposium "Psychiatry of Late Life" at St. Mary's Hospital, Montreal, October 1982.

It may provide insights to look behind the adoption of a functional test of competence and ask what underlying principle or principles this establishes. For instance, adoption of such an approach recognizes that competence is not an "all or nothing" phenomenon. Rather, there is a spectrum or range of competence or incompetence and the decision as to where to draw the line dividing competence from incompetence may shift along this spectrum and may be far from clear in certain circumstances. Further, such an approach may, in both theory and practice, represent, introduce, and implement a more dynamic approach to the assessment of competence.

The reason for assessing competence is to ensure that the right to autonomy or self-determination of a competent person is respected. That is, the decisions of competent persons regarding themselves have priority. In contrast, other persons make decisions for incompetent persons, via the mechanism of third party authorization or *proxy consent.*§

It has usually been assumed that incompetent persons totally lack autonomy. However, Miller, in his article "Autonomy and Proxy Consent,"[24] suggests otherwise. Miller proposes that autonomy can refer to:

(1) autonomy as a feature of particular actions of persons, including decisions; (2) autonomy as a feature of a person's capacities; [and] (3) autonomy as a feature of interpersonal and institutional environments.[24]

The four senses of autonomy of action, the relevant form of autonomy in relation to consent to medical treatment, are described as "autonomy as free action; autonomy as authenticity; autonomy as effective deliberation; and autonomy as moral reflection.[27] The degree to which different models of "proxy consent" either augment or detract from autonomy in each of these four senses can be examined. Models for proxy consent can be categorized within one of six classes:[24]

1. Specific Authorization
2. General Authorization with Instructions
3. General Authorization without Instruction
4. Instruction[s] without Authorization
5. Substitute Judgment
6. Deputy Judgment

The analytical tools just described can be used to assess whether the proxy consent mechanisms outlined, promote or detract from different aspects of the autonomy of the incompetent person in various situations. For instance, persons who have made "living wills"# that are used to determine what treatment they will

---

§It is suggested that the term "third party authorization" is preferable to that of "proxy consent," because it more clearly identifies that what we may consent to on our own behalf may not be the same as that which we may authorize to be done to another person.

#The "living will" is a document (which may or may not be based on statutory authority), to be signed by adults, directing family and physician in case of terminal illness, both concerning palliative care and to avoid heroic measures or extraordinary means of treatment and permit natural death. See Legal Advisors Committee, Concern for Dying (1983). The right to refuse treatment: A model act. *American Journal of Public Health, 73,* 918.

be given after they have become incompetent, have had their autonomy respected to a greater degree than has the person to whom a "deputy judgment" (that is a decision made by a third party not appointed by the incompetent person and taken simply according to impersonal, objective criteria) is applied.

There are many other issues related to competence that will need to be explored in future research. These include, for example, whether the normal presumption in favor of life, which mandates that incompetent persons be given life or health preserving treatment, is rebutted when the need for that treatment arises from a suicide attempt and it is known that the person was competent at the time he or she decided to take his or her life and intended that result. The type of situation that could be examined here, is that of treatment of a terminally ill person who decides to commit suicide by running his or her car into the pylon of a bridge, what is sometimes called "rational suicide." Should such a person be treated, beyond palliative measures, when he or she is brought to the emergency room and is incompetent to refuse treatment? Can we argue that such patients are not "normal," incompetent persons, but a special group whose decisions when competent prevail, that is, the effect of competence continues? Alternatively, are they members of a group with respect to whom the presumption in favor of life and the requirement, therefore, that life-prolonging treatment be administered, is rebutted?

Another issue that needs consideration and research is whether the legal doctrine of factual competence that, at present, depends only on assessment of the cognitive functioning of the person, should be expanded to take into account emotive functioning. Difficulties can arise when a patient suffers from emotional malfunction, but is cognitively competent. For example, a paranoid patient who is cognitively competent may refuse treatment because of emotional malfunction in the nature of intense and irrational fear of psychiatrists and, thus, as a practical result, be denied access to care.The difficulty with recognizing emotional malfunction as a form of incompetence in the cognitively competent person, is that it could constitute, or be used as, a major derogation from respect for the right to autonomy of the person. The doctrine of autonomy accomodates the recognition of irrational and even stupid decisions, because, if it is not possible to make such decisions, autonomy has no real meaning. How, then, would we draw the line between respecting this latter class of decisions and not those that have been classified as being the result of emotional malfunctioning sufficient to amount to functional and factual incompetence? It may be possible to make acceptable and valid distinctions in this respect, and what may be needed is a more precise delineation of the effect of emotional malfunction in relation to competence. However, we need to tread warily in this regard, lest we seriously detract from the right to autonomy.

INVOLUNTARY HOSPITALIZATION: DANGEROUSNESS TO ONESELF OR OTHERS

Interdiction or commitment, in the sense in which that term is used in the above section, must be distinguished from involuntary civil commitment, that is, involuntary or compulsory hospitalization, which is the subject of this section. Involuntary hospitalization, the process referred to as "close treatment" or "*cure fermee*" within Quebec law, or involuntary civil commitment in the United States and common law provinces of Canada, operates from a basis that requires a finding that persons to be committed are dangerous to others or themselves, including through a failure to care for themselves, which threatens imminent and serious physical harm.[25,26] The procedural and technical rules surrounding involuntary civil commitment are complex in most, if not all, jurisdictions. Because these rules operate to deprive a person of liberty they must be stringently interpreted and strictly applied. Such rules will not be examined here.

Rather, the first point to be made is that involuntary hospitalization is not synonymous with, and is not necessarily related to, incompetence on the patient's part to consent to or refuse treatment. This becomes clear when the nature of the principle basis on which involuntary hospitalization may be ordered, dangerousness to oneself or others, is emphasized. A person can be dangerous but still understand the nature and consequences of accepting or refusing certain treatment, that is, he or she is competent to consent to treatment or to refuse it. However, it used to be thought, and it still is thought in some jurisdictions and by some persons, that involuntary hospitalization automatically carries a right to treat the committed person in what is regarded as the most medically appropriate way. It was argued that it is illogical to confine a person compulsorily and then not to treat that individual. This approach has been considerably modified, particularly in the last 5 years, and now the more common attitude is that competence is the primary governing criterion in deciding whether persons, including those who are involuntarily hospitalized, have a right to refuse treatment. In short, competence is to be assessed separately from dangerousness. This use of a competence criterion to determine the rights of involuntarily hospitalized patients to refuse treatment, has been criticized. It is claimed that the practical results of applying the two tests of dangerousness and competence cumulatively, is a situation in psychiatric hospitals of patients "rotting with their rights on."[27] This would occur if a competent patient refused treatment and, because of this refusal and the effects of not having treatment, the patient continued to be classified as dangerous and hence continued incarceration was held to be justifiable.

There has been much written on the concept of dangerousness and its predictability and that debate will not be explored in any detail in this chapter.[28] Clearly, this is a very difficult and contentious area. Is past dangerousness a reliable predictor of future dangerousness? Are the people whom we characterize as being dangerous any more likely to act dangerously than any other member of the population? Who has the burden of proof of dangerousness and to what standard must it be proved? There is a trend in some jurisdicions, Canada being one of them, to follow the approach developed in American case law, which requires "clear and convincing evidence" of dangerousness.[29] This is a standard that rests between the highly demanding criminal one of proof beyond a reasonable doubt, and the more lenient civil standard of proof on the balance of probabilities. One may well ask whether there is any real difference in practice between such varying standards of proof, although nice theoretical distinctions can be drawn. However, the making of such distinctions and their application in practice serve, at the least, to underline the seriousness, for the person affected, of a finding of dangerousness and have an educative function in this regard.

It is essential to have a constant and conscious awareness of the fact that involuntary hospitalization is a very serious matter. Like interdiction, it carries social and personal stigmatization and it is one of the few exceptions, in modern western legal systems, to the rule that incarceration of a person can only be subsequent to conviction for a criminal act. It is a grave decision to involuntarily hospitalize a person and there has been increasing realization of this gravity. However, there may be different attitudes in this respect, for instance between different regions of a country. There are two ways in which such differences are exhibited: first, the grounds on which, and procedural ease with which, involuntary hospitalization may be ordered, may vary in their width and stringency from state to state, or province to province. Secondly, in some regions of a country, the percentage of patients in psychiatric facilities who are involuntarily hospitalized may be high as compared with other regions.¶

It is also worth mentioning that although there may be risks in not involuntarily hospitalizing a person, there may also be risks in doing so. Consequently, especially when the basis for involuntary hospitalization is the patient's dangerousness to himself or herself, rather than to others, risks associated with his or her involuntary hospitalization should be given full weight. For example, when the reason for hospitalizing a person is because of fear that he or she will commit suicide if left at liberty, this risk would need to be balanced against any risks of death involved in hospitalizing that individual. In one case that was brought to my attention, a man had a heart attack and died in attempting to resist involuntary hospitalization. Of course, it is not always easy to predict what the risks of involuntary hospitalization will be, but the reason for raising this matter is to draw attention to the fact that there are risks as well as benefits in all courses of conduct and the widest possible spectrum of these risks should be considered in making a decision whether to involuntarily hospitalize a person.** This comment is not intended to be stiffling of action on the part of psychiatrists, or to paralyze decision-making founded on considered professional judgment that takes into account any required basis on which, and the situation in which, the decision must be made and other relevant factors. Rather, it is simply meant to articulate and to focus attention on the fact that the risks of both intervening and not intervening must be considered.

Finally, just as less restricive alternatives to global interdiction or commitment have been devised (see p 63) less drastic measures may suffice in situations in which involuntary hospitalization is, at present, the only form of compulsory intervenion available. For instance, "*cure surveillee*," that is some form of compulsory surveillance, or reporting on the part of the patient may in some cases be sufficient and would, in all likelihood, be a less invasive, less intrusive alternative to involuntary hospitalization, as far as respect for the rights of the patient is concerned. Such an alternative, however, is not at present generally available and has not been favored in at least one jurisdiction where it was suggested that it should be implemented.[30,31] But, failure to formally establish an institution does not necessarily mean that the same results cannot be achieved in practice. In one case a psychiatrist solved the problem of maintaining surveillance over a patient who became dangerous to his family when he failed to comply with his drug treatment regime, by arranging for the patient's unemployment benefit cheques to be sent to the hospital, making it necessary for the patient to pay

---

¶There do not appear to be any reliable statistics available for Canada, in this respect, but there are indications that this may indeed be the case. I am indebted to Dr. Charles Cahn, Director of Professional Services at the Douglas Hospital, Montreal and of the Canadian Psychiatric Association, for discussion of this matter with me.

**In one Quebec case, a patient in a psychiatric hospital was assaulted by another patient with serious injury resulting. Such risks are not negligible and should not be ignored. See *Cineas v. Hopital Louis-H. Lafontaine* (unreported, Quebec Superior Court, no. 05-022493-777, June 27, 1979, Colas, J.).

weekly visits to the hospital. As always, one should consider whether such an approach is ethical and legal. Among other factors, this will depend on the balance of harms, risks, and benefits it involves in comparison with the alternative courses of conduct, including the possibility of no intervention, which are available.

INVOLUNTARY DE-HOSPITALIZATION

Unlike involuntary hospitalization, involuntary de-hospitalization has not been the subject of much discussion or research until very recently. Involuntary de-hospitalization is an increasingly difficult and serious problem, particularly in relation to the elderly and especially in relation to elderly psychiatric patients. Situations of involuntary de-hospitalization would include the discharge of patients who do not wish to be de-institutionalized, or who object to being transferred to another institution. Among such patients are persons who have nowhere else to live, or who need care but of a lesser intensity than that provided in the institution in which they are patients, or for whom further therapy would serve no useful purpose but who need custodial care. Sometimes such patients can include those who do need and could benefit from psychiatric treatment,[††] but a political and policy decision by a government can cause them to be involuntarily de-hospitalized.

Some jurisdictions have proceeded with large scale de-hospitalization of psychiatric patients. This has been a particularly striking undertaking in Italy where it has been achieved by passing legislation that will lead to the closing of large traditional psychiatric hospitals.[32] De-hospitalization of psychiatric patients has also been increasing in the United States. This has been carried out pursuant to a general policy against custodial care and of rehabilitation and reintegration of mentally ill or retarded persons into society.[33] The legal basis used to implement this policy is that it is contrary to a patient's fundamental constitutional rights to incarcerate him or her unless this is justified under the police power (as it would be for convicted criminals) or by the *quid pro quo* of treatment.[34] Consequently, when treatment is not possible, continued involuntary hospitalization of at least the nondangerous patient, and possibly, even the dangerous patient, is unconstitutional.[§§] In short, it is not so much that de-hospitalization of these patients has been justified, but rather continuing to hold such patients in mental hospitals is contrary to their rights and unjustified. The recognition of civil liberties inherent in such an approach and of the harms as well as benefits of involuntary hospitalization is essential and to be welcomed. But, while this recognition is welcome,

---

[††]It should be recognized that a statement that somebody "needs" psychiatric treatment, is a value judgment. However, it is submitted that when the apparent benefits of treatment clearly and, at least somewhat objectively (objectivity also contains a value judgment component), outweigh its apparent harms, it is possible to say there is a need for that treatment.

[§§]Some lower court decisions indicate that even dangerous patients cannot be held under a civil (as compared with a criminal) commitment order without treatment. (*Rouse v. Cameron*, 373 F. 2d 451 (1966) and *Wyatt v. Stickney*, 325 F. Supp. 781 (1971); 334 F. Supp. 1341 (1971); 344 F. Supp. 373 (1972)). The United States Supreme Court has not yet ruled on this issue.

implementation of a consensus that there should be emphasis on patients' rights and civil liberties does not necessarily lead to welcome outcomes. For instance, one such outcome could be involuntary de-hospitalization in circumstances where this is harmful to the patient. An explanation of how paradoxical results like this can occur, in that an approach meant to do good can cause harm, is described well by Mollica:

> On the one hand, policy planners fought for the humanization of mental-health institutions, so that those institutions could provide adequate and effective care. One the other hand, the same planners often sought to reveal the corrupt nature of public institutions in order to bring about their total destruction.[33]

Further, the harms involved in de-hospitalization may not have always been given sufficient weight. Moreover, emphasis on legal analysis may sometimes have clouded or suppressed proper analysis of the ethical issues involved. It may be, also, that it has suited governments and administrative authorities to emphasize the benefits to patients of de-hospitalization and not its detriments and risks (for instance, homelessness or lack of financial or emotional support), because, in the current difficult economic circumstances, there is a substantial cost-saving for health care systems that adopt a policy of de-hospitalization.

It bears repeating with respect to the foregoing discussion that political and policy decisions or approaches alter the decision-making situation in which patients find themselves, in that their range of available options can change with such decisions or approaches and that these can be implemented in various ways, including through the use of law. Thus, in the United States the administrative authorities have not, as has resulted in practice in Italy, compulsorily de-hospitalized psychiatric patients. Rather, by way of case law, the option of de-hospitalization has been provided to patients (and, it could be added, to institutions, although it is provided more indirectly) for whom it was previously unavailable and this has resulted in increased de-hospitalization.

A further problem relating to de-hospitalization that is raised in the context of the present discussion concerns the issue of consulting elderly persons regarding decisions affecting their hospitalization or institutionalization. Not infrequently, I receive enquiries about the right to transfer an elderly patient from an acute care hospital to some less expensive institution. One of the disturbing factors found in some of these cases is that the old persons themselves have not been consulted. To some extent they are being seen as "packages" to be picked up and delivered to a suitable destination, rather than as persons.[35] Packages do not have decision-making rights, are not self-determining, and need not be consulted; persons do, are, and must be, respectively. There is great danger in such an attitude, as there is in any attitude that exhibits that there has been depersonalization of a patient. Further, as a matter of law, it could be argued that to the extent that the nature of the accomodation provided constitutes part of a patient's treatment, then the person must consent to any change in that accomodation. Such an approach is, however, subject to provisions in the law that enable physicians to discharge patients who no longer need hospitalization.[36]

The problem with respect to many elderly people is that there are no real or viable alternatives to their hospitalization, especially when their relatives refuse or are unable to accept them. In this respect, it should be considered what steps need to be taken to avoid the tragic situation of the abandonment of aged relatives in hospital emergency rooms, which is occurring in some parts of the United States. "[F]amilies that had been caring for the abandoned simply felt unable physically and financially to continue."[37] The lack of adequate support facilities for care-givers, for example, lack of adequate home-care programs, often contribute to such outcomes. But the reasons that families refuse to care for their aged members may be more complex. It has been suggested that institutionalization of elderly persons in North America may "meet a deep psychic need of the generation in control"[38] and may have roots in the fact that "an immigrant country distances itself from ancestors. Coming to America entailed a kind of abandonment of the aged... -- all for the sake of the young."[38] Thus the refusal of individual persons to care for aged family members may have been molded by societal attitudes and pressures. To the degree that this is true, the former may only change in response to change in the latter.

DECISIONS REGARDING MEDICAL TREATMENT

The above discussion leads us to a more general consideration of elderly psychiatric patients and decisions concerning their medical treatment. One of the main areas of law applying here is the voluminous one of informed consent. Consideration of this doctrine and whether it needs modification when it is applied to an aged psychiatric patient, is particularly important in a discussion of decision-making by such persons.

As has been pointed out, the approach taken in this chapter is to work from the legal rules and ethical principles that would be applicable in a "competent adult model" and then to determine the variations in these rules and principles that need to be incorporated to allow for the differences from that model in the situation being dealt with. The application of the doctrine of informed consent to aged persons in the context of psychiatric care will be dealt with in this way.

In considering what variations from the "normal" rules may be needed, it is necessary, first, to look at the purposes sought to be achieved by obtaining informed consent and to assess whether it is possible to achieve these in any given circumstances through compliance with the doctrine's legal requirements. If it is not, one must ask what alternative course of conduct is indicated as appropriate in terms of either achieving the same or similar aims or alternative aims that are justified in the circumstances. The aims sought in requiring that informed consent to treatment be obtained include protection of the right of autonomy and inviolability of the person and, perhaps behind these, relief of suffering as a more all-encompassing, global purpose.[39] When, for example, an aim of protecting a person's right of autonomy is impossible, because the person is mentally incompetent, giving priority to aims such as protection of the person, beneficence and above-all respect for life may be justified and the rules may need to be modified to accomodate this changed priority.

The elements of the doctrine of informed consent -- competence, information and voluntariness -- can then be examined. All of these raise special problems in relation to decision-making by and for aged persons in the context of psychiatric care. For instance, can third parties authorize the same range of interventions on their incompetent wards as the incompetent persons could authorize in relation to themselves if competent? Does the information given to an aged, mentally ill person need to be modified because it could cause that person harm? And, with respect to deciding whether consent is freely given, that is, is voluntary, what are the effects on a person of institutionalization and of feeling weak, powerless, frail, and dependent?

Assessment of competence and some distinctions between competence and incompetence have already been discussed (see pp 62-66). These could be characterized as intrinsic differences. But there are also other extrinsic differences that result from a finding that a person is competent or incompetent and some of these relate to informed consent. Competent persons have a right to decide for themselves whether they wish to have or forego certain treatment. Incompetent persons must have these decisions made on their behalf, but there are limits as to which decisions can be so made, and on what is an acceptable outcome of certain decisions. For example, although a competent person may give informed consent to participate in nontherapeutic medical research, third party authorization of such a procedure on an incompetent person would not be legally valid.[40]

Another distinction that can be relevant in decisions concerning treatment, and which should be superimposed on the competent/incompetent characterization, is that of whether the patient is terminally ill or not terminally ill. Often terminally ill patients are old, but neither the fact that they are old nor the fact that they are terminally ill should be directly taken into account in decision-making in which they are involved. However, some treatment that may be indicated as appropriate in a nonterminally ill patient, such as cardio-pulmonary resuscitation, may not need to be undertaken in a terminally ill patient when its effect is simply to prolong dying.[41] One of the difficulties here is to determine what is meant by appropriate or inappropriate treatment. The first point that can be made in this respect, is that appropriateness is not limited to medical appropriateness. Secondly, there is usually a value judgment, and sometimes a hidden one, involved in characterizing a certain course of conduct as either appropriate or not. Thirdly, whether treatment is indicated as appropriate depends on first, and overridingly, the patient's wishes, which are determinative if the patient is competent and which must at least be taken into account with respect to an incompetent patient. If the patient is incompetent, appropriateness will also depend on the usefulness of the treatment in terms of reducing pain or suffering, prolonging life, or curing a pathological condition (the latter of which, by definition, is not applicable in a situation of terminal illness, at least in relation to the terminal illness itself), and on the application of a proportionality principle. Applying a proportionality principle means that the benefits and harms involved in giving the treatment must be compared with the benefits and harms involved in not giving it. Where the harm involved in giving it (in terms of suffering inflicted by the treatment or prolongation of suffering not related to the treatment) outweighs any benefit the treatment could promise, then, under a proportionality principle, the treatment would not be indicated as appropriate, that is, it need not be given.[42]

One important point to note in relation to judging whether certain treatment is indicated as appropriate for any person, but particularly one who is either old or incompetent, is that health care professionals should consciously avoid both applying to the patient their own personal and subjective view of what constitutes a satisfactory quality of life and including this view as a criterion on which the decision whether or not to give treatment is based. This is not to exclude the possibility of employing a quality of life criterion in such circumstances, rather if this criterion is used, it must be assessed from the patient's point of view. What may be regarded as a totally unsatisfactory quality of life by a busy 30-year-old professional, is not necessarily so for an 80-year-old.

It is often claimed that it is too dangerous to allow decision-making to depend upon judgment as to quality of life, and there are strong arguments against allowing the use of such a criterion, not least of which is that precedents will be set that could easily be abused. Certainly, if we do use such a criterion it must be subject to appropriate limiting devices. One important example of such a device is the principle that requires that a quality of life criterion must be employed solely for the benefit of the person to whom it is applied. It is not uncommon to find decision-making in a medical context really reflecting outcomes meant to be of benefit to others, who can include the family of the patient, the treating staff, the hospital, or even the community in general. For example, how should the decision whether to give respiratory support to an incompetent elderly woman with advanced cardiac disease be taken? The sole fact of her incompetence should not be a basis for denying the treatment. Have we any evidence, such as a "living will," of this person's own perception of her quality of life, or can we exercise "substituted judgment" in this respect (that is, stand in the shoes of the patient and try to determine what she would think), and should we make a decision taking that judgment into account? In reaching a decision should we consider the suffering of the family in witnessing the progressive and serious physical and mental deterioration of their loved one? Is it relevant that we are short of medical resources and feel that these resources could be more profitably used? In order to retain at least a pretence of the priority that we purport to give to the principle of sanctity of life, many of these factors will not be able to be taken into account in reaching a decision whether to give or withhold treatment, at least not overtly. Is there a need for us to be more honest and open concerning the factors influencing our decision-making? Or would more openness be destructive and be introduced mainly as a means of dealing with any guilt we feel in relation to our decisions, rather than to benefit the patients who are affected by those decisions? Further, who should make these decisions? It is almost trite to add the postscript that such questions raise very difficult and complex issues.

One matter that arises in the context of medical care decisions concerning aged persons, and which has generally had inadequate attention paid to it in the past, is that of pain relief treatment. The subject of pain relief is an extensive topic and only a few points that may be of particular interest in the context of a discussion of decision-making by and for aged persons receiving psychiatric care, will be mentioned here.

For the purposes of definition and clarity, it might be worthwhile to characterize *pain* as a physical sensation, and the mental perception of physical pain and "pure" mental pain as *suffering*. Suffering may be viewed as a person's awareness of his or her own disintegration or of the threat of this or his or her loss of control over what happens to him or her.[43] It is proposed that a pre-eminent task for all physicians, but particularly perhaps for psychiatrists, should be to seek to relieve suffering in individual cases and to search for more effective ways of achieving this aim in general. Suffering may be more difficult to relieve than pain, but even pain may not always be relieved when it could and should be. The inadequacy of pain relief treatment in many clinical situations has been well documented recently.[44] It is suggested that there should be a malpractice liability for failure to take reasonable steps to relieve pain. Stated in other terms, this is to postulate a legal duty to act as a reasonably competent health care professional would act in the same circumstances with respect to the relief of pain, and that a failure to fulfill this duty would constitute actionable negligence. The content of this duty is novel. But the existence of a duty and the standard of care and competence it requires, parallels legal duties that exist within the health care professional-patient relationship with respect to all other medical care and treatment.[45]

The matter of decision outcome options being limited because certain treatments were not available or their availability was blocked in some way, has been raised (see pp 60-61). This is a particularly important consideration in terms of providing patients with the widest acceptable range of options with respect to pain relief treatment. The most stringent limitations surround the provision of pain relief treatment that may shorten life or situations where the health care professional is concerned about the patient becoming addicted to the pain relief drug. Part of the underlying cause for limiting access to certain pain relief treatments in such situations may be connected with the law. Fear of legal liability is the most obvious example, but there may be more subtle "legal" causes. It might be that the law is interpreted as delivering a moral message that certain pain relief treatment, for instance, that which could shorten life or where the patient is addicted, should never be made available. Any such messages need to counteracted.

The fear is often articulated with respect to allowing pain relief treatment that may possibly or even probably will shorten life, that active euthanasia can be masqueraded as pain relief treatment. This fear is not groundless and yet it is suggested that, at least for the terminally ill patient, pain relief treatment that is the only reasonable alternative available in terms of efficacy, should be allowed to be offered to a patient who needs it, even if it does risk shortening life. The "slippery slope," or dangerous, open-ended precedent that such an approach opens up is that once we acknowledge it is acceptable to shorten life in order to relieve pain, where do we draw the line between relieving pain and more general relief of suffering and should we draw such a line? Accepting that it is valid to shorten life to relieve suffering would be to validate active euthanasia, with which many persons strongly disagree. However, while it is true that pain relief treatment that may shorten life has some of the characteristics of active euthanasia, it is proposed that it is distinguishable. In giving pain relief treatment the primary aim is to relieve pain and not to cause death, whereas in euthanasia the aim is to shorten life in order to relieve suffering.[46]

Finally, in this discussion of decision-making relating to medical treatment of aged persons in the context of psychiatric care, it is worth examining a few examples of situations in which the rules that are normally applicable to general medical treatment decision-making, by competent adult patients, may need to be varied because the patient is aged or the medical care is psychiatric.

It is usually thought that the requirement that informed consent be evidenced in writing is protective of the patient who is required to sign the consent form, because the act of signing will make the person realize that he is entering into a serious undertaking. Some studies, however, have shown that aged persons who signed consent forms, later became disturbed and anxious because they could remember that they had signed a document, and that it was of some importance, but they could not recall the nature of the document. These patients became fearful that they had signed something that they should not have, which would have harmful results for them.[47]

Aged persons may also differ from younger ones in their perception of risk. There is a tendency for old persons to refuse risk altogether if they see this as a possible choice, but when risk is unavoidable they are no less risk-taking than younger persons.[48] Moreover, risk-taking options seem to be more acceptable to older persons after group discussion of the risks involved and if they perceive that they are not alone in the venture. Further,

[t]he option to make no choice is selected by the elderly more frequently than by those in younger age groups. This option is always available in research protocols and subjects must be free of coercion to participate even if their inherent tendency to select this option makes geriatric research more difficult to accomplish. However, in clinical treatment situations involving elderly pa-

tients, this tendency to avoid choice has ethical implications for the physician. Whether the decision not to decide is a manifestation of depression or an expression of an altered value system is a vitally important and problematic distinction. In the first instance, the option not to opt for treatment is not a decision at all but an avoidance of one. In the second instance, the option not to opt for treatment is a decision and should be respected as such. It may, in fact, represent a very brave and risky choice. When to intervene, paternalistically, in an effort to contravene a depressed patient's choice is a difficult judgment and deserves ... considered attention ....[48]

Thus, depending on how decision options are described and the situation in which they are presented, an old person's choice could be quite different. In this respect care should be taken that such knowledge is not used to manipulate the old person; rather, it should be employed to extend his freedom of choice. In other words, we need to be sensitive to the variations that may be required in the "normal" rules or approaches in order to promote the "best interests," in the widest sense of that term, of aged persons. We must make sure, however, that adoption of a "best interests" approach, while not being uninterested, is disinterested, and that it is not espoused as a cover for unacceptable paternalism.

Other differences that can be suggested as sometimes giving rise to a need to modify "normal" rules when aged persons are involved, include being sensitive to the possibility that older persons may have a different attitude to mental health care than younger persons. Such differences need to be taken into account by health care professionals. For example, telling an old person in a general medical ward that it would be a good idea if he or she had a psychiatric consultation may, in itself, cause distress or even harm to him or her, because "the act of calling in a psychiatrist [may]communicate a threat to the patient of being labelled mentally incompetent or insane."[49] This is not meant to indicate that such a suggestion should not be made to the old person, but it should be made only after having properly assessed the risk of harm involved.

PSYCHIATRISTS ROLE IN DECISION-MAKING REGARDING MEDICAL TREATMENT

The above discussion leads to a consideration of what should be the role of psychiatrists with respect to decision-making regarding medical treatment. The article by Perl and Shelp from which the quotation just cited was taken, merits detailed study in this respect, as it "red-flags" several important issues.

The first question addressed is why and when are psychiatrists called in for a consultation by other physicians. It is suggested, that:

[s]ometimes nonpsychiatric physicians turn to their psychiatric colleagues for help and guidance with morally troublesome cases. In these contexts, psychiatrists are not necessarily seen as moral arbiters; rather, we believe they are regarded as experts in mediating and resolving conflict, both intrapsychic and interpersonal. The primary physician is often acutely aware of the patient's psychic distress and of the interpersonal tensions that accompany the medical-

moral problems. The psychiatrist is expected to fill a mediating role, often with a mandate to resolve the situation in a particular direction, to persuade the patient or family to act in a certain way.[49]

A second issue is what effect do psychiatrists have on medical treatment decision outcomes. In discussing three case studies, the authors of the article demonstrate how psychiatric consultations can be used to coerce patients towards certain decision outcomes regarded as appropriate by their treating physician, by lending authority to the latter's decision. They suggest that:

[i]t would seem imprudent for the psychiatrist ... to lend authority to another physician in influencing a patient's decisions so as to conform to that physician's desires when the patient is competent to choose among morally defensible options.[49]

The basic proposition espoused is that psychiatric consultation may be used to mask moral dilemmas in medicine:

Confusion has arisen in some professional circles and in the public mind about the proper role of the psychiatrist in medicine and society. Being an expert in the science of human behavior tends to be equated with knowing which behavior is morally right. Psychiatrists are customarily called in to render opinions on what are, in fact, ethical and legal questions.[49]

Further, the psychiatrist may be seen "as a guardian of the psychosocial and holistic approach to the patient, and by implication, as being more approachable than other physicians on moral questions as well."[49]Not the least of the dangers involved in adopting such an approach is that it helps to perpetuate the mind-body duality that has bedevilled medicine.[43] Moreover,

[t]here is a danger in artificially demarcating physicians' roles in this way. If the psychiatrist is seen as more humanistic, is the surgeon less so? Such an approach militates against, rather than in favor of, the biopsychosocial unity of medicine.[49]

The authors conclude that "it appears to serve no legitimate purpose for medicine to mask moral choices as psychiatric problems -- that is, as merely belonging to another field of medicine."[49]

It is clear that the psychiatrist's role in decision-making by the patient is complex, delicate, and open to abuse, but, at the same time, if used properly, can be enabling for and protective of the patient and promote the patient's interests. Further study and analysis of the proper scope and function of the role are needed.

Much has been written about the value of psychiatric consultation in the general medical setting. Little has been said, however, about what is outside the proper role and expertise of the psychiatrist. The temptation is great for the psychiatrist to assume the role of moral guide or moral decision maker. But the psychiatrist's mission has traditionally been one of helping patients arrive at decisions autonomously, of providing the opportunity to discuss and explore complex issues and feelings in a nonjudgmental setting.[49]

CONCLUSION

It has recently been suggested that the explanation of our inability to contain health care costs (for example, in the United States these have risen from 5 percent of the Gross National Product in the 1950s to over 10 percent in the 1980s) is that we are not identifying the true cause of their increase.[50] It has been proposed that the reason that we are spending more on health care is not just that there is more health care and more expensive health care technology available, nor that the system is abused, nor that it is being over-serviced or over-used.[50] Rather, our increased spending may be a method we are using to affirm the worth and rights of the individual, when the recognition of that worth and of those rights seems to be particularly threatened by the bureaucratization of society.[50]

If the above analysis is correct, it may have implications for our treatment of aged persons. To the extent that we make adequate health care, and possibly in particular mental health care,[##] available to aged persons, we may be expressing a value that is relevent to every member of our society, namely, that you count as an individual, as a person in your own right. Likewise, to the extent that we fail to provide health care to the aged we may be making the converse statement. Consequently, we cannot afford to judge the issues raised by this discussion of decision-making by and for aged persons in the context of psychiatric care, in isolation, whether that isolation consists of limiting the discussion within health care disciplines, or within medicine and law, or to consideration only of aged persons. One reason that a more comprehensive approach is needed is that both medicine and law have symbolic functions. Although this symbolism arises from a particular situation, for instance, from the context of the current discussion, it has much wider ramifications. If we kept this in mind we would be less surprised about some of the community reactions that occur in response to medical decision-making and that health care professionals may sometimes find inappropriate. Such reactions may be to the symbolic ramifications of a decision, rather than to the substance of the decision itself. In short, the health care system may be carrying a burden of symbolism expressing what we think of ourselves, of our neighbours, and of our society.

The symbolic function of the law may be regarded as its superego. Within the context of the same analogy, it is appropriate to mention the development of a method of legal analysis that is described as the use of a psychoanalytic probe of

---

[##]The reason that the provision of psychiatric care may bespeak a greater concern for the individual, is that to the extent that the need for such care is less obvious than for physical care, it is being provided because of true concern for the person and not for ulterior motives. Such motives could range from saving ourselves the discomfort and guilt of observing the suffering of uncared for persons, to political reasons such as attracting votes. See Daube D (1966). Trasplantation: Acceptability of procedures and the required legal sanctions. In Wolstenholme GEW & O'Connor M (Eds): *Ethics in Medical Progress: With Special Reference to Transplantation.* London:J.A. Churchill Ltd., p 188 (note the principle of "hidden mutilation" Daube proposes: that we will tolerate intentionally inflicting harm, if the damage we cause can be hidden).

law and jurisprudence to discover the law's unconscious -- its real origins, purposes, functions, aims, and effects.[51] Thus, we are not only looking at what is sometimes called the "black letter" law, the direct expression of the law, perhaps its conscious, but also above this to the law's symbolism and below it to its deeper origins. In other words, psychiatrists may psychoanalyze individual patients, some jurists are seeking to psychoanalyze legal systems. Analysis at all of these levels of law and their mutual integration are important in the further development of humane, health-promoting, beneficial, and just health care law and health care systems to which that law relates.

In conclusion, one reason that discussion of a topic such as "legal and ethical aspects of decision-making by and for aged persons in the context of psychiatric care" may become increasingly important, is because this could be representative of areas where some self-analysis could give rise to valuable and important insights. We may purport to espouse some values overtly, but our attitudes, decisions, and conduct with respect to what we as a society, as professionals, and as individuals are willing to do for weaker and needier members of our community, may reflect rather clearly and directly the adoption of other inconsistent values. We need to know that this is the case, if, in fact, it is.

ACKNOWLEDGMENT

I wish to express my appreciation to my research assistant, John Kennedy, for assistance in preparing these footnotes.

REFERENCES

1. Somerville MA (1980). Medical interventions and the criminal law: lawful or excusable wounding? *Vol. 26. McGill Law Journal*, 82, 89
2. Civil Code of the Province of Quebec, art. 14
3. Engelhardt HT Jr (1984). Shattuck lecture -- allocating scarce medical resources and the availability of organ transplantation: some moral presuppositions. *The New England Journal of Medicine, 311*, 66
4. Individual's Rights Protection Act, R.S.A. 1980., c.I-2, (Alberta) (For Example)
5. The Human Rights Code, R.N.S.B. 1973, C.20 (Supp.), S.N.B. 1976, C.31, and S.N.B. 1979, C.41 (For Example)
6. Rawls J (1971). *A Theory of Justice*. Cambridge, Massachusetts:Belknap Press, p 136 et seq
7. Fried C (1974). *Medical Experimentation: Personal Integrity and Social Policy*. Amsterdam:North-Holland Publishing Co., p 107 et seq
8. Toulmin S (1982). Equity and Principles. *Vol. 20. Osgoode Hall Law Journal* (1) 1
9. Schoeman F (1982). Relationships: children's compentence and children's rights. *IRB A Review of Human Subject Research, 4(6)*:1
10. Somerville MA (1981). Structuring the issues in informed consent. *Vol. 26 McGill Law Journal*, 740
11. Civil Code of the Province of Quebec, art. 246 (For Example)
12. Public Health Protection Act, R.S.Q. c.P-35, sec. 42

13. Holder AR (1977). *Legal Issues in Paediatrics and Adolescent Medicine.* New York:John Wiley & Sons, pp 145-148
14. Civil Code of the Province of Quebec, arts. 325-336
15. R.S.A. 1980, c.D-32
16. R.S.A. 1980, c.D-32, secs. 9, 10
17. Marlett NJ. Issues of Competence and the Dependent Adults Act. Public Guardian's office (Alberta), p 9 et seq
18. R.S.A. 1980, c.D-32, sec. 4(1)
19. R.S.A. 1980, c.D-32, sec. 6(3)
20. R.S.A. 1980, c.D-32, sec. 10
21. Roth LH, Meisl A, & Lidz CW (1982). Tests of competency to consent to treatment. *Americal Journal of Psychiatry, 134,* 279
22. Dyer AR (1982). The dynamics of dependency relationshops: informed consent and the non-autonomous person. *IRB A Review of Human Subjects Research, 4(7),*1
23. R.S.O. 1980, c.262, sec. 1(g)
24. Miller BL (1982). Autonomy and proxy consent. *IRB A Review of Human Subject Research, 4(10),*1-7
25. Mental Patients Protection Act, R.S.Q. c.P-41, sec. 11 (For Example)
26. Mental Health Act, (Ontario), R.S.O 1980, c.262, sec. 14
27. Gutheil TG (1980). In search of true freedom: drug refusal, involuntary medication, and "rotting with your rights on." *Americal Journal of Psychiatry, 137,* 327
28. Awad R (1979). Involuntary civil commitment in Ontario: the need to curtail the abuses of psychiatry. *Canadian Bar Review, 57,* 250
29. *State v. Addington,* 588 S.W. 2d 569 (1980), at p 570
30. Nova Scotia Psychiatric Facilities Review Board: Annual Report, 1980, pp 12-13
31. Nova Scotia Psychiatric Facilities Review Board: Annual Report, 1981, p 4
32. Tranchina P (January 1981). Current issues in Forensic Psychiatry. Special Report, Movement for Democratic Psychiatry, Florence, Italy, 5th International Congress on Law and Psychiatry, Banff
33. Mollica RF (1983). From asylum to community: the threatened disintegration of public psychiatry. *The New England Journal of Medicine, 308,* 367, 371
34. *O'Connor v. Donaldson,* 422 U.S. 563 (1977), 45 L. Ed. 2d 396 (1976), 95 S. Ct. 2486
35. Somerville MA (1985). The law and mental health care for competent and incompetent elderly persons. In AG Awad, HB Durost , WO McCormick, & HM Meier (Eds): *Disturbed Behavior in the Elderly.* New York: S.P. Medical and Scientific Books
36. Health Services & Social Services Act, Quebec R.S.Q. c.S-5, s.4 (For Example)
37. "Deserting the Aged" (March 6, 1983). *The New York Times,* p 49
38. May WF (1982). Who cares for the elderly? *The Hastings Center Report, 12(6):*31, 31-33
39. Somerville MA (1982). Correspondence. The nature of suffering and the goals of medicine. *New England Journal of Medicine, 307,* 758-759
40. Somerville MA (1980). Randomized Controlled Trials and Randomized Control of Consent. *1 Health Law in Canada,* 58
41. Somerville MA (1982). The Dying Elderly Person: Issues in Palliative Treatment and Care. *3 Health Law in Canada (4),* 74
42. Law Reform Commission of Canada Working Paper No. 28 (1982):

Euthanasia, Aiding Suicide and Cessation of Treatment. Ottawa, Supply and Services Canada, pp 58-59

43. Cassell EJ (1982). The nature of suffering and the goals of medicine. *New England Journal of Medicine*, 306, 639

44. Angell M (1982). The quality of mercy. *New England Journal of Medicine*, 306, 98

45. Somerville MA (1982). Correspondence. Inadequate treatment of pain in hospitalized patients. *New England Journal of Medicine, 307*, 55

46. Somerville MA (1984). Pain and Suffering at Interfaces of Medicine and Law, Reports, 6th World Congress on Medical Law, Ghent, Balgium, August, 1982, vol. I, p. 246; 10 Jus Medicum 133

47. Lawton MP. Psychological Vulnerability of Elderly Subjects. In Protection of Elderly Research Subjects. Summary of the National Institute on Aging Conference, July 18-19, 1977, DHEW Publication No. (NIH) 79-1801, p 6, at p. 12

48. Ratzan RM (1982). Cautiousness, risk, and informed consent in clinical geriatrics. *Clinical Resources, 30*, 345, 351

49. Perl M & Shelp EE (1982). Psychiatric consultation masking moral dilemmas in medicine. *New England Journal of Medicine, 307*, 618, 620

50. Jellinek PS (1982). Yet another look at medical cost inflation. *New England Journal of Medicine, 307*, 496, 497

51. Weisstub DN (1978). The theoretical relationship between law and psychiatry. *International Journal of Law and Psychiatry, 1*, 30

DISCUSSION QUESTIONS

1.   What is the relationship of the law to ethics? Should laws be determinative of what constitutes ethical behavior and vice-versa? Is all ethical behavior legal and are all laws ethical in either their formulatin or application?

2.   A client, Mr. Smith, was admitted to a mental health institution by his family who stated that he had "been making threats towards his family, sometimes saying that he'd kill them all." Following examination, it was determined that Mr. Smith really was not dangerous either to himself or others and plans were made to discharge him. When told, Mr. Smith claimed, "I want to stay, I might get angry again and do something rash." Should discharge plans continue? In considering your answer follow the decision-making tool included in Chapter 1.

3.   Should *all* elderly individuals be guaranteed the right to health care?

4.   What kind of evidence would you need in order to prove the "dangerousness" of a client?

5.   In general, do you think that elderly clients give up any rights when they are admitted to nursing homes? Which rights might be most frequently involved? Do they need, if they are competent, to consent to giving up any such rights or is this an automatic consequence? How can you, as a health professional, strive to insure the autonomy of competent elderly clients?

6. A client is unable to manage personal financial affairs but otherwise seems to be an alert individual. This client runs the risk of fractures if a fall should occur. An order is written to restrain the client while awake but the client refuses. Should the restraint be applied anyway? Follow the decision-making process included in Chapter 1 in considering your answer.

7. How can the health team work together to assess the competency of a client? What kind of information would you seek in your assessment?

8. Should the required standards for professional behavior be guided principally by external agencies (e.g., special laws or administrative agencies) or should the control remain with the individual professions?

9. Examine the professional codes in the Appendix and discuss how the various professions address the requirements for ethical behavior. Discuss how the codes can serve as guidelines in decision-making concerning ethical issues.

10. On one piece of paper list the adjectives that come to your mind when you think of elderly clients and, on another piece of paper, those that come to mind when you think of psychiatric clients. Discuss how the factors you have listed might be relevant to or affect ethical aspects of decision-making concerning these persons. Are there any areas of potential conflict between the two lists, when both would apply to the same person?

5

Spencer Eth
J. Wesley Robb

Informed Consent:
The Problem

Spencer Eth, M.D., is an assistant professor of psychiatry at the UCLA School of Medicine and a clinical assistant professor of psychiatry at the University of Southern California School of Medicine. His specific academic responsibilities include the teaching of ethics to psychiatric residents. He has presented and authored articles centered on psychiatric issues in childhood and ethical issues in psychiatric practice.

J. Wesley Robb, Ph.D., holds appointments as a professor of moral philosophy and professor of bioethics at the University of Southern California. Teaching responsibilities include courses in bioethics. Dr. Robb has authored several books, including *An Inquiry into Faith* and *The Reverent Skeptic.* He has served as the president of the American Academy of Religion (1967-1968) and has served as a chaplain in the United States Navy.

Drs. Eth and Robb examine the philosophical, legal, and clinical aspects of informed consent. They discuss issues such as autonomy, beneficence, paternalism, and exceptions to informed consent. A lengthy section on competence is also included. Throughout the chapter there is emphasis on the area of mental health practice and a variety of cases are cited.

Informed consent has its roots in the age-old history of the doctor-patient relationship.Through the years consent has grown in importance, not only to physicians and their patients, but to attorneys and philosophers as well. The essential contributions made by the three fundamentally dissimilar professions create a serious obstacle in the exploration of these concepts -- the lack of a perspective

ETHICS IN MENTAL HEALTH PRACTICE
ISBN 0-8089-1738-2

and terminology common to medicine, law, and ethics. Physicians and mental health practitioners treat disease with the goal of enhancing the patient's future well-being. This clinical orientation is empirical, scientific, and prospective. The law intercedes after an event has occurred.The legal objective is to right a perceived wrong in court using an adversarial, retrospective system of precedents and procedures. The subject matter of philosophers is timeless, and the approach is reflective. Ethical discourse maintains an introspective focus. Recently, startling advances in high technology medicine have contrasted with publicity over examples of unethical experimentation. The public has become acutely aware of patient's rights, consumerism, and malpractice litigation. Meanwhile, scholarly writings on applied ethics proliferate while general trust in the medical and legal professions erodes. It is therefore timely and appropriate to examine consent within a framework and language encompassing all three modes of thought.

PHILOSOPHICAL ASPECTS

Consider the well-publicized case of a 26-year-old quadriplegic woman who wished to refuse consent for all medical care, including food, as a way to term- inate her life.She petitioned for a court order preventing the hospital staff from performing tube feedings against her will and from administering any treatment other than hygiene and pain relief. The patient had had herself admitted to the county hospital's psychiatric ward because she was unable to actively kill herself and did not want to expose her friends to prosecution for aiding her suicide.The Chief of Psychiatry testified that he considered her competent, though not able to make a good decision because she was suffering from depression. He would not permit her to starve in the hospital, even if it meant instituting force feeding. He stated that medical ethics commanded him to preserve lives, not end them.[1]

Interestingly, an equally dramatic case had an entirely different outcome. A 27-year-old severely burned man refused life-sustaining therapy stating: "I do not want to go on as a blind and crippled person." This time the psychiatrist ac- knowledged his right to die, though ultimately the patient chose not to exercise it. Dr. H. Tristram Engelhardt commented, "It is not medicine's responsibility to pre- vent tragedies by denying freedom, for that would be the greater tragedy."[2] How is it that equally ethical physicians can come to opposite conclusions on critical issues? As we will see, the mandates of physician beneficence and patient auto- nomy are often in conflict over consent.

The Oxford English Dictionary defines consent as a voluntary agreement to or acquiescence in what another person proposes or desires; that is, compliance, con- currence, or permission. The word itself derives from the Latin *cum* (with) and *sentire* (to feel or to think) to form, to feel with or think with. Consent is thus etymologically close to the word "consensus." Although not explicitly mentioned in the Hippocratic Oath, by Maimonides, or by other pre-19th century medical au- thorities, the importance of consent is now widely recognized.The right of each patient to learn of his or her diagnosis and the alternative treatments is a fun- damental ethical principle of patient care. The Patient's Bill of Rights adopted by the American Hospital Association is unambiguous in this regard.[3] The phi- losopher Paul Ramsey considers informed consent to be a cardinal canon of loyalty joining the physician and patient together in medical practice and clinical investigation.[4] Two prominent psychiatrists, Redlich and Mollica, assert that: "Informed consent is the basis of all psychiatric intervention and that without it no psychiatric intervention can be morally justified".[5] These sentiments accurately reflect the ethical priority assigned to consent, though they fail to consider the sources of consent's significance or the associated controversies.

Most philosophers agree that the ethical basis for consent is the natural right of man to freedom or liberty. As Robert Veatch states:

> Liberty is a fundamental principle, either an inalienable right endowed by the creator or simply a rational necessity for founding a moral system, (and is) an essential part of the social covenant.[6]

John Stuart Mill during the last century wrote: "Over himself, over his own body and mind, the individual is sovereign."[7] Another favored term for this concept of freedom or liberty is autonomy. The word first applied to the Greek city-states whose citizens made their own laws, as distinct from those held under the control of some conquering force. Today we also speak of autonomy when individuals have some degree of power to control their own actions or destinies, without infringing on the rights of others. As Veatch makes clear, autonomy depends on freedom from restraint and access to knowledge and resources necessary for action. In a medical situation, an autonomous patient retains both the right to accept or refuse treatment and the right to information.

Autonomy is therefore seen as a necessary attribute for the full status of personhood, and so holds a strongly positive value. In addition, the consistent application of consent functions to protect the individual, since an autonomous person is the one best able to maximize his or her own welfare. This point is stressed by John Stuart Mill who states "that he shall not do with his life for his own benefit what he chooses to do with it. He is the person most interested in his own well being."[7] There are also secondary benefits to society since consent enhances public trust and promotes the self-scrutiny of doctors.

The ethical rule that autonomy be respected is predicated on the assumption that the patient is a moral agent who has the capacity for free choice. However, some psychological theories regarding an individual's decision-making apparatus preclude recognition of the patient as a moral agent. If the behavioristic model of the nature of man is taken seriously philosophically, then free choice is replaced with the view that behavior is determined by genetic endowment and past reinforcement history. Since the person's actions are viewed as responses subject to control, the moral recognition involved in the respect for a patient's autonomy is clouded by a theoretical psychology that denies the notion that individuals are moral agents free to choose their own destiny. In contrast, a humanistic psychological model stresses the reality of an autonomous self that must be respected as an important aspect of the doctor-patient relationship. Certainly from a common-sense moral point of view, a strictly deterministic model for human behavior and decision would deny holding an individual responsible for his or her own behavior. Fortunately most of us relate to other persons in ways that belie our theoretical structures and the specific issue of the rights of patients is no exception.

Another relevant moral value given positive weight is beneficence. The aim of altruistic beneficence is to act to confer benefits to another. Doing good is the ethical justification for certain types of paternalism, which lies at the heart of the Hippocratic tradition. Here the focus is on the patient's needs, not the patient's rights. First and foremost the patient needs to be protected from harm. The analogous model for paternalism is, of course, the caring parent who insists on doing what is best for the child. The inherent conflict arises from the frequent disagreements between what the physician believes the patient needs and what the patient actually claims to want. Those who promote paternalism point to the fact that the regressive pressures of illness produce the associated "sick role." This creates a situation in which the physician rightfully plays the parental role while the patient adopts a quasi-child stance, thereby assisting health care acquisition.[8] Others have firmly dissented, stressing the distinction between the authoritative and authoritarian physician.[9] With regard to psychiatric patients, some have argued the extreme paternalistic position, justifying intervention on the belief that the mentally ill lack the ability to discern or act in their own interests. Thus, psychiatric patients are seen to require not only protection from harm but benevolent therapeutic control as well.

Jay Katz has succinctly defined the central ethical problem of informed consent:

(It is) the conflict created by uncertainties about the extent to which individual and societal well-being is better served by encouraging patients' self-determination or supporting physicians' paternalism...reflecting a thorough-going ambivalence about human beings' capacities for taking care of themselves and need for care-taking.[10]

Many medical controversies can be reduced to the core conflict of autonomy versus beneficence. For instance, in his article on informed consent, LaForet castigates the term as a fraud:

Informed consent is a legalistic fiction that destroys good patient care and paralyzes the conscientious physician...The integrity of the physician continues to represent the most effective guarantee of the rights of the patient.[11]

For Dr. LaForet the doctor-patient relationship of "trust and mutual respect" ensured optimal medical care, since it allowed the physician to do what is best for the patient. Whether this statement conveys historical truth or fantasy is subject to debate. But it is clear that an extreme position of paternalistic beneficence does not represent a moral consensus or the current legal reality.

We contend that autonomy is at the core of personhood and has priority value. Its encroachment must be defended by overriding considerations. Autonomy might be legitimately compromised by paternalistic beneficence when the autonomous decision-maker is laboring under false information, undue influence or is incompetent to choose. Another possible circumstance, as illustrated by the case histories, would be when the autonomous decision favors an act that would result in an irreversible harm. It has been suggested that a reasonable and ethical view of the patient's limited autonomy is defensible and must include the clinical realities of the doctor-patient relationship, particularly in cases of serious illness. In such instances, it is argued that the response of the physician should be one of beneficence, fully cognizant of the tension between compassion for the well-being of the patient and the patient's right of autonomy.

An act utilitarian approach is widely practiced in medicine, in which the decision for action is determined by the effects or utility that follows a particular decision. Since each situation is different, there are no binding rules that can apply in every circumstance; each situation must be considered on its own terms. The heart of the ethical dilemma is not whether a physician accepts a primarily pragmatic ethic concerning compromising patient autonomy, or chooses to follow a more absolutist or deontological ethic respecting patient self-determination.

Rather the issue is whether the physician squarely faces and struggles with the conflict between these two ethical positions. The physician who adopts the pragmatic view without questioning the ethical adequacy of such a notion can easily fall prey to an opportunistic style of expedient decision-making that is neither professionally responsible nor ethical.

The philosopher David C. Thomasma argues that the principle of respect for persons involves two moral duties: "The first is to respect the self-determination or autonomy of others...the second is to help restore that autonomy or help establish that autonomy when it is absent."[12] In this view the principle of beneficence will often take precedence over autonomy, particularly in those cases where the patient is confused or otherwise incapacitated. Of course there is the danger of lapsing into extreme paternalism. Thomasma tries to protect himself from this charge by suggesting that autonomy is "the goal of treatment" and not an inherent right when an illness inhibits the patient's ability to make clear decisions regarding his or her own care. The judgment of the patient's ability to weigh the crucial factors involved in medical care is viewed from Thomasma's perspective as a judgment involving the conflict between the patient's right and the patient's well-being, the latter taking precedence. This suggests that physicians will use their discretion conservatively, weighing all of the known factors in making the decision in the patient's best interests.

It is difficult to defend an ideal representation of the physician in everyday clinical practice. From our perspective, patient autonomy should be a basic principle of medical practice and when it is violated the onus of responsibility to justify a countervailing judgment rests with the physician, who has elected to set aside the patient's fundamental right to determine his or her own care. Though the mechanisms of legal action are burdensome, such provisions are available to assure that the physician's judgment is warranted and that the patient has an advocate. In such instances it might be possible to fulfill the ethical responsibility of both respect for the patient's rights and a beneficent action that will serve the patient's best interests.

LEGAL ASPECTS

The asymmetric nature of the therapeutic dyad has been apparent to medical, legal, and ethical commentators. Psychiatrists have recognized that the development of a curative transference, essential to successful psychotherapy, depends on the patient's tendency to relate to the physician in ways fundamentally inappropriate to the exercise of equality. The law considers this treatment alliance as falling within the class of fiduciary relationships in which one person (patient) invests another person (physician) with a special trust and confidence. The physician accepts the responsibility to act in good faith for the benefit of the patient. The physician is thereby constrained to remain skillful, caring, and loyal.

Many implications follow from the assumption of a therapeutic relationship. For instance the patient retains the right to terminate the treatment at any time and for any reason unilaterally. The physician, on the other hand, may withdraw only if precautions are taken to assure continuity of care. This point is especially pertinent to the treatment of hateful or suicidal patents.[13] It should also be well known that sexual activity between patient and physician, under the guise of treatment, is wrong. Regardless of the patient's consent, sexualizing the relationship is inherently exploitative.[14] Psychiatrists need to be wary of maintaining social contacts with patients, even if it does not seem to be harming the treatment. In the case of Landau vs. Werner, a psychiatrist began seeing a patient outside of session in order to help resolve an erotic transference. The patient eventually made a suicidal act, and the psychiatrist was held blameworthy for breach of trust.[15]

The concept of a fiduciary relationship imposes a burden on the physician for any misrepresentation of the treatment by commission or omission. There can be no such caveat as patient beware, for patients can always assume the physician is on their side. From a legal perspective, "Informed consent is meant, then, to force the doctor to give the patient knowledge that will make him or her an equal bargaining partner."[16] Consent is seen to encourage independence in the treatment process, thereby lessening the asymmetry of the doctor-patient relationship. The widest application of voluntary informed consent promotes equity and fairness by moving in the direction of a contract among equal's model of interaction. But the adoption of a contract model, to the extent that it is feasible, diminishes the fiduciary responsibility of the physician and ignores the corresponding dependency of the patient. Further, doctor-patient transactions frequently concern life and death decisions that are qualitatively different from the choices involved in purchasing a used car. We believe that informed consent expresses the affirmative duty of the physician to preserve autonomy by encouraging knowledgeable decision-making. This requires the disclosure of sufficient information in the consent process.

The legal requirement for patient consent to medical care was first derived from the law of civil battery. Technically, a battery is an intentional, unauthorized touching.There need be no intent to harm, for the act itself is a wrong regardless of the consequences. By extension it is a battery to perform a medical procedure or treat a patient without first obtaining consent. The landmark case in this regard is Scholoendorff vs. New York Hospital, in which a fibroid tumor was removed from the patient during an operation purportedly for diagnostic purposes. Justice Benjamin Cardozo's 1914 decision has been quoted repeatedly:

> Every human being of adult years and sound mind has a right to determine what shall be done with his own body; and a surgeon who performs an operation without his patient's consent commits an assault, for which he is liable in damages.[17]

Although historically significant, the principle of battery has come to be applied to situations in which no consent has been obtained. One psychiatric example involved an institutionalized catatonic schizophrenic who became pregnant by another patient. An abortion was performed without consent, and a suit for assault and battery followed.[18]

The modern trend is to regard the provision of information as a requirement of health care providers. Hence the failure to inform adequately constitutes negligent nondisclosure. Here the patient has consented to the procedure, but has done so without sufficient knowledge of the risks involved. The particular term "informed consent" was first used by the Kansas Supreme Court in 1960 in Natanson vs. Kline. In that case a woman suffered injuries from radiation therapy for breast cancer. Consent was obtained and the treatment was properly performed; however, the consent was invalid because the patient had not been fully informed of the possible serious side-effects. Although predictaed on negligence rather than battery, the court's decision stressing patient autonomy greatly resembles Cardozo's of a half-century before:

(It) follows that each man is considered to be master of his own body, and he may, if he be of sound mind, expressly prohibit the performance of life-saving surgery, or other medical treatment. A doctor may well believe that an operation or other form of treatment is desirable and necessary, but the law does not permit him to substitute his own judgment for that of the patient by any form of artifice or deception.[19]

Negligence requires that the following conditions are fulfilled: that the physician had a duty toward the patient that was breached, directly resulting in damages. Therefore, legal action under the negligence doctrine must be based on an inadequate or invalid consent (the breached duty), permitting the patient to undergo a procedure that causes actual harm. The failure to disclose a risk that does not materialize, though morally wrong, imposes no legal liability since no damage occurred. Here the law ignores the ethical insult perpetrated by the omission of important information. Joseph Goldstein laments that the legal system fails to:

> recognize that a citizen can be wronged without being harmed, that his dignity as a human being has been violated and that an assault has taken place the moment the deceiving authority commences therapy... even if beneficial.[20]

The intent, then, of the legal remedy of an award of monetary damages is to compensate the victims for the expenses, pain, and suffering arising from their injuries and not to redress the moral wrong.

The central issue in negligent consent is:

> to define the extent of disclosure that is required so that physicians will have some idea of how to fulfill their duty, and patients will have some idea how to determine if their right to information is being denied.[21]

Since the goal of disclosure is to enhance the patient's autonomy in medical decision-making, full disclosure would seem ideal. It was, however, immediately recognized by the court in Cobbs vs. Grant that although "the patient has an abject dependence upon his physician for the information upon which he relies in reaching his decision...the patient's interest in information does not extend to a lengthy polysyllabic discourse on all possible complications."[22] The answer to the question "How much information is necessary and sufficient?" is usually "all of the material facts." A material fact is one that has significance for the reasonable patient in deciding to consent. Whether a particular fact is material can be determined according to two very different standards, which will be discussed in turn.

In a series on informed consent, published in the *Journal of the American Medical Association* in 1970, great emphasis was placed on the then prevailing community or professional standard approach.[23] This community standard measures the physician's duty to disclose by what a "reasonable medical practitioner would make under the same or similar circumstances."[19] In order to prove that the physician withheld facts that are usually mentioned, the patient would need to establish the actual practice in the community. This requires testimony from a physician familiar with local medical customs. For instance, trial witnesses stated that it was not the practice of surgeons in Wilmington, Delaware to warn thyroidectomy patients of the risk of damage to the laryngeal nerve. Therefore, under the community practice standard of informed consent disclosure, the defendant surgeon was not guilty of negligence for failing to mention this potential hazard, despite the patient's subsequent injury.[24]

Discomfort with this community standard arose. As the Wisconsin Supreme Court held:

> The duty to disclose or inform cannot be summarily limited to a professional standard that may be nonexistent or inadequate to meet the informational needs of a patient...the duty of the doctor is to make such disclosures as appear reasonably necessary...to enable a reasonable person...to intelligently exercise his right to consent or refuse.[81]

The responsibility of the physician is to disclose not what other physicians are mentioning, but what patients want to know. As such there is no requirement for medical testimony to establish the necessity of disclosure. It is the significance of the risks that are relevant, not the medical consensus. The courts are clear that the justification for expanding disclosure of information is the ethical priority of self-determination. In Cobbs vs. Grant the court overturned the community practice standard as, "irreconcilable with the basic right of the patient to make the ultimate informed decision regarding the course of treatment to which he knowledgeably consents to be subjected."[22]

The material risk standard is well articulated by Justice Spotswood Robinson in Canterbury vs. Spence. In this case a 19-year-old man became paralyzed following a laminectomy. The court explained its rationale in establishing what has become known as the Canterbury rule:

> The patient's right of self-decision shapes the boundaries of the duty to reveal. The scope of the physician's communications to the patient, then, must be measured by the patient's need, and that need is the information material to the decision. (A) risk is thus material when a reasonable person, in what the physician knows or should know to be the patient's position, would be likely to attach significance to the risk or cluster of risks in deciding whether or not to forego the proposed therapy."[25]

There is a serious methodological difficulty in ascertaining a particular patient's sense of material risk. A physician can never be sure if a danger is one that the patient wishes to know about unless that patient is asked. Operationally this would force the physician to present all possible risks to every patient. Some court decisions have appeared to invest physicians with mind-reading abilities in decoding each patient's unique desires. "The doctor-patient relationship is a one-on-one affair. What is reasonable disclosure in one instance may not be reasonable in another."[27] Reference to a "reasonable person" avoids this dilemma, although it is still ambiguous how this "reasonable person's" views are unmasked, and how the physician can compensate for the nonreasonable person's erosion of autonomy. Veatch suggests that the "reasonable person" can be approximated by asking a group of lay people whether they would want to be informed of a specific risk.[6] If five percent or more desire to know, then that constitutes a risk that should be disclosed. It then becomes the duty of the nonreasonable patient to communicate a special need to know.

American jurisprudence rests on a foundation of heterogeneous and evolving judicial rulings and statutory provisions. Jurists in several states have pointedly rejected the Canterbury doctrine as fostering malpractice actions, restraining physicians, and discouraging compliance with treatment. The prevalent trend is to combine the material risk and professional standards in an effort to preserve both patient autonomy and physician discretion.[28] A thorough state-by-state analysis of the legal requirements of disclosure can be found in Rosoff's 1980 text.[29]

A difficult question in all informed consent cases is to establish whether the patient would or would not have agreed to the procedure had additional information been supplied. If the patient would have consented anyway, then the resulting injury was not the result of negligent consent and the necessary proximate cause fails to be established. Two approaches are possible to resolve this causation issue. The subjective test is based on whether that particular patient would have consented or not, regardless of whether the patient's rationale is idiosyncratic, unsound, or even psychotic. One potential danger inherent in this standard is the tendency for plaintiffs to argue that they would certainly have refused treatment and attempt to justify that position post hoc. Although this subjective standard is most individualized and consequently most cognizant of autonomy, it is in disfavor relative to the alternative objective test.

In the objective standard the critical question is reformulated to: What would the prudent or reasonable patient, operationalized as judge or jury, have decided in that situation? Unfortunately, though, this rule adopts a form of a "community of patients" standard and fails to honor individuality. In effect physicians would share with Mr. Smith what a reasonable patient would want to know, not what Mr. Smith wants to know. Although an improvement over disclosing only what a consensus of doctors would reveal, this standard requires further refinement in order to serve the moral priority. Canadian courts have also wrestled with the "causation issue," without making a substantive advance from the American position.[30] It would seem wise then to adopt a set of rules that can accommodate the strict demands of ethics. In so doing, both subjective and objecive tests are met and autonomy is maximally fostered.

There are several exceptions to the rule requiring informed consent, which may serve as an affirmative defense in court. A true medical emergency, where the patient is unconscious or unable to respond, confers presumed consent for a lifesaving intervention. In that case it can be assumed that if the patient could consent he or she would certainly do so. If possible, a proxy consent should be secured from a spouse or close relative, but emergency treatment cannot be delayed while searching for a relative. A more limited exception to specific consent involves a situation in which consent is implied. For instance a general consent to surgical procedure will allow the surgeon to proceed with a minor extension if indicated. It would be ludicrous to forego an opportunity to readily correct a small problem during the course of an operation.

For psychiatrists the concept of tacit consent permits ongoing psychotherapy without the burden of obtaining consent before each session. Consent for the psychiatric treatment remains in force until the patient raises an objection. Finally, the government is empowered to take action intended to protect the public. Governmental consent can establish quarantines and vaccination programs. This form of obligatory consent covers protective interventions, but could never compel a citizen to confer a benefit onto another. Consequently there are no mandatory blood or organ donation programs.

The law does provide for proxy or vicarious consent for dependent children by parents, guardians, or the court. Minors are considered incapable of giving consent in every jurisdiction, except for treatment of certain specified illnesses, such as venereal disease or drug addiction.[31] Although third party consent for treatment of the child is universally accepted, a procedure designed to benefit another person requires additional justification. For instance a court permitted kidney transplantation between 7-year-old identical twins living in the same home, because trauma to the donor may have resulted from the death of her sister.[32] But another court disallowed the donation of a kidney from an institutionalized, retarded schizophrenic to his sibling since there was no evidence that any interest of the patient would be served.[33] However, other conflicting decisions suggest that no clear set of rules is in force.

Consent for the involvement of children in medical research is fraught with controversy.[34] In many ways children are biologically different organisms from adults, so that extrapolation from adult findings is invalid. Experimental data must be obtained from children directly, lest they become scientific orphans estranged from medical progress. Because the young subject is legally and often psychologically incapable of consenting, some alternative mechanism is necessary.[35] Extending the parental right to offer consent for the child from the treatment situation to a research context seems unacceptable for dangerous, nontherapeutic studies. Fortunately, low risk/high benefit research of the type most relevant to clinical child psychiatry is generally felt to be permissible.

Another exception to informed consent is the doctrine of therapeutic privilege. Therapeutic privilege holds when the physician believes that revealing information poses a serious threat, so that disclosure is medically contraindicated. For instance, in cases of serious illness or extreme distress, a full explanation might alarm the patient to the point that he or she would be unable to make a decision, follow the treatment prescribed, or be psychologically harmed. Under these circumstances a physician may exercise discretion and withhold information. A California court has operationalized the limited applicability of therapeutic privilege to:

> When a doctor can prove by a preponderance of the evidence he relied upon facts which would demonstrate to a reasonable man the disclosure would have so seriously upset the patient that the patient would not have been able to dispassionately weigh the risks of refusing to undergo the recommended treatment.[22]

The decision to rely upon a claim of therapeutic privilege is a serious one, perhaps best made after consultation with another physician. As Judge Robinson warns: "The privilege does not accept the paternalistic notion that the physician may remain silent simply because divulgence might prompt the patient to forego therapy the physician feels the patient really needs."[26] It must be abundantly clear that disclosure constitutes a significant threat of harm to the patient. Under these circumstances disclosure might be made to the patient's spouse or close relative, or a waiver of disclosure might be sought from the patient. Underlying therapeutic privilege is the critical distinction between withholding information and deception. Lying is rarely the legal, ethical, or clinical preferred choice. Physicians ought to strive for truthfulness even when full truth is too dangerous.

CRITERIA FOR COMPETENCE

Informed consent presupposes autonomy in decision-making, which itself is dependent on mental competence. "Competent persons possess both the right and the ability to give informed consent; incompetent persons have neither the requisite ability nor the right."[36] Although this principle can be clearly stated, defining and determining competency are immensely complex tasks, frequently pitting lawyer against doctor. Consider the problems associated with this general definition: "Competence is a legal concept dealing with a mental capacity or ability of a person to perform an act," such as giving informed consent to treatment.[37] Competence, as a legal concept, must be adjudicated by a court. The court is forced to judge a person's mental capacity to make a treatment decision, a subject far afield from its usual domain of ascertaining criminal or civil guilt. Further, the court's finding must be either one of competence or incompetence, contrary to the clinical reality of a spectrum of intermediate abilities. The consequence of a court determination of incompetence is enormous, as only the court-appointed guardian of an incompetent patient can provide a legally binding consent.

Under common law, all adults are presumed to be competent to consent until a court declares otherwise. Historically the age at which an incompetent minor becomes a competent adult has varied from 13 to 21 years, and to the present no consensus age has emerged. Since a juvenile is by law incompetent, the Supreme Court has ruled that a parent may commit a minor to a mental institution against the child's wishes. Because the parent has consented, the hospitalization is considered voluntary.[38] In a medical context, competence is assumed for all conscious adult patients. A patient does not automatically become incompetent because of mental illness, retardation, or any other disease. However, lack or loss of competency can and does result from a variety of circumstances, including the temporary influence of toxins, the more long-lasting effects of functional psychiatric disorders, and the chronic incapacitation of primary degenerative brain diseases. From a clinical perspective, the critical concerns are the diagnosis and treatment of conditions affecting mentation, such as delirium, psychosis, and dementia. Ethicists and attorneys are much more interested in the concomitant erosion of autonomy and the need to determine whether the patient has sufficient capability to consent.

The most common trigger for questioning a patient's competence is noncompliance with a treatment recommendation. It is as though the failure to cooperate with a physician means that the patient does not comprehend the benefits of accepting the treatment or does not appreciate the dangers of refusing to consent. The result is a Catch 22 situation for patients rejecting treatment. Patients are considered competent and treated if they consent, and are deemed incompetent and treated anyway if they refuse. Although medically expedient for the patient declining life-saving treatment, this tautological criterion for competence has been ridiculed by the court:

> Until she changed her original decision and withdrew her consent to the amputation, her competence was not questioned, but the irrationality of her decision does not justify a conclusion that Mrs. C. is incompetent in the legal sense. The law protects her right to make her own decision to accept or reject treatment, whether that decision is wise or unwise.[39]

Decision-making depends on competency, and competency must be defined and determined in a manner acceptable to physicians, lawyers, and philosophers. All demand a reliable standard that balances autonomy and beneficence. There are several possible competency standards of varying stringency; each is justifiable, internally consistent, and reliable. The choice would depend on the public policy goals for the specific purpose for which the standard is to be applied. Although a psychiatrist can accurately describe a patient's mental status, this empirical finding alone does not establish competency. The core issue for the court is where to draw the line between allowing the patient to make a decision and giving that responsibility to someone else.

Competency is an especially vexing problem in psychiatry, where so many patients appear to be marginally competent. Some have suggested that the determination should be based on an assessment of the patient's overall abilities. Abernethy proposes that:

> the standard for finding a patient not competent to refuse treatment should be no less than generalized incompetence, including clear evidence that a patient is uninformable on emotionally neutral issues and cognitively incapable of making ordinary decisions on matters unrelated to the crisis at hand.[40]

However, a functional test fails to recognize that a patient may be globally capable, but yet at the same time be quite unable to offer competent decisions specifically about medical care. Further, this standard would work to exclude the majority of beneficient paternalistic interventions.

An alternative standard is based on cognitive ability. This test reflects the patient's comprehension of a procedure and its consequences. Modifications of this standard are in wide use, despite its limitations. The cognitive standard admittedly places great value on rational thought as the proper justification for actions. Yet, many observers note that even competent patients lack impressive comprehension. Many patients go through the formalities of the consent process without comprehending critical information. The late editor of the *New England Journal of Medicine* has written: "Chances are remote that the subject (of a clinical study) really understands what he has consented to."[41] Consent forms are also an obstacle. Five representative surgical forms were examined by applying standardized readability tests to them and it was discovered that to understand these forms with some degree of comprehension would require an upper division or graduate level university education.[42] The problem is compounded in multilingual, multicultural clinical settings. Most courts do not require proof that a patient understood, only that information was disclosed in a manner and at a time so that the patient could have understood. As Judge Robinson ruled: "The physician discharges the duty when he makes a reasonable effort to convey sufficient information although the patient, without fault of the physician, may not fully grasp it."[26]

We will present a spectrum of tests of competence based on a cognitive standard. These five tests, derived from several authors, range from one that is biased strongly in favor of patient freedom to another that markedly serves patient protection.[43-46] The first test deems a patient competent if he or she is able to express consent or refusal of treatment. The patient need only evidence a choice in order to have that preference honored. This test gives all but the unconscious, mute, or unintelligible patient control of the treatment. If the patient can unambiguously indicate yes or no, his or her wishes will be followed. The test relies exclusively on the signal, not on the attendant thought processes, and thus is overinclusive of patients whose decision-making abilities are critically impaired. Certain extreme patient advocates, who always take the patient's literal word as the rightful command, have argued for this test.[47] Nearly all physicians, however, and most ethicists and attorneys will firmly reject it as precluding beneficent interventions.

The second test considers patients competent if they have the ability to understand the elements of the consent process. This test only weighs the capacity to comprehend, not actual comprehension of the relevant material. A method to determine if the patient has that capacity is to evaluate the patient's handling of information of equivalent complexity during the mental status examination. The application of this competency test by the court can be inferred in the case of *In re Yetter*. Mrs Yetter was a 60-year-old schizophrenic who had been hospitalized for two years. A breast mass, felt to be cancer, was discovered on physical examination. Mrs. Yetter refused to consent to a biopsy and possible surgery on the basis of psychotic thinking. She claimed falsely that her aunt had died from such surgery and that treatment would interfere with her ability to have babies. The judge ruled Mrs. Yetter competent to decline medical care:

> Are we then to force her to submit to medical treatment because some of her present reasons for refusal are delusional and the result of mental illness? Upon reflection, balancing the risk involved in our refusal to act in favor of compulsory treatment against giving the greatest possible protection to the individual in furtherance of his own desires, we are unwilling now to overrule Mrs. Yetter's original irrational but competent decision.[48]

Psychiatrists have also supported this second test. For instance, Culver and colleagues will hold a patient competent to decide about a particular psychiatric treatment if the following criteria are met: (1) "the patient knows that the physician believes the patient is ill and in need of treatment," (2) that "this particular treatment may help the patient's illness," and (3) "the patient knows he or she may be called upon to make a decision regarding this treatment."[46] A decision based on an irrational belief or an irrational desire should be respected. Hence a patient exhibiting psychotic denial is still competent to reject treatment. Unlike the Yetter court, Culver would disregard this test for delusional patients who wish to forego livesaving procedures. Although this exception permits paternalistic action when it is most needed, it is logically inconsistent to alter the standard according to the gravity of the decision.

The third test characterizes competency as an actual understanding and use of the relevant information discussed in the consent process. The patient must participate actively in order to comprehend and consider the essential material. As such, inadequate intelligence, language skills and deficits in attention, processing, and memory can all result in incompetence. The practical advantage of this test is that it reflects an integral consent activity that can be reliably measured by examination. But the test has been criticized as circular since the question of competence ultimately rests only on the understanding of the consent information provided and not on any abilities unrelated to the patient's illness and treatment situation.

The fourth test defines competency as a decision based on rational reasons. There is some disagreement in the literature whether "rational reasons" is to mean demonstrating good judgment or relevant and recognizable conclusions. Demanding good judgment causes most deluded, thought-disordered, manic, and severely depressed patients to be judged incompetent, removing from them the right to consent or refuse treatment. Rational reasons can also be construed as the patient having acceptable premises and a conclusion related to these premises. The patient should be able to justify the conclusions even though they do not precisely follow from the premises. If this test allows for false premises and *non-sequitur* logic, then it comes to closely resemble the second test. The practical difficulty with both the fourth and the second tests is ascertaining the patient's actual thinking about the specific treatment issue. Silent, noncooperative, and evasive patients create insurmountable problems in determining competency according to these tests.

The final test equates competency exclusively with a decision favoring a reasonable outcome. The patient must be able to appreciate other perspectives and make a mature treatment choice. A patient who experiences denial, lack of insight, or concrete thinking may be barred from the consent process. Although this standard would enable a Jehovah's Witness from refusing a blood transfusion, it would exclude far too many psychiatric patients from participating in their own care. This test is unacceptably paternalistic. Assuring beneficent action cannot justify the sweeping deprivation of autonomy for the mentally ill. There is no consensus standard for competency to consent. Each case generates its own array of unique factors that require a separate and thoroughgoing analysis. However, the general issues explored above provide a framework for determining when the patient's right to decide may be ethically, legally, and clinically compromised.

Following a court determination of incompetence, a guardian is appointed. Preference is usually given to the spouse or next of kin to exercise the patient's right through substituted consent. When family members are unavailable or unsuitable, the court will choose someone to serve as guardian, conservator, or patient advocate. Occasionally the court will make the treatment decision. A recent development has been the suggestion that persons might wish to nominate a guardian in the event that they became incompetent. For instance, patients with mild Alzheimer's disease could select their own future guardians, thereby retaining some indirect control of later treatment. Childress has characterized this procedure as "past consent."[49] A timeless example is Odysseus' command that his men bind him to the mast and then stuff their ears with wax while sailing past the captivating Sirens.Odysseus ordered the sailors not to untie him, regardless of what he subsequently said. Odysseus' past consent overruled his future, incompetent demands. Two unanswered questions with this procedure are: how can the original instructions be validated years later, and under what circumstances can the instructions be changed?

Some have suggested that subjects or patients be routinely screened for competency. Miller and Willner propose that all potential research subjects be given a questionnaire as part of the consent process to ensure that the information presented has been understood. Repeated failures would disqualify a person's consent from being accepted.[50] Eth and Eth express the need to safeguard the consent process in research involving self-destructive psychiatric patients. They would call upon a nurse to serve as a monitor to veto consent that is a manifestation of masochistic tendencies.[51] Other possibilities include consent auditors, advocates, or trusted advisors. The difficulties with these systems are that the patient's privacy and autonomy are threatened and that investigations are impeded. Except for extraordinary research, such as psychosurgery, these procedures have not been adopted.Schwarz, a psychiatrist, has published a checklist for the routine evaluation of patient capacity to consent to treatment. He recommends that chronic patients be reassessed on a regular basis.[52] Although consent forms for psychotropic medications are in common use, these forms have generally not included sections documenting patient competence.

VOLUNTARY AND INVOLUNTARY TREATMENT

Voluntary implies a free choice without undue influence or coercion. Undue influence can include any excessive reward or irrationally persuasive technique.

Coercion covers those situations in which threat or forceful manipulation is applied. There is a gray zone where pressures can diminish though not negate free will. Shakespeare warns in Act 5 of *Romeo and Juliet*, "tempt not a desperate man." Surely the duress of illness is such that free choice may no longer be possible. An eminent gastroenterologist has observed:

> Indeed, I doubt if any physician care for any patient can ever get really informed consent from the patient; the patient-physician relationship is, or should be, so strong as to make the likelihood of free consent about the same as that of prisoners.[53]

Psychiatrists are well aware of the power of a transference reaction in the doctor-patient relationship. In this context a patient may make decisions that seem out of character for that individual. Courts have given considerable weight to the disadvantage inherent in the patient's transference-laden, trusting relationship with the physician. For instance an infirm, elderly patient gave a substantial gift to her physician. The transaction was voided by a court perceiving the physician's ulterior motives and the patient's undue influence. Appelbaum and Roth urge clinicians to consider not only the transference and psychodynamic elements of the patient's personality, but the nature of the information exchanged and the effect of the consent process milieu as well.[54]

The concern over voluntariness is underscored when the patient is suffering from a serious psychiatric disorder. In addition to the direct effects of the mental impairment itself on cognition, affect, and personality, there are significant secondary consequences of chronic hospitalization. Institutionalization can promote the iatrogenic effects of low self-esteem, inertia, and diminished effectiveness in decision-making. Recognition of these ills led to the deinstitutionalization and community psychiatry movements.[55] These issues were directly addressed by the court in the case of a state hospital inmate who signed a consent for experimental psychosurgery. An attorney, Kaimowitz, sued to prohibit the procedure. Since the patient had been involuntarily confined for 17 years, the judge concluded that: "The very nature of incarceration diminishes capacity to consent."[56] A patient population particularly vulnerable to the infantilizing effects of institutionalization is the mentally retarded. For certain patients there may be no practical alternative to the appointment of a guardian, who must delicately balance the patient's expressed wishes with the patient's actual needs in determining a course of action.

Civil commitment or involuntary psychiatric hospitalization is legally based on the joint determination of mental illness and dangerousness, not on the competency to make rational decisions. Although these areas of function may overlap, they are not congruent. A finding of incompetence does not alone justify commitment. Psychiatric hospitalization without consent must be accomplished in full accord with the local laws and procedures governing this action. Otherwise, the psychiatrist is in jeopardy of being charged with assault, false imprisonment, and malpractice. The controversies surrounding involuntary hospitalization have been argued from psychiatric, legal, and ethical perspectives in detail.[57, 58]

The recent legal thrust in favor of autonomy and civil liberty has prompted a distinguished psychiatrist to complain: "The rights of the mentally ill to be treated and protected are being set aside in the rush to give them their freedom."[59] A majority of psychiatric professionals would favor tipping the balance in the direction of beneficent paternalistic intervention when autonomy is severely compromised by mental illness. This is especially true and compelling when patients represent a danger to themselves or others. Preventable suicide is a potent argument for the temporary abrogation of liberty. In many instances, treated patients will later express grateful appreciation for involuntary hospitalization, literally thanking the doctor for saving their lives. In a sense this represents "future consent."

The courts have been forced to define the limits of the patient's right to refuse treatment. In 1972 the court was asked to intervene to force a seriously injured Jehovah's Witness to accept a blood transfusion. The patient lucidly told the judge, "I'm willing to take my chances. My faith is that strong. I wish to live but with no blood transfusions." The judge declined to order a transfusion.[60] However, a competent patient's treatment refusal may have to be balanced against other interests. For instance patient autonomy may need to be compromised by the state's interest in preventing suicide, as in the case of the quadriplegic refusing food. Several times the court has had to consider the needs of innocent third parties, such as the dependent children of a parent refusing livesaving treatment. These cases raise complex issues that preclude generalizations or simple rules.

Courts have also had to decide whether guardians have the same power to refuse treatment as do competent patients. In the famous Karen Quinlan decision, the New Jersey Supreme Court held that her parents, as guardians, could choose to remove the irreversibly comatose patient from her respirator, even if death resulted from the discontinuation of that life support.[61] More recently the Massachusetts high court ruled that the guardian of an elderly institutionalized retardate could deny the patient chemotherapy for a form of incurable leukemia, because the suffering caused by the treatment was not worth the relatively brief remission it might induce.[62] The court indicated that the guardian's goal is to choose the action the patient would select if competent.

As difficult as it is to define the medical patient's right to refuse treatment, it is even more problematic in psychiatry. The outcomes of these cases center on questions of whether the mentally ill patient is truly competent to refuse treatment and of what constitutes an emergency situation requiring involuntary treatment. As Perr contends, it seems contradictory that those already judged to be impaired in their capacity for autonomy by their confinement to a psychiatric hospital may still retain the right to refuse treatment necessary to reestablish full autonomy.[63] Michels has suggested several possible arguments to justify the psychiatric patient's right to refuse treatment. For example the constitution guarantees the right to free speech and prohibits cruel and unusual punishment.[64] However, these arguments seem more relevant to extreme cases, such as experimental treatment with prisoners. Another group of arguments rely on the right of privacy and the fundamental notion of the inviolability of one's own body.

Two landmark decisions have clarified when the right to refuse treatment is or is not legally justified, and outlined the steps to be taken when the assumed right to refuse treatment is denied. In *Rogers vs. Okin*, a Massachusetts federal court found that "civilly committed patients in the state have a right to refuse all psychiatric medication except in emergencies."[65] If that right is to be revoked, the patient must be declared incompetent and the appointed guardian then must be given consent. The emergency exception is defined as "substantial likelihood of, or as a result of, extreme violence, personal injury, or attempted suicide."[65] In a later review, the Appellate Court ordered the District Court to broaden its definition of an emergency and devise a less complex method for determining competency. In *Rennie vs. Klein*, a New Jersey federal court stressed the importance of disclosing possible medication side effects in the informed consent process. Again the court allowed for an emergency exception to consent for behavior that "creates danger to the patient himself or to others in the hospital."[66] Involuntary patients can be declared incompetent, but only after a review by a patient advocate.

Knotty problems arise when a prisoner may benefit from psychiatric treatment in the prison setting. Although not incompetent, the incarcerated prisoner, like the institutionalized patient counterpart, may have his or her ability to offer voluntary consent impaired. Such might be true if transfer to more favorable quarters or even release were contingent on accepting a certain form of treatment. One clearly suspects situations involved in experimental behavior modification program for sex offenders in the Connecticut Correctional Institute.[67] The prisoners were informed that participation in the program would determine whether parole would be granted or denied. In another case a federal appeals court struck down an Iowa treatment protocol involving apomorphine as an aversive stimulus. The court indicated "that the Eighth Amendment also may protect mental patients from certain forms of enforced 'treatments' which have been imposed over their objection and which are really punishments in disguise."[68] However appropriate, nonpunitive treatment administered without threat or bribe can be given over the objections of a prisoner. For example, no violation of federal rights occurred when a prisoner/patient was injected with fluphenazine against his will.[69]

The issue of the right to refuse treatment has been accentuated with the advance and now customary use of psychotropic medication. Further legal action can be confidently predicted. Although conventional psychotherapy and other forms of milieu treatment are not physically invasive, it can be argued that they are psychologically intrusive and thus could infringe on the right to privacy principle. It would seem that the right to refuse treatment is more easily exercised by the hospitalized patient when the nature of the care afforded is purely verbal. Unfortunately, the mentally ill patient's right to reject treatment efforts conflicts with the committed patient's right to be treated. This dilemma has found no comfortable resolution.

CLINICAL ASPECTS

The most stringent available rules governing informed consent are those suggested for use in clinical research involving human subjects.[70] These federal guidelines follow the 1947 Nuremberg Code embedded in the court opinion of the trial of World War II physicians for crimes against humanity.[67] The Code specifies that voluntary consent is absolutely essential. A subject of human experimentation must have sufficient knowledge and comprehension of the elements of the procedures involved as to enable him to make an understanding and enlightened decision. The Nuremberg Code requires information about: the nature, duration, and purpose of the experiment; the method and means by which it is to be conducted; all inconveniences and hazards reasonably to be expected; and the effects upon health or person that may possibly come from participation.

Physician and researcher abuse of patients and subjects was later uncovered in the United States, though not of a magnitude comparable to the concentration camp experiments.[71] Federal intervention was inevitable as the scandals implied an unwillingness of some medical scientists to adhere to the ethical codes and an inability of the profession to police itself.[72] Governmental guidelines were codified by 1971 and revised a decade later based on the work of the National Commission for the Protection of Human Subjects of Biomedical and Behavioral Research.[73] Research protocols must be first approved by the local Institutional Review Board. The current federal standards are precise and encompassing in their informational content. It is safe to assume that if these research requirements (outlined below) are met, then the informational needs for routine clinical practice will be exceeded, precluding a later finding that consent was incomplete.

The consent process is a dyadic transaction between physician and patient predicated on personal discussion; consent is more properly negotiated than obtained. Informational disclosure may begin with and should always include a description of the illness, including diagnosis, in language accessible to the patient. Informed consents have been voided by the courts because a patient has failed to understand such key words as mastectomy or laminectomy. Since several of the current psychiatric diagnoses are new, special care must be taken to explain fully the nature of these disorders to the patient.[74]

Psychiatrists are frequently sensitive to the impact of revealing certain diagnoses. The mention of "schizophrenia" may overwhelm a patient with associations to former images of incurability and life-long institutionalization.[75] For these patients, familiar terms may need to be redefined in light of current knowledge and prognostic optimism. This approach is preferable to the deceptive alternative of inaccurately substituting euphemistic phrases for the true name. The use of "thought disorder" for schizophrenia or "slow" for retardation is as much a disservice as the former practice of referring to cancer as a growth, in the misguided though well-intentioned attempt to mystify and relieve the patient.[76] It may be uncomfortable for physicians and patients alike to confront serious illness, but it is of course unavoidable. Psychiatrists above all are committed to the wisdom of overcoming fear in order to face and cope with reality.

The discussion of the illness naturally leads to a description of the recommended procedure, such as a further diagnostic test or a particular treatment. Obviously a reasonable patient would want to learn about the purpose, nature, cost, and intended benefits. It is best to avoid false assurances, which can be easily misheard as unintended guarantee.The hoped-for benefits must be weighed against a survey of risks and consequences. This area of the consent process has proven to be intensely controversial. The dispute centers on the advisability of warning patients of an improbable risk of injury. For instance in the Canterbury case, the surgeon chose to withhold information about a 1 percent chance of paralysis.[26] He reasoned that it would needlessly frighten his patients, causing some to forego the benefits of surgery. The circuit court of appeals held that by so doing the physician violated the patient's right of self-determination. In another case the risk of gastroscopic stomach puncture estimated to be less than 1 per 2000 was deemed disclosable.[77]

On close examination, the law is seen to contain a myriad of different and frequently contradicting opinions. As Annas has noted, the lists of risks that must be mentioned overlaps considerably with a list of risks that need not be disclosed.[67] For that reason, only generalizations are possible. It is safe to assume that any risk of serious bodily injury or death, however slight, ought to be stated. Any novel or innovative practice, that is procedure or treatment employed by a minority of physicians, may require the same prudent disclosure and consent form as a medical experiment. A safe rule to follow is that the more unorthodox the treatment the more information should be divulged. For routine practice, risk disclosure can be less inclusive. After long deliberation a Boston City Hospital committee decided that any risk expected to occur with greater than 1 percent frequency should be mentioned.[67] Others have suggested 2 percent or 5 percent frequency for nonserious risks.[6] It would seem that physicians are not obligated to reveal trivial risks or risks that are universally known.

These rules have direct applicability to psychiatric work. Several notable cases underscore the importance of maintaining a standard of knowledge and responsibility commensurate with that practiced by other psychiatric specialists. For instance it is clear that the risk of fracture in unmodified electroconvulsant therapy should be conveyed to the patient. Failure to mention this potential danger, followed by its occurrence during a course of treatment, is an invitation to a successful law suit.[78] Another example of nondisclosure involved a psychiatrist who gave a telephone discharge order to an electroconvulsant therapy patient. The psychiatrist prescribed a sedative without warning the patient or family about precautions. The patient was severely burned by his cigarette, and the psychiatrist was held liable.[79] Currently a consensus is emerging that the risk of tardive dyskinesia from treatment with neuroleptics warrants mention.[80] Since all patients taking neuroleptics are susceptible to tardive dyskinesia, it would seem best to warn each patient before beginning nonemergency treatment or when continued use becomes indicated.[81]

An essential element of information disclosure is a description of the alternatives to the recommended procedure or treatment. One choice is always no treatment, and this option mandates a description of the natural history and prognosis of the condition. In order to evaluate each alternative, the patient must be presented with the same kind of information as provided for the recommended treatment. As one judge wrote, "A patient should be told of the alternative possibilities and given a chance to decide what should be done before the doctor proceeds...the rule preserves the patient's dignity in choosing his own course."[82] Hence, a psychiatrist must reveal the existence of all creditable treatments, necessitating the perpetual maintenance of a specialist's level of knowledge. In today's practice that would translate into at least an awareness of neuroleptic and antidepressant medications of several different chemical classes and of psycho-neuroendocrine diagnostic procedures. A psychiatrist is duty bound to notify a patient of the availability of these options on referral to a consultant, even if the psychiatrist is personally unfamiliar with their use. Unaccepted or unethical forms of treatment need not be mentioned.

The informational component of the informed consent process is not complete until the physician has offered the patient an opportunity to ask questions and elicit additional information. Some patients will need to be encouraged and reassured that potentially idiosyncratic or embarrassing questions can be asked freely. Physician disapproval will have a stifling effect on the entire consent process. Occasionally a patient may wish to seek another opinion before agreeing to the recommended course of action. Other patients may consent immediately, but on later consideration decide to refuse treatment. Physicians must respect the patient's right to withdraw from treatment at any time and for any reason, without retaliation. If the physician cannot in clear conscience continue to treat under the terms dictated by the patient, then a referral to another physician should be effected. Abandonment of a patient leaves the physician on tenuous moral, legal and clinical grounds.

There have been a number of empirical studies of informed consent, most of which have investigated the effect of information disclosure. Unfortunately, few of the reports attempted to determine what physicians routinely tell their patients.[83]

However, there are studies of patient attitudes towards disclosure. For instance Alfidi and colleagues in 1971 wrote, "that a straightforward statement of complications will result in only a small percentage of patients (2%) refusing a special procedure (diagnostic angiography). We are convinced that the vast majority of patients desired this information.[84] Interestingly, in a 1975 study the same team showed that if patients were asked before being told of the risks, many would decline to receive the information.[85] It would seem that the fear of what the doctor might say has more significance than the consequences of what actually is told.

Other investigations have focused on patient understanding of the information released. For instance, testing memory for consent material has demonstrated poor recall of important data. In an often cited report, twenty cardiac surgery patients were questioned four to six months postoperatively.[86] Before surgery the informed consent had been given in a straightforward conversation between the patient and the surgeon. The authors believed that all patients understood the information given. Nevertheless, the patients subsequently forgot most of what they had heard and made conspicuous errors in their attempts to reconstruct the consent interview. The poorest scores were achieved in the category of potential complications. The patient who remembered the least was the patient who responded most authoritatively and expressed no doubts regarding recollection. One patient, whose informed consent conference lasted 24 minutes, stated: "All he did was lift up my shirt, put a stethoscope on my heart, and that was it.""[86] Although this study can be criticized because of the unacknowledged deleterious effects on memory of open heart surgery, the results suggest that information presentation does not imply successful information processing and retrieval.

Several reasons have been suggested for the poor recollection of consent material. The consent forms themselves can prove to be an impediment to understanding, especially when the language is too complex or there is a pressure of time. These issues are especially problematic for the less educated, lower socioeconomic strata patients. There are important psychodynamic considerations as well. Some patients will rely exclusively on their physician's advice, rendering the consent process a mere formality regardless of the content of the information disclosed. Other patients have already made up their minds before the discussion ever begins. For instance in an investigation of kidney donors, Fellner and Marshall found, "that most donors made an immediate decision when first contacted, preceding the acquisition of data required for an 'informed consent'."[87] Characterologic defensive styles, such as denial and repression, can greatly color both motivation for treatment and memory of consent. Goin, Burgoyne, and Goin showed the 12 of 20 patients having had a face-lift gave different reasons postoperatively than before for surgery; 9 could not recall any possible complications, and 7 admitted that they purposely did not think about the risks.[88] It is no wonder that of the 200 cancer patients surveyed, more than three-quarters endorsed "legal documents to protect the physician's rights" as the definition of consent form.[89]

A few studies have directed attention to the informational component of consent for psychiatric patients. Olin and Olin assessed the amount of understanding that 100 mental hospital patients had of the voluntary applications for admission they signed on entry.[90] Only 8 percent of private and state hospital patients were rated as being completely informed of the terms of the contract at the time of admission. Appelbaum, Mirkin, and Bateman interviewed a group of 50 newly admitted voluntary psychiatric in-patients.[91] Their data suggest that a large percentage of the patients were not competent to consent to their own admission, in part, because of their poor understanding of their legal rights explained during the consent procedure. In another study, 20 schizophrenic patients in an urban aftercare center, none of whom were retarded or organically impaired and all on psychotropic medication, were given an informed consent sheet about a new fictitious drug, Lamex.[92] On testing, 40 percent were considered not informed, and yet all agreed to take the new medication. Interestingly, when compared with patients on a medical floor, hospitalized psychiatric patients did not agree to participate in clinical research of either high or low risk any more often.[93] So it would seem that patients with all kinds of illnesses are prone to make arbitrary decisions about treatment, much as people are idiosyncratic when buying a car or voting. Importantly, the concern that full disclosure or risks would lead to increased refusal to accept care is not supported by the available empirical evidence.

There is recent controversy surrounding a backlash to the informational component of the consent process. The dispute has developed over its purported potential for inducing iatrogenic illness. For instance, Kaplan, Greenwald, and Rogers report two cases in which patients without known heart disease suffered myocardial infarction or arrhythmia about twelve hours after participating in an overinclusive informed consent for surgery.[94] Others have identified the inherent risk for a negative reaction analogous to the beneficial placebo effect.[95] Instead of the usual positive response arising from the comforting words of the physician, the patient becomes symptomatic by suggestion following the detailed enumeration of possible unpleasant side-effects. What patient prescribed a medication would comfortably comply with treatment after reading the package insert? Under these circumstances, one would need to obtain a consent for the consent.

These arguments imploring us to restrict consent because of certain improbable outcomes are overstated. Kaplan fails to establish that the consents were etiologically responsible for the subsequent cardiac complications.[94] And if related, might Kaplan's consent process rather than informational content be implicated? An encounter with a morbid physician obsessively dwelling on remote harms will induce anxiety and its ill-effects. However, we can imagine few iatrogenic difficulties arising directly from the doctor-patient relationship operating as it should -- with a sensitive regard to possible negative interactions. We firmly believe that the dangers in empathic sharing of information lie in disclosing too little rather than too much. The successful evolution over the past twenty years of physicians' attitudes toward truth telling with cancer patients documents the wisdom of a policy of honesty and openness.[96]

Signaling consent is an intentional act performed in an unambiguous manner. With the exception of consent to participation in clinical research, there are apparently no legal requirements for written consent. The consent process involves the sharing of information, decision-making, and indicating permission or refusal. A consent form is a document useful to remind the physician what to discuss, to record the transaction, to summarize the conclusion, and to provide evidence that the process occurred. In some states a signed consent form establishes the legal presumption that voluntary informed consent had been obtained. Since electroconvulsant therapy is controversial and associated with memory deficits, a consent form should be signed in the presence of a witness, preferably a spouse or close relative concurring with the treatment. Consent forms for psychotropic medication are becoming increasingly common. There is probably much to be gained in their use, especially in an era of major concern over tardive dyskinesia A few psychiatrists have recommended repeating the consent process and renewing the consent form at regular intervals.

In practice a note detailing the consent process can often substitute for a form. One or the other can be invaluable when the physician is called upon, perhaps years later, to prove that consent had been obtained. It seems advisable to document the entire consent process, including the reasons for believing the patient is competent and that consent was voluntary and informed. Physicians should realize that some courts will assume that whatever was written was all that was said. If such complete notes are inscribed, it seems prudent to ask the patient to sign them as well. The consent form can of course attest that the patient declined to be informed of the details of a treatment or that the patient requested to designate someone else to receive the information. As an editorial in the *New England Journal of Medicine* reminds us:

> Virtually the only way to obtain informed consent is through a conversation...the consent form must be recognized for what it is: nothing more than evidence that informed consent has been obtained.[97]

SUMMARY

The vulnerability of the mentally ill patient places a special responsibility upon the psychiatrist to be fully cognizant of the ethical aspects of the doctor-patient relationship. Issues of voluntariness and competence, as we have seen, are crucial, complex, and frequently misunderstood. Even psychotic, institutionalized patients may have moments of lucidity when they can think clearly and articulate their will, but this is all too often overlooked by the staff because the expression of the patient's preferences are momentary and are embedded in the context of psychiatric illness. Because they are perceived as abnormal, psychiatric patients often lose their rights. Although mental practitioners are taught to resist this stereotype, attitudes toward the mentally ill are a part of our cultural ethos and tend to affect professional attitudes and judgments. The best available protection against viewing the marginally competent psychiatric patient as an object, or in the language of Martin Buber, as an "it" and not as a subject, is to vigilantly respect the full meaning of consent.[98]

Because psychiatric patients are caught in the web of the diagnostic labelling of illness (in most instances justified but in some cases not warranted), it is difficult for them to extricate themselves from a situation that, by its very nature, often precludes the exertion of autonomy. Pharmacological agents, often necessary to control illness, dull sensibilities and alter one's rightful position as a moral agent. This is not intended to be a criticism of widely and appropriately practiced care of the mentally ill; it is only to point out the extremely vulnerable posture of the patient who is not in a position to exert his or her freedom of choice.

The consistent theme of this essay has been that respect for the patient's autonomy and the right to give consent and be fully informed about the nature of the illness and treatment are fundamental ethical principles that must be safeguarded. If it appears necessary to abrogate these principles, the evidence supporting the violation of these rights must be demanding and conclusive.

The respect for the integrity and personhood of the individual is deeply rooted in our philosophical, religious, and political heritage. The Kantian dictum that all persons must be treated as ends in themselves and not merely as means, as well as Mill's understanding of what constitutes liberty, stand tall in our western philosophical tradition. Likewise our Jewish and Christian religious heritages have consistently maintained that persons have been created in God's image, and thus each person is of intrinsic value. The founding fathers reflect our political legacy in their affirmation that persons have inalienable rights.

The major themes of this chapter have been consonant with the moral traditions of our western heritage. These values are also reflected in the ethical codes of the major health care professions.The interrelationship between our legal and ethical traditions is clear and the numerous judgments of the courts, cited in this paper, indicate that fact. At a time when the violation of human rights is widespread throughout the world, it is important that the health care professions conserve the preservation of the rights of those who are dependent upon us for care. Continued discussion and concern for the application of these principles to our professional conduct will assure that we will not misuse the unique trust that patients place in us. When it appears necessary to countermand the patient's autonomy, the provisions of the courts provide the ultimate means to serve the patient's best interests.

REFERENCES

1. Cummings J (December 18, 1982). Plea by patient for starvation barred by court. *New York Times,* p 8
2. White RB & Engelhardt HT (1975). A demand to die. *The Hastings Center Report 5(3),* 9-10
3. American Hospital Association (1975). *A Patient's Bill of Rights.* Chicago: American Hospital Association
4. Ramsey P (1970). *The Patient as Person.* New Haven:Yale University Press
5. Redlich F & Mollica RF (1976). Overview: ethical issues in contemporary psychiatry. *American Journal of Psychiatry, 133,* 125-136
6. Veatch RM (1981). *A Theory of Medical Ethics.* New York: Basic Books, pp 194, 202, 203
7. Mills JS (1983). On liberty. In S Gorovitz, R Macklin, AL Jameton, *et al.* (Eds): *Moral Problems in Medicine* (2nd ed.). Englewood Cliffs, New Jersey: Prentice-Hall, pp 46, 48
8. Parsons T (1975). The sick role and the role of physician reconsidered. *Milbank Memorial Fund Quarterly, 53,* 257-278
9. Freidson E (1970). *Professional Dominance: The Social Structure of Medical Care.* New York: Atherton Press
10. Katz J (1977). Informed consent -- a fairy tale? *University of Pittsburgh Law Review, 39,* 137-174
11. Laforet EG (1976). Fiction of informed consent. *JAMA, 235,* 1579-1585
12. Thomasma D C (1983). Limitations of the autonomy model for the doctor-patient relationship. *Pharos, 46 (2),* 2-5
13. Groves JE (1978). Taking care of the hateful patient. *New England Journal of Medicine, 298,* 883-887
14. Stone AA (1976). Legal implications of sexual activity between psychiatrist and patient. *American Journal of Psychiatry, 133,* 1138-1141
15. Dawidoff DJ (1973). *Malpractice of Psychiatrists.* Springfield, Illinois: Charles C. Thomas, p 39
16. Stone AA (1979). Informed consent: special problems for psychiatry. *Hospital & Community Psychiatry, 30,* 321-327
17. *Schloendorff v. Society of the New York Hospital,* 105 N.E. 92, (N.Y., 1914)
18. *McCandless v. New York,* 162 N.Y.S. 2d 570, (N.Y., 1957)

19. *Natanson v. Kline*, 350 P. 2d 1093; rehearing denied, 354 P. 2d 670, (Kan, 1960)
20. Goldstein J (1975). For Harold Lasswell: some reflections on human dignity, entrapment, informed consent, and the plea bargain. *Yale Law Journal, 84,* 683-703
21. Meisel A (1981). Informed consent: who decides for whom? In MD Haller (Ed): *Medical Ethics and the Law: Implications for Public Policy.* Cambridge, Massachussets:Ballinger, p 202
22. *Cobbs v. Grant*, 502 P. 2d 1 (Cal, 1972)
23. Holder AR (1970). Informed consent II. *JAMA, 214,* 1383-1384
24. *DiFillipo v. Preston*, 173 A. 2d 333 (Del, 1961)
25. *Scaria v. St. Paul Fire & Marine Insurance Co.*, 227 NW 2d 647 (Wisc, 1975)
26. *Canterbury v. Spence*, 464 F.2d 772 (DC Cir); cert denied 409 US 1064 (1972)
27. *Wilkenson v. Vesey*, 295 A. 2d 676 (R.I.,1972)
28. Miller LJ (1980). Informed consent: IV. *JAMA, 244,* 2661-2662
29. Rosoff AJ (1981). *Informed Consent: A Guide for Health Care Providers.* Rockville, MD: Aspen
30. Dillon JR (1981). Informed consent and the disclosure of risks of treatment. *Bioethics Quarterly, 3,* 156-162
31. Mills MJ & O'Keefe AM (1983). Legal issues in outpatient treatment. *Journal of Clinical Psychiatry, 44(6)(sec.2),* 33-40
32. *Hart v. Brown*, 29 Conn. Super. 368, 289 A. 2d 386 (1972)
33. *In re Pescinski*, 67 Wis. 2d 4, 226 N.W. 2d 180 (1975)
34. McCormick RA (Autumn 1974). Proxy consent in the experimental situation. *Perspectives in Biology and Medicine,* 2-20
35. Gaylin W (1982). The "competence" of children. *Journal of the American Academy of Child Psychiatry, 21,* 153-162
36. Roth LH (1982). Competency to consent for or refuse treatment. In L Grinspoon (Ed): *Psychiatry 1982: Annual Review.* Washington, DC: American Psychiatric Press
37. Smith SM (1983). Competency. *Psychiatric Clinics of North America, 6,* 635-650
38. *Parham v. J.R.*, 442 U.S. 584, 99 S. Ct. 2493, 61 L. Ed. 2d 101 (1979)
39. *Lane v. Candura*, 376 NE 2d (Mass App, 1978)
40. Abernethy V (1984). Compassion, control, and decisions about competency. *American Journal of Psychiatry, 141,* 53-58
41. Ingelfinger FJ (1972). Informed (but uneducated) consent. *New England Journal of Medicine, 287,* 465-466
42. Grunder RM (1980). On the readability of surgical consent forms. *New England Journal of Medicine, 302,* 900-902
43. Roth LH, Meisel A, & Lidz CW (1977). Tests of competency to consent to treatment. *American Journal of Psychiatry, 134,* 279-284
44. Fredman B (1981). Competence, marginal and otherwise: Concepts and ethics. *International Journal of Law Psychiatry, 4,* 53-72
45. Appelbaum PS & Roth LH (1982). Competency to consent to research: a psychiatric overview. *Archives of General Psychiatry, 39,* 951-958
46. Culver CM, Ferrell RB, & Green RM (1980). ECT and the special problems of informed consent. *American Journal of Psychiatry, 137,* 586-591
47. Herr SS, Arons S, & Wallace RE (1983). *Legal Rights and Mental Health Care.* Lexington, Massachusetts: Lexington

48. *In re Yetter*, 62 Pa. D. & C. 2d 619 (1973)

49. Childress JF (1982). *Who Should Decide? Paternalism in Health Care.* New York: Oxford University Press, p 87

50. Miller R & Willner HS (1974). The two-part consent form: a suggestion for promoting free and informed consent. *New England Journal of Medicine, 290,* 964-966

51. Eth S & Eth C (1981). Can a research subject be too eager to consent? *The Hastings Center Report, ll(4),* 20-21

52. Schwarz ED (1980). A revised checklist to obtain consent to treatment with medication. *Hospital & Community Psychiatry, 31,* 765-767

53. Spiro HM (1975). Constraint and consent -- on being a patient and a subject. *New England Journal of Medicine 293,* 1134-1135

54. Appelbaum PS & Roth LH (1981). Clinical issues in the assessment of competency. *American Journal of Psychiatry, 138,* 1462-1467

55. Karno M & Schwartz DA (1974). *Community Mental Health: Reflections and Explorations.* New York:Spectrum Press

56. *Kaimowitz v. Department of Mental Health,* Circuit Court for the County of Wayne, Michigan, July 10, 1973. Civil Action No. 73-19434-AW

57. Szasz TS (1983). *Law, Liberty, and Psychiatry: An Inquiry into the Social Uses of Mental Health Practices.* New York: Macmillan

58. Peszke MA (1975). *Involuntary Treatment of the Mentally Ill: The Problems of Autonomy.* Springfield, Illinois:Charles C. Thomas

59. Chodoff P (1976). Case for involuntary hospitalization of the mentally ill. *American Journal of Psychiatry, 133,* 496-501

60. *In re Osbourne,* 294 A. 2d 372 (D.C. Ct. of App., 1972)

61. *In re Quinlan,* 355 A. 2d 647 (N.J., 1976)

62. *Superintendent of Belchertown v. Saikewicz,* 370 N.E. 2d 417 (Mass., 1976)

63. Perr IN (1982). Refusing treatment -- who shall decide. *Bulletin of the American Academy of Psychiatry Law 10,* 233-247

64. Michels R (1981). The right to refuse treatment: ehical issues. *Hospital & Community Psychiatry, 32,* 252-255

65. *Rogers v. Okin,* 478 F. Supp. 134 (D. Mass., 1979)

66. *Rennie v. Klein,* 476 F. Supp. 1294 (N.J., 1979)

67. Annas GJ, Glantz LH, & Katz BF (1977). *Informed Consent to Human Experimentation: The Subject Dilemma.* Cambridge, Massachussets:Ballinger, pp 46, 116, 233, 279

68. *Knecht v. Gillman,* 488 F.28 1136 (8th Cir., 1973)

69. *Smith v. Baker,* 326 F. Supp. 787 (W.D. Mo., 1970)

70. Levine RJ (1981). *Ethics and Regulation of Cinical Research.* Baltimore: Urban and Schwarzenberg

71. Beecher HK (1966). Ethics and clinical research. *New England Journal of Medicine, 274,* 1354-1360

72. Jones JH (1981). *Bad Blood: The Tuskegee Syphilis Experiment.* New York:Free Press

73. U. S. Dept. of Health and Human Services (January 26, 1981). Final regulations amending basic HHS policy for the protection of human research subjects. *Federal Register, 46,* 8366-8392

74. American Psychiatric Association (1980). *Diagnostic and Satistical Manual-III.* Washington DC: APA

75. Kondziela JR (December 1983) Telling patients they are mentally ill. *Resident Staff Physician,* 63-70

76. Green RS (1984). Why schizophrenic patients should be told their diagnosis. *Hospital & Community Psychiatry, 35,* 76-77
77. *Cooper v. Roberts,* 220 Pa. Super. 260 A. 2d 647 (1971)
78. *Mitchell v. Robinson,* 334 SW 2d 11 (Mo., 1960)
79. *Christy v. Saliterman,* 179 NW 2d 288 (Minn., 1970)
80. Wettstein RM (1983). Tardive dyskinesia and malpractice. *Behavioral Science and the Law, 1,* 85-107
81. Deveaugh-Geiss J (1979). Informed consent for neuroleptic therapy. *American Journal of Psychiatry,136,* 959-962
82. *Jeffries v. McCague,* 363 A 2d 1167 (Pa., 1976)
83. Meisel A & Roth LH (1981). What we do and do not know about informed consent. *JAMA, 246,* 2473-2477
84. Alfidi RJ (1971). Informed consent -- a study of patient reaction. *JAMA, 216,* 1325-1329
85. Alfidi RJ (1975). Controversy, alternatives, and decisions in complying with the legal doctrine of informed consent. *Radiology, 114,* 231-234
86. Robinson G & Merav A (1976). Informed consent: recall by patients tested postoperatively. *American Thoracic Surgery, 22,* 209-212
87. Fellner CH & Marshall J R (1970). Kidney donors -- the myth of informed consent. *American Journal of Psychiatry, 126,* 1245-1251
88. Goin MK, Burgoyne RW, & Goin JM (1976). Face-lift operation: the patient's secret motivations and reactions to "informed consent." *Plastic Reconstructive Surgery, 58,* 273-279
89. Cassileth BR, Zupkis RV, Sutton-Smith K, *et al.* (1980). Informed consent: why are its goals imperfectly realized? *New England Journal of Medicine, 302,* 896-900
90. Olin GB & Olin HS (1975). Informed consent in voluntary mental hospital admissions. *American Journal of Psychiatry, 132,* 938-941
91. Appelbaum PS, Mirkin SA, & Bateman AL (1981). Empirical assessment of competency to consent to psychiatric hospitalization. *American Journal of Psychiatry, 138,* 1170-1176
92. Grossman L & Summpers F (1980). A study of the capacity of schizophrenic patients to give informed consent. *Hospital & Community Psychiatry, 31,* 205-206
93. Stanley B, Stanley M, Lautin A, *et al.* (1981). Preliminary findings on psychiatric patients as research participants: a population at risk? *American Journal of Psychiatry, 138,* 669-671
94. Kaplan SR, Greenwald RA, & Rogers A (1977). Neglected aspects of informed consent. *New England Journal of Medicine, 296,* 1127
95. Loftus EF & Fries JF (1970). Informed consent may be hazardous to your health. *Science, 204,* 11
96. Novack DH, Plumer R, Smith RL, *et al.* (1979). Changes in physicians' attitudes toward telling the cancer patient. *JAMA, 241,* 897-900
97. Vaccarino JM (1978). Consent, informed consent and the consent form. *New England Journal of Medicine, 298,* 455
98. Buber M (1958). *I and Thou* (2nd ed.). New York:Charles Scribner's Sons, p 11

DISCUSSION QUESTIONS

1. Briefly describe the relationship between liberty, automomy, personhood, and informed consent.

2. Give several examples when paternalistic decision-making could be morally justifiable.

3. Can a truly informed consent ever be obtained? What guidelines should be used in determining how much information to disclose?

4. Is lying to a client ever acceptable in health care practice? If so, when, and for what reasons?

5. Should psychiatric clients, hospitalized for nonpsychiatric reasons, be routinely screened for competency before attempting to gain informed consent for precedures? Do psychiatric clients have the option to refuse psychotropic medications?

6. Your client has signed a consent form for surgery to be performed tomorrow morning. The client tells you that, "I really didn't understand all of what the doctor said; but I suppose it is best to have this surgery since I'm on summer vacation now and will have some time to rest." What would you do in this situation assuming that you have graduated from school and are licensed? Utilize the decision-making tool included in Chapter 1 in formulating your answer.

7. You are preparing to dismiss a client who is going home on rather potent medications that have a variety of side effects. You know the client is sensitive to suggestion. How will you determine what to tell the client about the side effects of each medication?

8. You truly believe that a particular treatment would benefit your competent client. From previous documentation you know that the client will most likely refuse the treatment. Role play such a situation, pretending that you are the person responsible for obtaining the informed consent.

9. Examine and critique the various consent forms of your particular institution.

10. Do you feel that, in a teaching hospital, verbal consent of a client (in addition to the general consent which is signed upon admission), should be obtained before a particular student cares for that client?

6

Mark Sheldon

Some General Problems Related to Informed Consent and the Psychiatric Treatment of Children

Mark Sheldon, Ph.D., is an associate professor of philosophy and an adjunct associate professor of medicine and psychiatry on the Gary, Indiana campus of Indiana University. His teaching responsibilities have included, among others, courses in medical ethics, philosophy of the child, and death and dying. He has authored publications in journals such as *The Journal of the American Medical Association, Bioethics Reports*, and *The Journal of Social Philosophy*.

In this chapter Dr. Sheldon examines the issue of informed consent and the related issues of assessment of competence and coercion in the psychiatric treatment of children. He also includes a section on some of the general moral dilemmas faced by professionals engaged in the provision of mental health care.

The issue of informed consent and how it relates to the psychiatric treatment of both young children and adolescents will be examined in this chapter. Little has been written on this topic, though much has appeared that focuses on conducting therapeutic and nontherapeutic research among children.[1-4] Also, many articles and books have appeared that deal with children's rights issues.[5,6] More will be said about children's rights and about the distinction between research and standard treatment in relation to psychiatry and mental health, but first some preliminary remarks about the issue of informed consent.

An early article, "Dilemmas of Informed Consent in Children,"[7] by Anthony Shaw, M.D., deals with the problem of obtaining parental permission for children to undergo various surgical procedures. Shaw discusses a variety of different cases and concludes the following:

> If an underlying philosophy can be gleaned from the vignettes presented above, I hope it is one that tries to find a solution, humane and loving, based on the circumstances of each case rather than by means of a dogmatic formula approach.[7]

Shaw makes clear that he is indebted to Joseph Fletcher's *Situation Ethics*[8] for assistance in articulating his views on medical ethics, and it is clear that Shaw suggests that there is no other basis upon which these decisions can be made. In fact, at the conclusion of Shaw's paper he shifts from the issue of on what basis the decisions ought to be made to who should make the decisions, as though the second issue is an unproblematic substitute for the first. But clearly it is not, and the shift creates confusion in conceptualization of the issue. However, Shaw makes, in the following paragraphs, a point relevant to the purpose of this chapter:

> Who should make these decisions? The doctors? The parents? Clergyman? A committee? As I have pointed out, I think that the parents must participate in any decision about treatment and that they must be fully informed of the consequences of consenting and of withholding consent. This is a type of informed consent that goes far beyond the traditional presentation of possible complications of surgery, length of hospitalization, cost of the operation, time lost from work, and so on.
>
> It may be impossible for any general agreement or guidelines for making decisions on cases as the ones presented here to emerge, but I believe we should bring these problems out into public forum because whatever the answers may be, they should not be the result of decisions made solely by the attending physicians. Or should they?[7]

What is interesting is that Shaw regards the issue as so complex. Not only does he have difficulty in getting clear what ought to be the basis of a decision, but he also has very serious problems indicating which individuals ought to participate in making the decisions. His paper concludes with a question, but with a question to which an affirmative response would be very paternalistic; attending physicians should decide. It is as though Shaw presents the possibility that the situation is so complex (no clear basis for a decision is available, and it is not clear who should decide) that it is reasonable to conclude that perhaps the health care professional ought to have the ultimate determination. A claim of such thoroughgoing paternalism, even if apparently reached through elimination of alternatives, requires very close examination. Of course, this chapter intends to deal with the issue of psychiatric treatment, not surgical procedures, but the dilemmas that Shaw expresses in a sensitive and searching way are ones that cannot be avoided, and we will return to these.

MORAL DILEMMAS AND THE MENTAL HEALTH CARE PROFESSION

It is true that there are guidelines that have been set by professional groups and laws established by society specifying proper behavior, but it is also clear that the guidelines are incomplete and inadequate and do not begin to be equal to the enormous complexity of issues that confront the professional. The American Psychological Association (APA), for instance, in recent years has made attempts to come to terms with the problem of deception in psychological research.[9] There has been much discussion and criticism of this effort.[10,11] Clearly the laws and guidelines proposed by professional societies do not give adequate guidance and judicial decisions are often reversed. A good example of this is, in fact, the change in requirements involving informed consent in the ordinary practice of medicine, a change from a professional standard to a community standard.[12] Where before the "professional standard" involved a committee of professionals who appraised the practice of a peer to determine whether he or she acted in the standard manner (from their point of view), the "community standard" recognizes that lay persons sit in judgment on the practice of the professional to determine whether the patient has been informed adequately from their point of view. It seems clear that a mental health care professional confronts even more difficulties and uncertainties in this area.

In the APA's *Ethical Standards of Psychologists* the Preamble reads as follows:

> Psychologists respect the dignity and worth of the individual and honor the preservation and protection of fundamental human rights. They are committed to increasing knowledge of human behavior and of people's understanding of themselves and others and to the utilization of such knowledge for the promotion of human welfare....[13]

While this passage is addressed to significant concerns, what it does not make clear is which concern ought to be regarded as having primary importance: individual rights, people's understanding of themselves, or a consideration of general human welfare? What does seem to be true is that there is an assumption that, among all three, there is compatibility. Moreover, there is little in the remainder of the document to indicate any anxiety about the possibility of unresolved tension between these three concerns. For instance, there are times when a psychologist must determine whether information divulged to him or her by the patient, in the course of therapy, ought to be shared with the larger community. There might also be times when a concern for the protection of a child's privacy in cases of sexual abuse might necessitate withdrawing information from the larger community even when the community might be benefited by having such information. There are also questions that pertain to what the nature of the relationship is between parents and children. It certainly does not involve ownership of the child by the parent, but it is not clear what it does involve.

The section on ethical standards where one would expect to find discussion reflecting a recognition of the complexity of these matters, Principle 3: Moral and Legal Standards, is, in fact, quite limited in scope. It reads as follows:

> The psychologist in the practice of his profession shows sensible regard for the social codes and moral expectations of the community in which he works, recognizing that violations of accepted moral and legal standards on his part may involve his clients, students, or colleagues in damaging personal conflicts, and impugn his own name and the reputation of his profession.[13]

It is worth noting that in this passage the legal and the moral are mentioned together; there is no indication of any possibility that the two might be in conflict. This passage is also limited in relation to what one might expect to find in this section. For instance, one might expect to find discussion of such questions as what one should do when an adolescent requests treatment without the knowledge of parents when the law clearly requires such disclosure; or what one should do when parents have signed commitment papers for an adolescent who clearly, from the point of view of the psychiatrist, does not need such commitment; or what kind of judgment one ought to make regarding the wish of a 7-year-old to donate a kidney to her twin sister who will die unless she receives such a transplant?[14] It is very difficult to know what to do with cases of this sort particularly within the context of concern for community standards, rights of individuals, and the reputation of the profession. These same difficulties apply when one moves from specific cases involving particular psychologists and patients to broader areas of psychological research and inquiry. For instance, recent attempts of the APA to deal with deception in research indicates an approach involving peer review that focuses on the question of ends justifying the means -- a utilitarian justification in relation to an assessment of the value of the knowledge acquired, with the value of this acquired knowledge judged by other professionals, not laypersons.[9]

There seems to be some question, therefore, concerning the extent to which professional societies for mental health care providers assist their members in dealing with ethical dilemmas, or even encourage their members to be sensitive to the possible existence of such dilemmas. The American Medical Association (AMA), for various reasons, appears to be much more aware of the complex moral dilemmas that much of its membership confronts regularly. The Association has become increasingly aware of the need to encourage its members to be conceptually alert to these issues, and appreciative of their importance. Perhaps the AMA has become involved for defensive reasons, since the public and other professionals have felt much more prepared to contribute ideas about the goals of ordinary medical practice. There is not this same comfortable feeling of preparedness regarding the outcome of psychiatric therapy. More shall be said about this shortly. In any case, as far as the APA, for instance, is concerned, its advice to its members is basically cautionary: "moral dilemmas" are those that involve the questions of what to do with colleagues who advertise improperly, have sex with their patients, or misrepresent their qualifications. It is clear, however, that these are not moral dilemmas in the usual sense, that is questions that involve issues of right and wrong or conflict of rights. Instead, they are dilemmas concerned with how to dispose properly of colleagues who behave in ways regarded as unprofessional. Otherwise, moral dilemmas defined in the former sense are basically nonexistent and the professional is encouraged to maintain and not challenge community standards. That there may be difficulty in ascertaining "community standards" is not suggested. Yet, obviously this is a very basic problem. Also, this concern with a community standard appears to be in some conflict with the approach the APA takes to dealing with other problems, such as deception in research, where the evaluation of the knowledge gained in relation to the deception perpetrated is judged by a committee of other psychologists, not the larger community.

In any case, the concern of this section is to indicate the need of the mental health associations to begin to come to terms with the complex moral dilemmas that exist. The issue of deception in research has been mentioned. This is a sensational problem. An issue just as serious, but not as dramatic, is that of informed consent, and we turn to this issue, first in terms of a general perspective. Afterwards, children and the problem of consent for psychiatric treatment will be dealt with specifically.

INFORMED CONSENT

The problem of informed consent is an ethical issue that warrants close and sustained examination. Consider the following: Section 7 from the House Enrolled Act No.1830 of the Indiana General Assembly reads:

All patients or clients are entitled to be informed of the nature of the treatment or habilitation program proposed, the known effects of receiving and of not receiving such treatment or habilitation, and alternative treatment or habilitation programs, if any. An adult voluntary patient or client, if not adjudicated incompetent, is entitled to be informed of this right. An involuntary patient or client who wishes to refuse to submit to treatment or a habilitation program is entitled to petition the committing court or hearing officer for consideration of the treatment or program.[15]

According to this document, the right to refuse treatment is available to adults who are judged competent, and who have been fully informed to the extent that, if they do refuse, the refusal itself is based on adequate knowledge. This is a fairly stringent requirement, and one that has developed parallel to informed consent requirements in the practice of medicine, essentially going beyond informed consent to informed refusal. This is a development that has been applauded by some and criticized by others,[16] but, in any case, a large volume of significant literature has appeared on the issue.[17] What has appeared more slowly is literature dealing with children and informed consent, and that is what we turn to now.

CHILDREN AND INFORMED CONSENT

The House Enrolled Act, mentioned above, does not seem to make any special provision for children, and thus appears to include them in the category of incompetents. Various articles[1,4] have appeared in the last several years dealing with different perspectives on this issue, and different general points have been emphasized. Some writers[4,6] have stressed the importance of the family and warned against adversarial approaches that would threaten basic familial structures. Others[3] have distinguished between "consent" and "assent" arguing that while knowledge on the part of a child may not be possible or necessary, some sort of essential willingness to cooperate. They also stress the central significance for parental guidance and involvement. Another approach involves an emphasis on the importance of viewing each child individually to determine his or her level of competence. For instance, Adele Hofmann, pointing to broad differences among adolescence writes:

maturity, the most difficult element to measure, is best determined by such behavioral evidence as the frowning: An adolescent initiates his own health care contact...indicates that his medical affairs are to be confidential and gives good reasons...asks valid questions about his affairs...etc.[18]

The concerns and questions of a writer such as Hofmann are all significant, raising general problems about informed consent, not specific to psychiatric treatment. However, let's turn to the latter issue, that of informed consent in psychiatric treatment of children, by asking two questions: Is it proper to include children in the class of incompetents? And, is it meaningful to speak of informed consent in relation to the psychiatric treatment of children?

In response to the first question, the author wants to suggest that it is not right to regard children, as a class, as incompetent. First, it is true that children are not competent to make certain choices or certain judgments (for instance, the value of attending school), but it does not follow that they are "incompetent" to make other significant choices, such as who their friends will be. Also, children seem to exhibit different levels of dependability, awareness, and forethought. Therefore, what is important is to determine clearly what the issue of choice is, what the competence of the child is in relation to the topic, and then make a judgment regarding the child's qualifications to choose. It is also important to consider the educational capacity of the child regarding the particular topic, and his or her intellectual and emotional ability to grow to competency.

Also of interest is the fact that children historically have not always been viewed as incompetent. There are romantic and religious traditions that hold children as having a view of reality more accurate than adults. An example of a 19th century romantic poet who is a particular appreciation for the perspectives of childhood is William Wordsworth. Consider the following:

> The Youth, who daily farther from the east
> Must travel, still in Nature's priest,
> And by the vision splendid
> Is on his way attended;
> At length the Man perceives it die away,
> And fade into the light of common day.[19]

For those who view 19th century poetry as no longer representative of a significant perspective, the past decade has witnessed the very successful production of *Equus*, a play by Peter Shaeffer. The message bears a definite similarity to Wordsworth in an important sense, though somewhat more complex existentially. Dysart, the child psychiatrist in the play says:

> The normal is the good smile in a child's eyes -- all right. It is also the dead stare in a million adults. It both sustains and kills -- like a god. It is the ordinary made beautiful; it is also the average made lethal. The normal is the indispensable, murderous God of health, and I am his priest. My tools are very delicate. My compassion is honest. I have honestly assisted children in this room. I have talked away terrors and relieved many agonies. But also -- beyond question -- I have cut from them parts of individuality reputnant to the god in both its aspects. Parts sacred to rarer and more wonderful gods.[20]

It is apparent from this speech that there is some significant and compelling metaphysical sense in which the perspectives of the child are profoundly important, and profoundly competent (especially, it seems, in relation to the objectives of psychiatric therapy where, often, the compelling standard is a superficial sort of "appropriateness" rather than a perspective sustaining more meaning).

Pursuing this issue a little further, let's examine Morris Kaplan's discussion of *Equus* as he suggests a particular characterization of the aims and interests of psychiatry. He writes: "Both secular instrumental rationality and conventional modes of social behavior have been seen as diminishing the range of human possibility, and denying a deep need for transcendence...."[21] Referring to Heidegger, Kaplan continues: "Martin Heidegger has called ours a time of need: the old gods have died, and the new ones have not yet appeared. The need to orient one's self in relation to a transcendent source of meaning and value may be an irreducible aspect of the human condition."[21] Then, beginning to focus on psychiatry, Kaplan writes:

The absence of such orientation and the very denial of the need may be definitive of the culture of modernity. In relation to civilization and its discontents, psychiatry plays an ambiguous role. On the one hand, it recognizes the importance of nonrational factors like feelings, fantasies and dreams in shaping human life, and has explored the implications of ancient myth and ritual for understanding the human psyche. On the other hand, it aspires to the status of science, has allied itself with medicine, and can function as an instrument of adjustment to conventional norms.[21]

The implication of this point is that psychiatry has recognized a need for transcendence (it might be argued that science itself is an attempt at transcendence) but has redefined it in terms of integration -- integration of the human personality with itself, and integration of the human personality with society. It appears, however, that such a solution is inadequate. Such a notion of integration assumes a knowledge of the self and of society, at least to the point where identification of the self and of society can be affected for the purposes of integration. The perspective of the child complicates this issue, and increasingly in our society there is conflict between those who support an interest in children's rights and those who do not. Whether this is the result of the recognition that children presently appear to mature earlier,[22,23] or of the recognition that there seems to have been a possible failure of adult reason, or that the first is a result of the second, will not be discussed here. The author simply wants to recognize the pervasive poetic and existential critique of psychiatry in our society that sets out the perceptions and sensibilities of children as a possible sort of solution or salvation. A reflection of this, also, some would suggest, is the growth of alternative therapies where the intention seems to be to return to some original strong and healthy self, mythic in its qualities, possibly even, in some sense, a return to childhood. All of these considerations make it difficult to draw any simple conclusion regarding the competency of children, especially in regard to the psychiatric treatment of children.

The second question, whether it is meaningful to speak of informed consent in relation to the psychiatric treatment of children, raises a number of issues. First "informed consent" means minimally, "agreement," saying "yes," in some sense. But there is also the suggestion that something more in involved, that the patient must be given an opportunity to *decide*. This genuine deliberation requires information and understanding, and the source of the problem is of course that psychiatric treatment involves matters both highly technical and intellectually demanding. This suggests to some that informed consent is impossible to obtain in any legitimate sense, and that the interests of the patient are best served by having the professional decide for the patient. To take this point of view, however, is to confuse *difficulty of communication* with *impossibility of communication*. What happens, then, if one accepts the principle of the importance of informed consent? How does one actually apply it? That is, what criteria is objective enough for determining that a patient has understood the issues involved in a particular form of treatment, and how does one determine the necessary amount of information that must be imparted? What kind of sense can we make of these issues where children are involved, and why should we? First we will deal with the question of *why* we should.

As mentioned at the beginning of this chapter, much discussion has focused on the issue of informed consent and the way in which it relates to the involvement of children in research. The reason this point is referred to is because within the practice of psychiatry, one may argue, it is very difficult to distinguish between "treatment" and "research." The question is whether psychiatric practice is so well established, without internal or external disputation over methods and objectives of therapy, that it is possible to argue that one therapy is standard treatment and that another is experimental, actually involving the therapist in, for all significant purposes, research. Of course, in the sense of day to day practice, it is possible to make this distinction and describe certain therapeutic interventions and approaches as "standard" as opposed to "experimental" but the basis upon which one makes this distinction, substantively, is not clear. It appears that the ideological issues are overwhelming. True, these issues exist in physical medicine, as well, but the distinction between research and standard treatment is easier to establish in that realm.

What are the objectives of therapy? To obtain a "cure"? In what sense? Are the objectives, instead, to achieve a freedom that comes with knowing oneself, to be able to make choices neither obsessive nor neurotic? It has been suggested that patients ought to establish the objectives. But should all patients be able to establish such objectives? By what criteria can it be determined that some patients are competent to set such objectives, but others are not? What about the classifications of mental illness? The APA regarded homosexuality as a mental disorder, but it no longer does. What is the APA saying about homosexuality? That it was *wrong* in the past to regard it as a mental disorder? It would be quite peculiar for the AMA one day, to announce suddenly that they were wrong about cancer, that it is not a disease, after all. It is conceivable, of course, that some religious group might take a different view of cancer and suggest that it is not a disease, that it is actually a condition of and punishment for sin. The point being made is that it is not from members of the AMA that one would expect to hear such views expressed, and it is difficult not to be confused by the change in perspective of the APA.

The problem, of course, is that if one agrees with the points made regarding the characterization of psychiatric treatment as essentially experimental, both in terms of the knowledge base that underlies it and in terms of the objectives that one hopes to accomplish with it, then one is left with the very complicated ethical dilemmas that confront the person involved in research, dilemmas that are even more complicated when children are involved.

Let us agree, for the sake of argument, that psychiatric treatment is essentially experimental, is essentially, at least, the on-going application and evaluation of research, much more so than in physical medicine. In what category would this on-going evaluation of research fit -- therapeutic or nontherapeutic? This is a crucial question, especially as it applies to the involvement of children where the general consensus has emerged that children should not be subjected to nontherapeutic experimentation. It may be argued that the distinction between therapeutic and nontherapeutic is not relevant here, that while it may be that clearly the treatment is meant to benefit the individual receiving treatment, often unexpected behavior occurs, or a different explanation of behavior is given, or the patient views as acceptable what previously had been regarded as unacceptable. How all these possible outcomes relate to the patient under treatment is not at all clear, and even more confusing is the way in which these different outcomes relate to the next patient taken under treatment. But it is not my purpose to attempt a resolution of these dilemmas, only to indicate that they do arise and that they require further consideration.

There is yet another extremely significant issue that one must confront in dealing with psychiatric treatment and informed consent, the recognition of which underscores a further response to the question of why, in relation to children, it is very important to deal meaningfully with informed consent. The issue is that there exists in psychiatric treatment a great potential for coercion, the importance of which is heightened in relation to children.

In an article titled, "A Psychoanalytic Look at Coercion," psychiatrist Willard Gaylin points out that coercion is not always physical. He writes, "To understand coercion, then, one must understand that which threatens man. The threat to life or survival has traditionally been viewed as one of the ultimate threats...."[24] He continues, "All psychoanalytic models share the recognition of the early infant's equating of survival with love and approval."[24] Gaylin suggests that psychiatry can contribute an understanding of "these symbolic substitutes for survival."[24] He cautions that "any of these survival equivalents can be used to coerce a person"[24] and he suggests, therefore, that communicating directly with the unconscious constitutes an alternative kind of coercion. He writes: "The coercion would not simply involve forcing a person to do that which you will but rather forcing him through manipulation of his emotions to will that which you will."[24] Gaylin wants to argue that psychiatry can reveal to the public the overwhelming extent to which coercive practices are possible and even pervasive. Yet it is also his purpose to suggest that coercion is not entirely bad, and he indicates that it appears to be most acceptable within the context of the parent-child relationship. Otherwise, the profession that most seems to enjoy the privilege to coerce is medicine, and psychiatry, not only in a position to understand the dynamics of manipulative coercion, enjoys an identification with the field of medicine, as well.

Two concerns appear to emerge in Gaylin's paper, one fully articulated, the other suggested. The first is a concern about the nature of the contribution that psychiatry can make to an understanding of and protection from dangerous forms of coercion, and the second that psychiatry itself, with its understanding of the unconscious and its identification with medicine, is in a position to be particularly and dangerously coercive. It is not clear that Gaylin expresses the latter view in his paper, however, such a view can be constructed on the basis of the considerations that he raises. That psychiatry can have this sort of double-barreled power emphasizes further the importance of giving careful thought to the issue of informed consent prior to any sort of treatment of children. Children, according to Gaylin's admonitions, face a double potential threat -- from psychiatry and from the family. The family is mentioned because of the following consideration. Erving Goffman has used the notion of "total institution"[25] to refer to those institutions within which all aspects of a person's social life are connected and controlled. Goffman argues that prisons and mental wards are examples of such institutions. It may be possible to argue that, for the child, the family is just such a "total institution." This does not mean that the family is a prison or a mental ward (although it may be for some children), but that the relation of the young child to the family includes this sort of total dependency, or is as dependent in ways that are significant.

The conclusion that it seems possible to reach regarding the question of whether one can deal meaningfully with the issue of informed consent and the psychiatric treatment of children is that one can do so by giving careful attention to the problems that have been raised, in particular the status of mental health as a science, and the rightful position of the child in relation to abuse in society. On the one hand, for some children, it is not possible to avoid the question of what, ultimately, is the greater threat -- psychiatry and its methodological and ideological problems and its potential for manipulation and coercion or the family and its great power as a protected institution in society. It is possible that the family and the mental health professional are, regarding any particular child, working towards the same coercive end. Who is in a position to make decisions regarding the child's welfare given this matrix of potentially powerful coercive pressures? Interestingly enough, we are brought back to the sort of questions and concerns with which Shaw concluded his paper.[7] It is difficult not to think that some sort of advocate for the child is necessary as is required in many but not all court systems. The setting of qualifications for such a person requires considerable discussion, and the author cannot begin to do so here except to suggest that it should be a person fully knowledgable and aware of the sorts of concerns that have been indicated in this chapter.

Some individuals will counter this argument for the right of the child to have an advocate with concerns for the integrity and privacy of the family. It has been suggested, for instance, that "rights language," as applied to the family, inclines us to conceptualize the family as a contractual society of individuals.[6] The argument for the family continues with the notion that the idea of parental duties and responsibilities toward children (to love, protect, and educate, for instance) provides a better ethical framework on which to base such policy. In other words, what a child needs is not "rights," but trust, love, and care. Although the author supports this contention, it is not always the case that a child receives these, and a concern with "rights" is a concern to insure that the child will receive protection from someone. It does not ultimately matter whether the child, the parents, or the courts provide competent informed consent prior to the psychiatric treatment of children, but it is important that someone does. On the other hand, it is possible that, in the last analysis, where young children are involved, it does not make too much sense to talk about informed consent in relation to psychiatric treatment. It is possible that the notion, in this case, is not relevant, not intelligible, and not coherent. What does seem intelligible is to have psychiatrists, psychologists, social workers, psychiatric nurses, and other mental health care professionals committed to the welfare of the child. If it becomes finally necessary to indicate a preference for who is in the best position to determine the best interest of the child, a good argument can be developed in support of the well-educated, sensitive expert who values the special relationships of intimacy that families can provide -- those relationships where persons are valued because they are, rather than for the use to which they can be put. On the other hand, while families often provide this, they do not always; this is the problem. A final point might be that it is not an accident that it is difficult to discuss the notion of informed consent in relation to the psychiatric treatment of children since what might be ultimately indicated is some form of family therapy where the symptomatic child is not singled out for treatment. This would seem to be a situation where a particular approach to the problem is not only psychiatrically indicated but morally indicated, as well.

It seems apparent that this chapter has developed a defense of the thorough-going paternalism that Shaw left only as a possible question at the end of this paper. Also, what makes this even more problematic is that this defense has been developed in the context of a critique of the mental health care profession. In response, the author argues that hopefully this critique will lead to the sort of Socratic wisdom that will make it possible for the mental health care professional to see the needs of the child clearly, in relationship to family and society, without the encumbrances of his or her professional needs or scientific assumptions.

REFERENCES

1. Ackerman TF (1979). Fooling ourselves with child autonomy and assent in nontherapeutic clinical research. *Clinical Research, 27*, 345-348
2. Gaylin W (1982). The competence of children: no longer all or none. *The Hastings Center Report, 12(2)*, 33-39
3. Pence GE (1980). Children's dissent to research -- a minor matter? *IRB, 2*, 1-4
4. Schoeman F (1982). Children's competence and children's rights. *IRB, 4*, 1-6
5. Cohen A (1980). *Equal Rights for Children*. Totowa:Littlefield, Adams
6. Rothman DJ & Rothman SR (1980). The conflict over children's rights. *The Hastings Center Report, 10(3)*, 7-10
7. Shaw A (1973). Dilemmas of informed consent in children. *New England Journal of Medicine, 289*, 885-890
8. Fletcher J (1966). *Situation Ethics*. Philadelphia:Westminster Press
9. American Psychological Association (1981). *Ethical Principles in the Conduct of Research with Human Participants*. Washington, D.C. (draft copy)
10. Hunt M (September 12, 1982). Research through deception. *New York Times Magazine*
11. Soble A (1978). Deception in social science research: is informed consent possible? *The Hastings Center Report, 8(5)*, 40-46
12. *Cobbs v. Grant*, 502 P.2d 11 (Oct. 27,1972) (1983). In J Arras & R Hunt (Eds): *Ethical Issues in Modern Medicine*. Palo Alto:Mayfield Publishing Co.
13. American Psychological Association (1977). *Ethical Standards of Psychologists*. Washington, D.C., p 1
14. Lewis M (1981). Comments on some ethical, legal and clinical issues affecting consent in treatment, organ transplants, and research in children. *Journal of American Academy of Child Psychiatry, 20*, 581-596
15. House Enrolled Act No. 1830, Indiana General Assembly.
16. Laforet EG (1976): The fiction of informed consent. *JAMA, 235*, 1579-1585
17. President's Commission for the Study of Ethical Problems in Medcine and Biomedical and Behavioral Research: Making Health Care Decisions (Volume One: Report), 1982
18. Hofmann AD (1978). The right to consent and confidentiality in adolescent health care: an evolutionary dilemma. In EL Bandman & B Bandman (Eds): *Bioethics and Human Rights*. Boston:Little, Brown, pp 183-188
19. Wordsworth W (19674). Ode on intimations of immortality from recollections of early childhood. *Palgrave's Golden Treasury*. Oxford: Oxford University Press, p 310
20. Schaeffer P (1974). *Equus*. New York:Avon, p 74
21. Kaplan M (1975). Equus -- a psychiatrist questions his priestly powers. *The Hastings Center Report, 5(1)*, 10
22. Elkind D (1970). *Children and Adolescents*. Oxford:Oxford University Press
23. Elkind D (1981).*The Hurried Child*. Reading,Massachussets:Addison-Wesley

24.   Gaylin WA (1974). A psychoanalytic look at coercion.*Psychiatry, 37*, 3
25.   Goffman E (1961). *Asylums.* Garden City, New York:Anchor Books

DISCUSSION QUESTIONS

1.   What rights does a child or an adolescent have as a client in your institution? Are they different from those of adult clients?

2.   What types of data are obtained in assessing a child's competence within your institution?

3.   How are paternalism, coercion, and informed consent interrelated? What is the difference between strong and weak paternalism?

4.   Under what circumstances should an individual be approached about participating in nontherapeutic research?

5.   Respond to the question: What should one do when parents have signed commitment papers for an adolescent when no evidence exists that such commitment is needed? Utilize the decision-making tool described in Chapter 1.

6.   Role play obtaining an informed consent from a competent client. Use your institution's consent form and a medical situation of your choice. Discuss the types of communication techniques you used and whether or not they should be altered.

7.   Do you think it would be to the client's best interest if another health care professional, other than the one involved in direct treatment, would obtain the informed consent for treatment? What implications would this hold for professional practice?

8.   How can the health care team work together to assure that coercion of the client, by family or others, does not occur within the health care setting?

9.   What criteria might be used in the selection of a client advocate for a child? Which of these criteria would you say are the most important to consider?

10.   What types of ethical issues would be appropriate for referral to an ethics committee? What types of issues have been brought before your institution's ethics committee within the past year? Have any of these issues involved children?

7

Helen L. Morrison

Ethics and Values in the Evaluation And Treatment of Children: A Clinician's Viewpoint

Helen L. Morrison, M.D., a board certified general, child, and forensic psychiatrist, is founder and director of The Evaluation Center in Chicago, Illinois. She is a graduate of the Medical College of Pennsylvania and completed her child psychiatry training at the University of Wisconsin. She is a reviewer for the *American Journal of Psychiatry*, *The American Journal of Forensic Psychiatry*, and the *Journal of Forensic Sciences*. She has written over 45 scientific articles on topics in medicine and psychiatry and three books.

In this chapter, Dr. Morrison reviews the history of ethics in the evaluation and treatment of children. She discusses paternalism, advocacy, parental responsibility, and the legal doctrine of *parens patriae.* Other issues examined for their ethical implications include various aspects of the treatment of children using medications, behavior modification, and psychotherapy or agency consultation and the conflicts associated with public laws. She concludes the chapter by discussing the ethical implications of the use of children as research subjects.

This chapter will provide the reader with an overview of ethical issues and values inherent in the care and management of the child. The seemingly artificial distinction made between ethics and values represents the intricate complexities that challenge the individual in his or her capacity of responsible advocate, clinician, teacher, parent, or institutional representative.

Values are generally considered to include the concepts of models, standards, beliefs, criteria, examples, and goals. Ethics, often confused with the concepts that accompany the word "values", include the ideas of honorable, principled, prescriptive, moral, and proper.

The exceptional attraction evident in the current study of ethics and its relationship to children belies the recorded importance given this topic.[1-3] This past history is exemplified in this passage from Hooker:

> In detecting deception in the manner, the modes of expression and even the very tone of the voice, and sometimes, nay very often, people so far undervalue the good sense and shrewdness of children, that their deception is even ridiculously bungling and justly excites an honest indignation in the bosom of the deceived child. Every physician has seen the injurious influence of deception upon children. Deception is more frequently practicied upon children than upon adults and many seem to think that they have not the same right to candor and honesty in our intercourse with them. A child can appreciate fair and honest treatment as well as an adult can, and he has as good a right to receive it at our hands. He sometimes claims his right in terms and by acts not to be mistaken, and when it is taken from him, he shows his sense of the wrong by remonstrances and retaliatory language and by a system of rebellion to an authority that he despises as well as fears for its falsehood.[4]

THE PARADIGM

The "what is best" school of guiding ethical principles[5] has been criticized from multiple facets.[6-8] The controversy continues unabated.[9] From the perspective of Mill,[10] and adhering to the concepts of paternalism, the principle of liberty prohibits interference with freedom of action of an individual. Mill later expanded upon his views in his essay on Militarianism: that interference is permissible in protecting the naive from injury.[11] Theory aside, the clinician is only too aware of the controversies concerning techniques and models for evaluation and treatment of the child. No where is the controversy more obvious than in the distinction between control or treatment. The former has a goal of social conformity with laws and norms. The latter has as a goal of improvement of an afflicted individual. How does one assess this difference in, for example, the use of stimulant medication in the hyperactive child? Is the goal one of improving classroom behavior? Is the goal of one increasing attention so that learning can occur? Can one distinguish between the two goals? Are there two goals? Paternalism is simply defined as the custody or control of an individual, group, or society in a manner that suggests that of a father protecting or caring for his children. All of us are familiar with the concept as it relates to the acts of responsible caretakers to their children. Caretakers constantly justify their interference in the liberty of their children. Bullying, control, coercion, and priming are considered to be the obligation of the caretaker. We question to what extent a child may be able to conceive of their present or future interest. No one questions the constraint of liberty of action of the young child, whether the control is directed toward optimal development or whether the control is directed toward the prevention of harm or injury.

It is the lack of development or maturity that Mill addresses in his doctrines. Three-year-olds lack the cognitive awareness required for a completely logical decision. Despite the current flurry of action related to the rights of children and advocacy for children, it is easy for one to counter the claims that all acts of paternalism are immoral or unethical. This is especially true in the prevention of self-destructive acts. Thus, we have the concept of justifiable paternalism.[12] Restriction of the freedom of a child is a duty of a caretaker.[13]

What seems clear in concept is not so clear in practice. In the example above, the differentiation between control and therapy with the use of stimulant drugs reveals only that one intervention can serve multiple purposes. The exercise of paternalism has important moral limitations.[14] The contemporary emphasis on future oriented consent is that of what the child would, in the future, welcome, not what she or he may welcome in the present.[15]

The interests and the life of the child are protected in basic ethical guidelines. The child is thought to want basic supplies -- shelter, food, and security, regardless of what else they want. The interest of the child is clearly understood to be in a continual state of change. Caretakers are charged to shape those interests. This shaping is done in the context of the process of becoming autonomous and the development of the capacity for independent choice. In the context of parental consent, parents do not truly consent for the child. No child has chosen his or her caretaker. The child, therefore, has chosen neither the proxy nor the interest to be upheld by the proxy.[16] Just because the interest of the child is shaped by the caretaker, this fact does not justify all decisions made by the caretaker.

Multiple complexities surround any discussion of ethical behavior with and toward children. These complexities are not new. They are and have been based on the recognition that human and scientific progress are inherently incompatible. Despite the endeavors of the scientific method, the concept of detached scientific objectivity remains a mythical one. Scientific knowledge and progress is inseparable from the merger of personal and objective views.[17]

It seems a simplistic viewpoint that the foundations for good ethical treatment by a caregiver is based on the good person who becomes a caregiver. Despite medical school curricula changes, the training in ethical issues has been noted by several authors to have little effect. The greatest effect appears to be individual ethical makeup that a person brings to these courses. These courses can assist in some shift in self awareness of ethical issues. The lessons of the world are learned in the arena of reality, separate from the academic presentation of caregiving as successful, adequate, in control, and based on sound reasoning and scientific knowledge.[18]

How one reasons in an ethical manner is assumed to involve several essential elements. Identification of the recipient of care and the rights attendant to the recipient; the responsibilities and identification of the caregiver; the decisions to be made solely or in collaboration that will arise in the beginning, process of, or ending of care. The care question remains that of what ethical principles will guide the process of decision-making? How does one define their meaning? How does one justify the ethical principles? Does the caregiver embrace the values of society and its values in relationship to infants and children as individuals or as a future population group?

ADVOCACY

The greatest confusion for the caregiver in assessing the care issues of ethical decision is that of the concept of advocacy. Social action is the mission of child advocacy. Advocacy is based on the oft-heard phrase, "best interests" of the child. The assumption of common law is the doctrine of *parens patriae*: children are to be protected by society. Advocacy carries this doctrine to the requirement that the child as a powerless individual needs active proponents who will see to it that his or her rights will be protected. The advocate role finds conflict with the ethical role in this arena. A detailed discussion of this conflict is well beyond the scope of this chapter. The reader who is interested in this issue is referred to the volume by Melton.[19] For the purposes of this chapter, advocacy is separate and distinct from ethics. The reader is cautioned that this distinction is an artifical one.

GENETIC SCREENING

The ethical dilemmas prior to the birth of a child are no less complex that those attendant to the older age child. These dilemmas arise with conflict between the aims of medical care, the prevention of suffering, and the preservation of human life.[20] Scientific methods have advanced through the process of genetic screening sufficiently so that the risks or likelihood of suffering are more well known.[21] The ethical questions concern quality of life and the suffering of the parents compared to that of one who may never experience normality.

The establishment of genetic screening programs assumes that the development of a child is insured. It has also been assumed that screening will enable greater parental options, choices, and self-determinations. These are considered to be aspects of major benefits of the programs, responsible and informed decision-making concerning procreation. The questions of whether or not this is a constitutive right (which implies a correlative duty of others not to interfere in the exercise of these rights) is lost in the controversy surrounding the right to life. No one will state that parents have an obligation to bring as many children into the world as we are capable of procreating.[22] How are rights insured if this viewpoint is taken? The definition of "right" is found in terms of laws or rules that regulate or delineate relationships among individuals. In genetic screening, the genetic responsibility of the individual has been noted to involve several models. First, is the context of human genetics examined in relationship to parental responsibility. These include the encouragement of the development of the child, the nuturing, sustaining and supporting of the child, and preparation of the child for its role as a member of society. In the context of family, these responsibilities include preservation of the family welfare and propagation of its lineage and welfare. Both the common life of the individual and the common life of the family proceed within the common life of the society.

ABORTION

Safeguarding the interests of a child as a human individual is no more openly debated than in the context of abortion. There is an overwhelming amount of material written about the arguments on both sides of this issue. The issue is complex and seemingly insurmountable from theological, moral, ethical, and legal viewpoints. Even as one accepts as true the viewpoint of abortion as an immoral act the ethical issues remain unresolved. A consideration of selective abortion of fetuses with genetic abnormalities poses questions not applicable to the general question of abortion. Prenatal diagnosis through amniocentesis or chorion biopsy has drastically altered the questions of selective abortion.[23] The conflict of category of disease leading to a morally justified decision versus immoral deliberate infanticide is only beginning to be addressed by professionals involved in this process.

POST-NATAL LIFE

If one accepts as a rule the protection of life as the first duty of a caregiver, the neo-natal intensive care unit brings ethical issues to a critical forefront.[24] Basic questions of fairness, equity, right, wrong, responsibility, and accountability challenge the ethical principle. How does one interest the principle in the saving of an infant so severely damaged that no participation in human life beyond basic function is possible? Extraordinary supports for scarcely viable babies at the cost of independence have become transformed to ordinary support in many cases. The sanctity of human life is a concept that has directed ethical decision-making. Its principle has been utilized as final justification for the choices utilized in the decision-making in these cases. If a caregiver attends to the process of ethical decision-making, there is a caution to remember. The caution relates to understanding the effect of interaction between moral judgment and ethical principle. Prediction of mental deficit in a neonate is affected by the moral stance of the caretaker.[25] Will the decision-maker take the positions of "all (or none) must be saved?" Will the decision-maker utilize aspects of the question of encumbrance or worry of infant and family if the child is saved? Is there no limit to what must be done to preserve life? Ethical principles do not provide precise answers to these questions. Questions of values concerning the quality of life are also not answered by ethical principles.[26]

The decision to keep life no matter whether that life will be a fate worse than death must consider our acceptance of the responsibility we assume when we take into our hands the fate of human beings. Who is suffering? What will their lives involve or become? What means will justify what end? Whose interests will we serve? Is the condition treatable, partially treatable, or not treatable? Is treatment or withholding of treatment of free choice or by order of a court of law? These are questions to be asked and considered, individually and collectively. Despite the viewpoints of various practitioners, no explicit answers follow.[27] Infants have no capacity to understand their "rights" or "condition" or "prognosis." The ethical inquiry demands even greater consideration by the caregiver.[28]

ETHICAL ISSUES IN TREATMENT

Several volumes provide the reader of this chapter with great detail concerning the psychiatric treatment of children and their environments.[29-33]

No child is an individual when questions are raised as to diagnosis, intervention, and treatment. To consider an optimistic viewpoint, children usually have effective advocates. These may accompany roles assigned to parents. They may also involve juvenile court proceedings or custody or welfare proceedings.

The caregiver, assuming the role of advocate, may risk the alliance needed for adequate care of the child. Age of a child is not static. The developmental needs of the child demands that the caregiver continually assess the ability of the child to become more involved in the decision-making capacity previously given an advocate. Both mental and chronological capacities must be considered. Nowhere is this issue of assessment more critical than in the use of screening instruments. These instruments are ubiquitous. They have multiple characteristics. They have many negative components.[34] Inappropriate or inaccurate labelling, nonprovision of services once a label is applied, and refusal to acknowledge the limitations of screening programs are only a few of the ethical issues raised.[35]

In treatment, the ethical issues involve whether treatment is efficacious. If a treatment is not proven, the caregiver has an obligation of an ethical nature to evaluate or conduct research with a goal of providing effective treatment. The questions of risk and efficacy are no more critical than in the areas of use of medications. In a child, the risk of chronic effects, impairment, or damage become even more critical areas of inquiry.

Psychotherapy with children most commonly involves individual and family work. The ethical therapist cannot ignore questions related to the uncertainty of beneficial outcome, neglect or lack of concern about the parents, and the danger of subtle indoctrination of the child by techniques used in treatment. Imposition of the values of the therapist on the child and the family, potentially undermining the function of the child in the family, altering rules and authority or altering attitudes to more negative views, only jeopardizes the outcome for the child.[36]

A child brought for treatment is not equivalent to an individual who presents a need of intervention. The therapist structures the acute ethical issue. Imposition of values or beliefs of the therapist is not a prerogative regardless of the theoretical knowledge or length of experience accompanying credentials of the individual. If one accepts one goal of treatment as independence, the patient will have some protection from the therapist who could be seduced by the transference or confusion on the part of the therapist between personal and professional skill and power.

In behavior modification, this characteristic of power becomes more overt. The paradox is that abuse of power cannot happen. It does. To illustrate, control by a teacher of a classroom often utilizes behavioral procedure.[37] Tranquility or the search thereof has been used to justify behavioral methods. The goal of tranquility should be learning. If no improved opportunity is made for learning, no behavioral method is justified.

To complicate ethical matters, Public Law 94-142, Section 10 of the 1976 Education Act attempts to insure that the stigma of special education is minimal. Schools will ask their consultants to assist in removal of "difficult" students to other places. The consultant must question whether all possible alternatives have been adequately and thoroughly explored. The critical ethical question is: for whose benefit is the removal being done?

ETHICAL ISSUES IN THE COURTS

The legal status of children is evolving at a pace incomparable in our history. Juvenile courts were transformed into legal proceedings of due process in 1967 in the case of *In Re Gault*. The legal rights movement for children is becoming a focus of some mental health professionals.[38] Ethics and the courts are just beginning to confront often opposing goals.[39] These issues will demand the concern of any individual who must become involved in proceedings of this type. The professional, ethical individual is aware that the interests of the child are preferential to those of the adversarial legal proceeding, especially when this preference does not involve dangerousness or lack of truthfulness.

ETHICAL ISSUES IN RESEARCH

The Supreme Court has not address the issue of whether the law permits children to be subjects in research. The complications that accompany any research utilizing children as subjects are no more evident than with projects that offer no potential medical benefit. Some authors believe that "nontherapeutic" research is justified by the principle of humanity bearing minimal burdens if they are for the common good.[40,41] If risks are minimal or negligible, the research is considered justifiable by these individuals. The opposing view is that human subjects who cannot consent should never be used. No person should be simply a means to an end.

Protection of children in research projects is not legislated only by government or institutional regulations.[42,43] The researcher, like the therapist, must be concerned about the issue of undue influence, coercion, deception, and misleading information. Social ethics must be weighed against scientific ethics in any decision concerning moral dangers.

Coercion with children can include gift-giving, inappropriate use of authority, or inappropriate persuasion. Deceptions range from outright lying as to the purpose or sponsorship of a project. Researchers will use the excuse of research as a sobriquet for keeping a subject unaware of the true purpose of the study to avoid expected modification of subject responses.

In addition, children may be induced to act in situations that may diminish self-respect, despite the aura of "volunteerism" proposed by the researcher.[44]

What of the child who will be used in clinical teaching? Demonstrations have always been used as a method of imparting knowledge. Most simply, there should be minimum interference with the care of the child. Parents need to be informed as to presence of observers who could perhaps violate the statement of confidentiality.

How may one initiate awareness of the issues relating to research with children? Consent does not simply stipulate that a parent substitutes for a "voiceless" child. Minimal risk requirements demand that the child benefit to a greater degree than she or he could be harmed. The question of consent is the most highly debated and controversial questions relating to research with children. No greater ethical imperative exists beyond the protection of the child and his or her best interests.[45]

CLOSING STATEMENT

The best interest of the child is paramount to all that has been written in this chapter. No one, be he parent, guardian, evaluator or treater, teacher, child care worker, or administrator can ignore the tenent inherent in the ethics and values of our relationship to children.

REFERENCES

1. Fromm E (1947). *Man for Himself.* Canada: Holt, Reinhart, and Alenston
2. Dorsey JM (1974). *Psychology of Ethics.* Detroit, Michigan: Centre for Health Education
3. Ebling FJ (1969). *Biology and Ethics.* Proceedings of a Symposium held at the Royal Geographical Society, London, 26 and 27, September, 1968. London: Academic Press
4. Worthington H (1984). Truth in our intercourse with the sick. *Hooker Worthington, Physician and Patient.* New York:Baker and Scribner, p 357-382
5. Clements CD & Sidir RC (1983). Medical ethics assault upon medical values. *JAMA, 250,* 2970-2971
6. Churchill LR & Cross AW (1983). Letter to the editor. *JAMA, 250,* 2971
7. Steffen G (1983). Letter to the editor. *JAMA, 250,* 2972
8. Howe K (1983). Letter to the editor. *JAMA, 250,* 2972
9. Veatch RM (1981). *A Theory of Medical Ethics.* New York:Basic Books
10. Mill JS (1956). *On Liberty, l859.* New York:The Liberal Arts Press
11. Mill JS (1957). *Utilitarianism, l863.* (Edited by Oskar Priest). New York:Bobbs-Merrill
12. Macklin R (1982). *Man, Mind and Morality. The Ethics of Behavior Control.* Englewood Cliffs, New Jersey:
13. Dworkin G (January 1972). Paternalism. *The Monist, 56,* 64-83
14. Lidz D, Meisel A, Zerubavel E, *et al.* (1984). *Informed Consent: A Study of Decision Making in Psychiatry.* New York:The Guilford Press
15. President's Commission for the Study of Ethical Problems in Medicine and Biomedical and Behavioral Research. Splicing Life. A Report on the Social and Ethical Issues of Genetic Engineering with Human Beings, 1982
16. Brody H (1981). *Ethical Decisions in Medicine* (2nd ed). Boston:Little, Brown and Company
17. Roberts C (1974). *The Scientific Conscience: Reflections on the Modern Biologist and Humanism.* Fontwell Sussex:Centaur Press Limited
18. Cabot R (1926). *Adventures on the Borderlands of Ethics.* New York: Harper and Brothers
19. Melton G (1983). *Child Advocacy: Psychological Issues and Interventions.* New York:Alenum Press
20. Twiss SB (1974). Ethical issues in genetic screening: models of genetic responsibility. In D Bergsma (Ed): *Ethical Social and Legal Dimension of Screening for Human Genetic Disease.* New York:Stratton Intercontinental Medical Book Corporation
21. Goodall J & Evans R (1979). Dilemmas in the management of infants and children. In G Scorer & A Wing: *Decision Making in Medicine: The Practice of Its Ethics.* London:Edward Arnold, pp 83-98

22. Fletcher J (1976). *Moral Responsibility*. Philadelphia:The Westminister Press, p 112
23. Harris H (1975). *Prenatal Diagnosis and Selective Abortion*. Cambridge, Massachusetts:Harvard University Press
24. Jonsen AR & Garland MJ (1976). *Ethics of Newborn Care*. San Francisco, University of California: Health Policy Program and Berkeley, University of California, Institute of Government Studies
25. Scorer G & Wing A (1979). The control of the beginning of life. *Decision Making in Medicine: The Practice of Ethics*. London:Edward Arnold
26. McAllister JB (1955). *Ethics with Special Application to the Medical and Nursing Professions*. Philadelphia:W. B. Saunders, pp 352-368
27. Goodall J & Evans R (1983). Dilemmas in the management of infants and children. In DW Pfaff (Ed): *Ethical Questions in Brain Behavior. Problems and Opportunities*. New York:Springer-Verlag
28. Pfaff DW (1983). *Ethical Questions in Brain and Behavior. Problems and Opportunities*. New York:Springer-Verlag
29. Levine M (1972). *Psychiatry and Ethics*. New York:George Brazeller
30. (1982). *American Journal of Orthopsychiatry, 52*, 518-529
31. Koocher P (1976). *Children's Rights and the Mental Health Professions*. New York:John Wiley & Sons
32. Rosen C, Rekers A, & Bentler M (1978). Ethical issues in the treatment of children. *Journal of Social Issues, 34*, 122-136
33. McCartney J & Beauchamp TL (1981). Ethical issues in pediatric treatment and research. *Journal of Pediatric Psychology, 6*, 131-143
34. Rosenthal R & Jacobson J (1968). *Pygmalion in the Classroom: Teacher Expectation and Pupil's Intellectual Development*. New York:Holt, Rinehart, Winston
35. Silverman M & Silverman M (July 28-August 4, 1962). Psychiatry inside the family circle. *The Saturday Evening Post*
36. Fieldsteel ND (1982). Ethical issues in family therapy. In M Rosenbaum (Ed): *Ethics and Values in Psychotherapy*. New York:The Free Press, pp 258-268
37. Smith MB (1967). Conflicting values affecting behavioral research with children. *American Psychologist, 22*, 377-382
38. Schetky H & Benedek P (Eds) (1980). *Child Psychiatry and the Law*. New York:Brunner/Mazel
39. Lafon U (September - December 1976). The interviewing and questioning of children and adolescents by the police and legal authorities: from an anxiety-creating theme to the search for a code of ethics. *International Child Welfare Review*. No. 30-31, 63-68
40. Ramsey P (1970). *The Patient as a Person*. New Haven:Yale University Press, pp 1-58
41. McCormack SJ (Autumn 1974). Proxy consent in the experimental situation. *Perspectives in Biology and Medicine, 18*, 2-20
42. Frankel S (Spring 1979). Social, legal and political responses to ethical issues in the use of children as experimental subjects. *Journal of Social Issues, 34*, 101-113
43. Thomasma C & Mauer M (1982). Ethical complications of clinical therapeutic research on children. *Social Science & Medicine, 16*, 913-919
44. Rosenthal R & Rosnow RL (1975). *The Volunteer Subject*. New York: John Wiley
45. Eys J (1978). *Research on Children: Medical Imperatives, Ethical Quandries and Legal Constraints*. Baltimore:University Park Press

DISCUSSION QUESTIONS

1.   The author states "The best interest of the child is paramount...." What does that mean? How is that determined?

2.   A 14-year-old boy is brought to the psychiatric hospital by his mother who wants him hospitalized and treated. She states he talks back to her, fights with her, and disagrees with everything she says. She feels she cannot control him. Discuss the ethical issues regarding involuntary hospitalization of minors, confidentiality, responsibility to the client, and commitment to the client's good.

3.   Discuss the ethical issues of informed consent for the administration of drugs or treatments to minors. Can a child have the capacity to be autonomous? What affects his or her capacity?

4.   You are asked to assist in informing parents of the result of an amniocentesis that shows the fetus is genetically abnormal. What are the ethical issues for the parents, the fetus, and the treatment team?

5.   Psychological testing, IQ assessment, and psychiatric evaluation of children may result in labelling. Discuss the ethical responsibilities of the mental health care provider regarding labeling for the "best interest" of the child.

6.   A severely emotionally disturbed child is "mainstreamed" into the class-room of a public school under Public Law 94-142. You are asked to assist the school in providing the best education for this very disruptive child. What ethical questions must beconsidered regarding what is best for the child?

7.   A new medication has been developed for the treatment of autistic children. You are asked to assist in the administration of the medication to children on a research ward. Discuss the ethical issues involved in your discussion to partici-pate in the research.

8.   A high school psychology class would like to visit a local adolescent psy-chiatric treatment unit to learn first hand from patients about mental illness. It is up to you to agree to the visit. What ethical issues might you consider? What fac-tors influence the clients' capacity to consent to the visit?

9.   Write a child's Bill of Rights for psychiatric clients.

10.   Discuss the ethical issues involved in the court ordered psychiatric evalu-ation of a juvenile.

8

Domeena C. Renshaw
Mary Patricia Ryan

Ethics, Values, and Sex Therapy

Domeena C. Renshaw, M.D., F.A.C.P., a physician and psychiatrist, and professor in the Department of Psychiatry at the Stritch School of Medicine, Loyala University in Chicago is a nationally recognized authority in the field of sexual medicine. She has written and published extensively on the evaluation and treatment of sexual problems. She is the founder and director of the Loyola Sex Clinic.

Mary Patricia Ryan, R.N., Ph.D. is a registered nurse and associate professor of mental health nursing, Niehoff School of Nursing, Loyola Univeristy. She was a Kennedy Fellow in medical ethics at Harvard University.

In this chapter the authors discuss how ethics and values impact on the subspecialty of sexual medicine. They describe a code of ethics recently developed for sex therapy. They present some of the ethical dilemmas one confronts in sexual medicine and how one might resolve them. The chapter concludes with a description of the considerations, options, and actions of a working ethics committee.

Sex therapy as a method of treatment on a large scale has only evolved in the past 25 years. The "father" of sex therapy is generally accepted to be William Masters, M.D., a gynecologist who researched human male and female sexual responses in a scientific laboratory setting. Upon the knowledge gained he evolved a two week brief sex therapy method that dealt with biological and psychosocial factors as well as with partner interactions.[1,2] It was highly successful and easily duplicated in the original St. Louis 14-day format as well as in a large variety of modifications. Did Dr. Masters abide by the American Medical Association's Principles of Medical Ethics? That document is brief, sweeping, and nonspecific:

Preamble: The medical profession has long subscribed to a body of ethical statement developed primarily for the benefit of the patient. As a member of this profession, a physician must recognize responsibility not only to patients, but also to society, to other health professionals, and to self. The following Principles adopted by the American Medical Association (AMA) are not laws, but standards of conduct which define the essentials of honorable behavior for the physician.

Most considered that Dr. Masters was highly ethical in his research and treatment, respectful of his volunteers and of his patients. He made a positive contribution to medicine and the public although the sexual nature of his work raised millions of eyebrows. He, his associates and his family had much criticism to withstand. His work has since been duplicated and, therefore, scientifically validated in the United States and abroad. Also scholars have sought to integrate new sexual knowledge into traditional ethics.[3]

The two weaknesses, however, in this program were (1) the high cost of treatment and (2) the highly publicized use of sexual surrogates. Each has spawned poorly qualified profit-seeking "sex therapists" and "body therapists." While the field of sex therapy is new and small, there is already polarization around ethical issues such as competence and a behavioral code. There is no U.S. subspecialty of Medical Sexology. There are no nationally accepted standards of education or of clinical expertise for sex therapists. For these reasons an in depth volume was written to address ethical issues specific to sex therapy.[4]

Associations of sex educators, researchers, and therapists have been formed on the east and west coasts and in Washington D.C. Their strength and solvency have varied. All have been multidisciplinary, attempting to represent and respond to the many levels of skills and practices of their members.

In April, 1979, the American Association of Sex Educators, Counselors, and Therapists (AASECT) adopted a code of ethics, largely adapted from that of the Masters-Johnson Reproductive Biology Research Foundation, St. Louis, Missouri of March 1978. Students or trainees in sexology are not exempt from these principles. To ensure education and clinical competence for the protection of patients and of professionals who refer them for sex therapy the following is noted in the AASECT Code:[5]

1. Prerequisites for practicing sex therapy include professional and educational and demonstrated competence in a psychological or biological clinical field and additional prescribed training in the treatment of sexual problems.
    a. Sex therapists have earned an educational degree equivalent to a master's degree or doctorate in human sexuality or in a field related to the practice of sex therapy, such as psychology, social work, medicine, psychiatric nursing, and counseling.
    b. Competence in another primary discipline such as psychology, psychiatry, and marriage counseling is not equivalent to competence in sex therapy. Those trained in such related disciplines bring professional experiences and insights that provide a foundation upon which sex therapy training can be added.
    c. Training in sex therapy must always include supervised experience in the conduct of sex therapy.

2. Sex therapists and sex counselors should possess expertise in a number of specific areas:

   a. Sex therapists and sex counselors should possess basic information in the following areas:
      1. Sexual and reproductive anatomy and physiology
      2. Developmental sexuality (from conception to old age) from a psychobiological perspective
      3. Dynamics of interpersonal relationships
      4. Sociocultural factors in sexual values and behavior
      5. Marital and family dynamics
      6. Ethical issues in sex therapy and sex counseling

   b. Sex therapists and counselors should be knowledgeable about and possess clinical skills relevant to the following areas of diagnosis:
      1. Sexual disorders
      2. Psychopathology
      3. Techniques of evaluation and referral

   c. Sex therapists should possess knowledge and clinical skills relevant to the following:
      1. Techniques and theory of sex therapy, including several different models
      2. Techniques and theory of psychotherapy, including several different models
      3. Principles of outcome evaluation. Sex counselors should have background knowledge of these areas but are not expected to possess clinical skills related to the practice of sex therapy and psychotherapy.
      This does not mean that every sex therapist or sex counselor must be able to provide the full range of treatment

3. Sex therapists and sex counselors should recognize the necessity and benefit of professional growth by participating in continuing education, reading professional journals, and attending scientific meetings. Sex therapists and sex counselors should maintain knowledge of current developments in their field.

4. Credentials alone do not give evidence of full competence. The proof of competence is the ability to provide skilled, responsible service to clients.

AASECT has, for several years, published a booklet categorizing professionals as either therapists or educators and helpfully listing them by state. Since 1979 this organization has certain requirements such as treatment-training hours for members to be listed. However, there is no examining board for either category. In fact early AASECT listing required little more than a small fee. Their booklet, therefore, poses a dilemma unless the referring professional happens to know the listed professional personally.

Irregular or unacceptable activity in sex therapy rapidly translates into headlines. Recently the program "Sixty Minutes" televised an expose on therapist-patient sex providing useful public education. It is, however, very difficult to prosecute malpracticing "sex therapists" because patients hesitate to press charges due to the highly sensitive and private nature of a sex problem.

"Therapists" may easily obtain fancy diplomas, which are often handed out to registrants at weekend sexuality workshops, but "one workshop doth not a therapist make." Therefore, a referring professional must attempt to check a sex therapist's credentials, and also tell the patient to use good common sense, preserve their own basic moral values in sex therapy, and not be coerced to behave in ways that make him or her uncomfortable. Sexual loveplay should be private and done at home only. Patients who are referred by their primary physician can be invited to check back routinely after 12 weeks or sooner if they have doubts about the ethics or effectiveness of the sex therapist.

VALUES IN SEXUAL MEDICINE

Some professionals state that neither the therapist nor the patient's own values have a place in the therapeutic process. They argue that the patient comes to the sex therapist with an identified sexual problem and the only duty of the therapist is to help the patient resolve the problem. However, they would probably admit upon questioning that each patient does have religious, moral, or cultural values and that these must first be understood for diagnostic purposes then respected in treatment. Beyond that, "values-neutral" therapists believe that the therapist has no right to impose his or her values on the patient or indeed to even explore or examine the patient's values. Much of such reticence arises from the behaviorist movement in psychology under the leadership of B.F. Skinner, which underplayed the influence of attitudes upon actions.

Skinner contended that behavior change alone is important. If a behavior needed to be extinguished or reinforced, the coach (therapist/trainer) may reward or punish that particular behavior so that it appears more and more frequently or appears less and less frequently. Skinnerians consider what goes on inside the subject (animal or person) to be unimportant. The emergence of the desirable behavior or the extinction of the undesirable behavior is the therapeutic goal. The coach (therapist/trainer) does not enter into the process except in dispensing the reward or punishment. Behavior modification reached its peak in the 1960s and has since been incorporated into the therapeutic approaches of many disciplines: psychology, psychiatry, preventive medicine, and sexual medicine are some of those. It is no longer used by many professionals in its pure behavioristic form yet the values-free (or values-neutral) stand taken by the coach (therapist/trainer) is still being adopted. Behaviorism conflicts with a patient's ethical choice to bring thinking and feeling together (as his or her attitude) before sexual behavior (verbal or physical) is expressed. Thought and time are needed for attitudes to change.

This may cause confusion or a clinical stalemate. Because of the Skinnerian posture that a therapist's beliefs and professional values do not enter into the therapy sessions, values are not discussed in training or supervision, on the assumption that values are safely tucked away during the therapy session. Frequently a therapist says that he or she was appalled by a certain sexual story told by the patient but listened to the facts and gave no response -- positive or negative -- and did not even question how the patient felt about the situation. For competent clinical treatment, a patient's reaction (then and now) to the life event is essential, both to promote growth through awareness of the impact and for considering current ramifications for the patient.

Should values enter into a therapist's relationship with a patient? Is a values-neutral posture humanly possible? How do patient's values enter into the therapy sessions? What should be done by the therapist about the patient's values? These questions will be discussed in the following sections.

What is a Value?

A value is a perception of worth that an individual (or a group of individuals) places on an object, an idea, or an attitude. This worthiness leads oneself to "ought" or "should" demands on oneself in relation to the value and to suffer discomfort when these demands are not met. Uustal states that values are general guides to behavior or standards of conduct that each person endorses and tries to live up to or maintain. Values also provide a frame of reference through which each person integrates, explains, and appraises new ideas, events, and personal relationships.[6] Values are not seen directly. One can only infer them from the verbal or nonverbal behavior of the individual. Values are part of the unique personality in the innermost center of the being as shown in the act of choice.[7]

Values are not biologically endowed but are socially learned through explanation, moralizing, modeling, being rewarded or punished, identifying with a person or group, and manipulation. Many of these teaching methods are used in the family and reinforced in church, school, and life settings. They occur almost imperceptibly as part of daily living, generation after generation. Seldom other than in planned revolution or for indoctrination purposes does anyone take the time to discuss values. Are there value priorities? How do these affect behavior? In the area of sexual medicine, the latter is a most important question because sex and values are inextricably bound and need to be discussed so that the patient can clarify and connect what it is that helps or hinders his or her sex functioning. Only in understanding discomfort due to shame, guilt, or inhibitions can the patient come to terms with a values behavior conflict, so that sexual satisfaction is experienced. If a man has learned that kissing and petting are for teenage experimentation only and have no part in a marriage bedroom, marital and sexual conflict may result if his wife values foreplay.

Values clarification theory [6,8,9] offers an approach that attempts to help individuals sort through, analyze, and set the priorities of their own values. Barry[10] states that values clarification tries to help people begin to act in a way that is consistent and consonant with their own values. Values clarification is concerned primarily with the process of valuing. Raths, Simon, and Merrill[8,9] states that there are three main parts in clarifying values: (1) choosing, (2) prizing, and (3) acting. Seven steps are related to these three headings. They are:

1. Choosing freely.
2. Selecting from alternatives.
3. Choosing after consideration of the consequences of each alternative.
4. Being proud of and happy with the choice.
5. Being willing to affirm the choice publicly.
6. Making the choice part of one's behavior.
7. Repeating the choice.

Everyone would agree that a value should be chosen freely. It is commonly recognized that children learn and accept their family's values until the time that they begin to explore other alternatives and accept new values. To choose among alternative values is perceived as a great contributor to adolescent turmoil. Frequently, however, as an adolescent or a young adult, one goes from one peer group to another, accepting other peoples' values and trying to live up to others' values only to find them not useful in carrying out his or her own goals. The individual then experiences a growing sense of uncertainty, frustration, and confusion. Many of these individuals seek out professional help for the discomfort which they are experiencing.

If the individual has completed the first three of the seven steps successfully, then movement is made to *prizing* a value. A sense of contentment and happiness is experienced after the choice is made and the individual is ready to stand publicly for the chosen value. This may be with a family member, friends, or with strangers such as at a public meeting or in the classroom. The value is, therefore, first prized by the self and then shared, when appropriate, with others. Choosing and prizing are necessary steps in valuing, but do not in themselves complete the valuing process unless there is action.

The individual must show in behavior that there has been a shift from insight to behavior. What is the purpose of choosing and prizing unless one does something about what is valued? The last step includes consistent acting upon a value; for example, if one says that truth is valued but no effort is made to act consistently in the direction of prompting truth, others will begin to question whether one values truth.

APPLICATION OF VALUES TO SEXUAL MEDICINE

Personal Values

The therapist must not only be aware of his or her own values but must have gone through the process of values clarification so that personal values are recognized and accepted as such. If a therapist does not do this, there is danger of values unconsciously guiding not only a therapist's behavior but the behavior of the patient. When deliberate values clarification has occurred, the patient then is able to begin the process of valuing so that he or she may choose, prize, and act in ways consistent with chosen life's goals.

Professional Goals

Most sex therapists are professionals and come from disciplines that have developed codes of ethics. The codes reflect the values that have been adopted by the profession to serve as standards that guide the conduct of its members. Values do not exist in a vacuum. They are not like a mantle that is thrown on when one is engaged in professional activities. Professional values are a reflection and expansion of early learned personal values. If the professional has only a dimly perceived concept of how to act and has not internalized professional as well as personal values into the self, little satisfaction will occur and commitment to the profession may be difficult. Indeed, discomfort, anger, apathy, or destructive clinical responses could occur because of the inability of the sex therapist to see that professional acts belong to the self. Service interactions always involve the interdigitation of the values of the giver and the receiver of health care. Personal values of responsibility and competence direct behaviour. Satisfaction follows if action is consonant with values.

Program Values

From the above, one can see that sex therapy programs per se cannot have values; people do. But programs should have philosophies, policies, or goals of therapy, which can be stated and discussed by those who direct them and dispense the services. The professionals who practice in a sex therapy program must consent to demonstrate professional behavior that reflects the values held by the leaders of that profession as important in working with patients who seek help with a sexual problem. The professional who enters a sex training program may request a statement of policy before making a commitment to that program for the purpose of a values choice.

The following sections constitute a beginning list and include brief discussions of professional values that could be reflected in a policy statement of a sex therapy program or practice.

RESPECT FOR PERSONS

Respect for persons and treating each individual with dignity is one of the most important values that a professional must exhibit in behavior. Recognizing that there is a person who is suffering and needs help is important. There is no place in sexual medicine for a professional who collects facts and makes decisions without recognizing and understanding the patient as a person worthy of respect.

RESPONSIBILITY AND ACCOUNTABILITY

Just as the professional must be responsible for his or her actions, the patient or couple must be expected to take responsibility for their actions. "Cure me" or "fix her" are frequent pleas heard in sex therapy. Yet many patients do not wish to change themselves. The therapist and patients must each value full respective accountability for therapy and implementation. Each will then work responsibly to pursue the goals agreed upon in dispensing and using therapy. A caution is that each patient must take responsibility for change in self. A helpless stance of "take away the discomfort" is seductive. Patients change themselves, therapists only facilitate that process of autonomy.

Total dependency in sex therapy without perceived responsibility to actively participate rarely achieves change. This may be seen particularly in couples when only one of the partners presents a symtom while the other is symptom-free and blames the other, without cooperating in treatment to change. There is no un-involved partner in the dyadic sex act, which the therapist must reflect, suggesting responsible cooperation from the symptom-free partner to prevent sabotage, and then dealing with adjustment to the change of both partners being symptom-free.

CONFIDENTIALITY

Much of the material that is gathered in sex therapy from an individual or couple seeking help is of such a sensitive nature that it has previously been shared with few if anyone at all. The professional must be aware of the confidential nature of the information and protect the privacy of each individual or couple.

A word of caution is necessary in working with couples. The professional must not assume that all the material has been shared with each other. The therapist needs, therefore, to ask each individual if the given information has already been shared with the partner. If not, whether he or she wishes to do so.

There may be secrets that have not been shared and the individual may not be comfortable to share at the time. The therapist must respect the confidentiality and not betray the confidence. There are occasions when the patient may be relieved to share as much as possible and the therapist can offer to assist by being present when the patient feels ready. Coercion to share a secret before conjoint therapy can proceed is abuse of the unequal situation of a vulnerable patient who has entrusted a confidence only to have it's exposure become a condition of help.

OPEN COMMUNICATION

Open communication is valued for several reasons. It certainly facilitates the resolution of a problem in therapy. The honest relating of discomfort, symptoms, and the patient's opinions about casual connections helps the therapist to understand and plan for possible resolution of the problem. If a couple is seeking help, open communication between them is an important indicator of how well each partner relates and participates in the expression and resolution of conflicts. Incomplete, guarded, or inaccurate communication may indicate a lack of trust or a fear of closeness. The nonverbal as well as the verbal forms of communication are to be recognized and regarded by the therapist, who must not concentrate on the spoken word only and ignore behavior signals that indicate that change is occurring.

HEALTH CARE

Health, defined as living up to one's potential, is a value that is inherent in the very foundation of medicine. Sexual medicine is no exception. If a patient is suffering discomfort over a perceived sexual symptom, the professional value is to assist the patient of any age, to strive toward achieving an optimal potential of sexual health. At the same time, general health is carefully checked to understand whether physical or chemical factors may be causative of the sexual symptoms presented. The patient may not perceive a request for sex therapy as valuing total health care but the value is there nonetheless -- the desire to maintain an optimum level of functioning.

SEX EDUCATION

The professional must value the healthy expression of sexuality, realizing that there are many and varied socially sanctioned means, but also endless misinformations and inhibitions that have been learned. Therefore, accurate updated scientific sex education becomes an essential cognitive pathway to change and growth seen as a therapeutic goal.[4]

INFORMED CONSENT REGARDING TREATMENT AND A PATIENT'S RIGHT TO DECIDE

Inherent in any therapeutic relationship with patients is the value of patient autonomy. Each individual has the right to decide what will happen to him or her. Particularly in sexual medicine, the patient has the right to decide what they feel comfortable doing. Since the patients in sex therapy are, almost without exception, competent adults, the therapist must value and respect the patient's participation and decisions in the therapy sessions.

The therapist must recognize the ability of the patient to make decisions based on information that is given by the therapist in terms of what is needed by the patient. The need for information is determined by both the therapist and patient. When a couple is being treated, the therapist should be aware of undue pressure of one partner upon another and the use of coercion in seeking help, i.e., for sex therapy or for divorce. Recognition of such pressure can be acknowledged and an honest agreement worked out that indeed each individual will agree to participate in sex therapy. There may be a hidden agenda (to be recognized also) that "even sex therapy will not make me change so leave me alone." Discussion of such a therapist concern may allow the sabotage to surface in therapy so both partners may make a decision as to how to adjust or cope with the resistance.

JUSTICE FOR PATIENTS AND THERAPISTS

Justice is valued by the therapist in order to ensure that each individual is treated with fairness. Problems of labelling (aged, mentally ill, mentally retarded, minority) should be looked at to insure that neither patients nor therapists determine the treatment based on a label but rather on the presenting symptoms and the skills of the therapists.

OPTIMUM INGREDIENTS IN A FAMILY, A MARRIAGE, OR A SIGNIFICANT RELATIONSHIP

Caring/Sharing/Altruism/Order/Consistency. Particularly in treating couples who present sexual problems, caring, sharing, altruism, order, and consistency as values becomes important in assisting a patient's long range adaptation and growth. These values are also a part of open communication, of sex education, and of values transmission but they need extra emphasis in the building of durable relationships. Normal anger may convey noncaring to each other in a troubled relationship. The professional seeking to clarify that anger does not negate positives. Expression of each partner's underlying values of caring, sharing, and altruism as specifically noted in their relationship may be recapitulated to promote conflict resolution. Supportive relationships are considered health-promoting and include family, marriage partners, and enduring friendships.

Trust. Trust is basic to a positive long term personal relationship or a new therapeutic relationship. Without mutual interpartner trust minimal work can be done to resolve the presented sexual problem. The professional and the patient must value and have trust in each other for positive change to occur. Trust may take more time to develop with some persons. No one can go further or faster than their own values allow them.

Humor/Play/Relaxation. Recognizing that tensions are diffused by laughter, playfulness and "re"-creation, the sex therapist values and encourages their expression in a couple's relationship. Sexual problems often make a couple tense and fearful in the bedroom. They then forget to laugh, relax, or play. Valuing humor and playfulness allows the therapist to discuss with the patient or couple whether humor and play would be useful to them. Explicit permission and suggestion to "relax and enjoy" may be very helpful and start the patient or couple on the road to accepting and valuing relaxation. They may not have previously thought of it as important to them!

Competence in Self-care, Talents, Skills, Schooling, Social Exchange. The professional values that each patient seeks to reach optimum knowledge and skills in the area of sexuality. Also in reaching his or her potential in education, in a job and in social expression and relatedness.

Conformity to the Law of the Land. This is a basic value to be regarded by every professional individually and for the program policy. This will include standards of practice, licensure of personnel as well as mundane issues such as fire codes, medical records, etc.

Values Transmission. Transmitting values is the right and responsibility of every parent for their minor offspring. This may enter the sex therapy arena when a patient's history reveals that there was no sex education or negative messages were given during early learning about the place of sexuality in a relationship. There may also be questions from patients (usually when they have accomplished a change to health) about how they may protect and assist their young not to have similar sex problems later. The sex therapist can then discuss and explore with them their options, suggesting sex education readings for parents and age appropriate readings for children.

CONTINUING EDUCATION FOR PROFESSIONALS

Knowledge is valued by every competent professional as necessary for growth. So too in the very young field of sexual medicine. Reading, clinical training, attending workshops, etc. will retain competence in the field, affirmed by also sharing in discussions, writing, and giving lectures. Contained in this value is an obligation to recognize and report confirmed incompetence of sex therapists who harm patients and discredit the field. Research in sexuality is rudimentary but is being done. Treatment innovations can be shared, as they evolve, to improve patient care.

Ethical Issues in Sexual Medicine

Ethics is the study of good conduct. The word is derived from the Greek word *ethos*, which means good mind. Ethical conduct has been supported by codes or principles in medicine since the time of Hippocrates. The AMA was formed for two purposes: (1) to draw up a code of ethics, and (2) to formalize medical education. The first AMA Code of Ethics was written in 1846. In 1957 the code was clarified to be standards not laws. There were ten principles. In 1980, the AMA board approved a revised Principles of Medical Ethics that contains seven laws. Among the principles that would have direct bearing on sexual medicine are the areas of physician competence, confidentiality, ensuring best intests of the patient, and honesty.

Lief[11] stated "Ethical issues in sex counseling in many ways are like those of medical care...." There are similarities and additional special concerns that come up in sexual counseling that need further discussion.

PATERNALISM

Paternalism is the concept that the professional is better qualified than the patient to define "benefit" and "harm." In this view, values such as honesty and patient autonomy are not considred important but are judged a benefit in some cases, a harm in others.[12] It is especially important in sex counseling that the therapists engage the patient in all discussions and decisions that involve that individual. There is a possibility, especially when working with a couple that one partner may be left out of the decision-making or may be coerced into making decisions that are not fully accepted by that individual.

If the professional codes are taken seriously, the therapist will respect the freedom of the person to act on his or her own values as long as such actions do not directly and significantly restrict the freedom of others to choose freely.[13] This does not mean that one adopts a consumerism position in which the information or facts are given to the patient and the therapist withdraws and expects him or her to make the decisions without clarification of facts or discussion of consequences of possible actions.[12]

The ideal position for the sex therapist would be that of advocacy. The patient is given the information and the therapist and patient discuss the significance and consequences of the options available for resolution of a perceived problem. The patient makes decisions based on the discussion. In the advocacy position, the therapist can give an opinion as long as it is explicitly stated that it is a personal opinion and may not be the opinion of the patient. Only when the patient understands the problem through discussion with an expert (in this instance the sex therapist) can he or she freely choose the course of action that best meets his or her interests.[12] The therapist should be aware of falling into the trap of "values imperialism,"[13] which is imposing one's own values out of self-interest. At no time should a therapist act out of self interest over the best interests of the patient. Values imperialism is easily hidden under the mantle of paternalism. Both give the message: "Authority knows best."

DECEPTION

Deception is a problem that may arise in sex therapy sessions as in any branch of medicine. Withholding of information may be perceived as desirable by a paternalistic therapist when the information is viewed professionally as having negative or harmful consequences. When a couple is in sex counseling, the problem of deception may come up. The therapist should clarify that while respecting the confidentiality of what is shared in one-to-one sessions he or she will not participate in collusion against, or deception of, the partner. Keeping a secret confidence is difficult and also different from active deception. Together they set up the treacherous "Scylla and Charybdis" of conjoint therapy.

In practice at Loyola Sex Clinic, the two most common secrets relate to private masturbation and to an extramarital partner. Diagnostically if there is no sexual symptom alone (during masturbation) or with a lover, it changes the diagnosis of the symptom from global to selective. Secret masturbation is easily dealt with by openly assigning the therapeutic task to masturbate at home and discussing it with both. Prognostically the deception about another sex partner differs because it may greatly impede progress in improving a couple's relationship because the energy and time of one is directed elsewhere. It also makes a mockery of conjoint therapy. The patient who reveals the secret is told these facts and that the secret will be held in confidence. The partner having the extramarital affair is asked either to delay therapy till later or to suspend contact with the lover during treatment so that sincere efforts can be made to improve the marital bond. The partner with the secret must also expect the responsibility of answering any direct questions that emerge from the spouse in conjoint sessions regarding time away or the lover. Coercion by a therapist to reveal a secret affair is poor practice, may be for a therapist's need, and a values impositin upon a suggestible patient. It has been known clinically to lead to a suicide attempt in one or both partners, to separation or divorce.

If a therapist uses deliberate deception in the therapy sessions it may limit the rights and responsibility of patients. Rights are personal and can be waived by the patient. If the patient is deceived by a sex therapist it may be adjudicated that the consent that was previously obtained to a waiver of personal rights by the patient cannot any longer be effective. Deceptive practices are, therefore, subject to whatever legal liability would obtain in the absence of consent.[14]

INFORMED CONSENT/RIGHT TO DECIDE

The patient is entitled to information before making decisions and the results of tests that were done. Englehardt[13] says that sex therapists are limited by two constraints:

(1) the recognition of the right of persons to do as they choose as long as their activities do not directly diminish the similar rights of others, and (2) the recognition of our woeful lack of knowledge concerning which sexual activities or life styles are likely to maximize general happiness.

Englehardt differentiates life-style choices (aesthetic choices) from ethical choices. He states that the only strong cases of moral degeneration are those that involve the use (or abuse) of others without their consent.

The therapist also has a special moral obligation to inform patients that therapist suggestions on behalf of particular life styles or behaviors are more aesthetic than moral. Patients cannot go further or faster than each of their value systems allow them.[15] The therapist has an obligation to give such warnings in order to avoid the possibility of coercion by the therapist whose particular opinions or suggestions regarding sexual life styles might be interpreted as medical facts.

Englehardt concedes that the therapist has a right not to agree to help a patient adjust to a client-chosen sexual life-style even in the therapeutic context. However, this statement would be difficult to defend, other than in an initial evaluation to set up a therapeutic contract. Once therapy is under way and new facts emerge, the therapist may not abandon the patient even if the patient describes behaviors that the sex therapist considers wrong or bad. Values differences must be discussed and a consultation or therapist transfer (by mutual consent) could be effected in a professional and caring way if the sex therapist feels too uncomfortable to continue.

DOING NO HARM/EXPLOITATION

The taboo against sexual relations between therapist and patient is deep and widespread. It goes back to the Hippocratic Oath:

Into whatever houses I enter, I will enter to help the sick, and I will abstain from all intentional wrong doing and harm, especially from abusing the bodies of man or woman, bond or free.[16]

Coercion or sexual exploitation is significant when therapist-patient sexual relations occur and there may be harmful consequences rather than help. Englehardt states that the burden of proof that exploitation has not occurred would fall on those persons who wished to approve such patient-therapist relations.

It might be argued that a similar burden of proof will fall upon a sex therapist who sponsors, recommends, or refers a patient to a sexual surrogate. This new and controversial modality is defended as being -- "an ethically permissable way of establishing a therapeutic environment."[4] Should the surrogate "therapist" be bound by the patient-therapist sex taboo? There are no standards, requirements, or licensure for sexual surrogates.

Another type of exploitation, namely financial exploitation, occurs when the therapist continues to treat beyond the level of professional competence or uses inappropriate treatment or gadgetry for primary monetary gain or to retain a patient for longer than is necessary.

SEXUAL SURROGATES

This remains the most emotional, sensational, and controversial ethical issue in the field of sexual medicine. In guarded language the Masters-Johnson Institute includes the following segment in their second volume on ethical issues:[4]

Although controversial, the use of partner surrogates in sex therapy may be an ethically permissible way of establishing a therapeutic environment, when conducted in a responsible manner. If partner surrogates are to be used at all, it should be understood that the partner surrogate is not a sex therapist; surrogates should understand that their role is not that of either sex therapist or psychotherapist; and sex therapists working with partner surrogates must exercise diligence and concern for protecting the dignity and welfare of both the surrogate and the client.

a. Persons functioning as partner surrogates should receive special education in matters related to client confidentiality.

b. If use of a partner surrogate is contemplated, the sex therapist should be highly sensitive to the client's values.

c. Sex therapists working with partner surrogates have a strong responsibility to discuss in depth with these persons and their clients the possible social, psychological, physical, and legal risks pertaining to their roles.

d. Before employing a partner surrogate who is married, consent should be obtained from the surrogate's spouse.

e. Before providing a partner surrogate for a client who is married, consent should be obtained from the client's spouse.

f. In some jurisdictions, the use of partner surrogates may be counter to existing laws. In these circumstances test cases may appropriately be sought or sex therapists may work toward changes in the law. (p 415)

An interesting note is that the AASECT Code of Ethics (1980), repeats, word for word all but point "f" above. The significance is that the use of sur- rogates may indeed be considered, in some jurisdictions, to violate professional and public ethics. The advice of seeking change in existing laws by surrogate test cases was not followed in St. Louis. Instead the (Masters-Johnson) Institute settled out of court when threatened by an ex-surrogate. Acting ethically, in the interest of patient confidentiality, Dr. Masters preferred to settle out of court rather than have a media headline fiesta. If local laws regard "paid for sex" (surrogate) as prostitution, the referring professional may have to face charges for the referral. AASECT, therefore, does a disservice to its members by the omission of this clause.

Dr. Masters had originated the idea of formalizing the use of sexual surrogates as a special way to help men with sex symptoms, but abruptly discontinued their use after the legal problems. While anyone may try to sue for anything, theoretically, an uninformed spouse may have a case against a referring therapist for alienation of affection by sending the patient to another partner specifically for sexual contact. Again, theoretically, a surrogate may be married or as yet undivorced, and her (or his) partner may similarly regard the therapist as alienating affection and causing "loss of consortium," which belongs in the marital unit. Therefore in the Masters-Johnson ethical issues segment (1980) they suggest that consent be obtained from the spouse of the surrogate to be used as a referral sex partner. In 1984 a Baltimore judge ruled a surrogate guilty of prostitution, although she claimed to have been "trained" as a sexual surrogate. The higher courts have not yet heard the case.

Perhaps the first recorded sex surrogate story is to be found in the Old Testament (Book of Kings 1:2-5) where King David attempted to salvage his potency and his throne by bringing to his quarters "a young virgin ... a damsel fair who cherished the King and ministered to him ... but the King knew her not." It was a self-help sex therapy failure. Sleep tumescence studies today may have altered the course of history. However, in those distant days, power to rule seemed linked to sexual potency (possibly to offspring). Adonijah replaced David as King.

Today sex therapists still argue the pros and cons of surrogate therapy.[15,17,18] Has sex therapy been tried and found ineffective? Has solo all men or all women brief group sex therapy been tried?[19] There are today numerous effective alternatives for someone whose partner refuses to participate in couples sex therapy. Therefore, why use radical therapy (surrogates) when simpler help is available. An analogy is why do a radical mastectomy when an excision biopsy is indicated? Some struggle against the "sacrosanct monogamous marriage assumption," saying it is too limiting, therefore, surrogate use is defensible.[17] Others seriously question the use of surrogates for sexual symptoms that are potentially reversible with solo therapy, fantasy, and self-stimulation.[15]

The selection, education, and values of surrogates themselves, and why they choose this behavior, are all additional ethical questions still unanswered. Despite an almost missionary zeal verbalized by card-carrying surrogates, they are careful to avoid calling themselves therapists since they are unlicensed and use terms such as "body workers" or "body counseling." Payment for offering the self as a sex object to a stranger (patient), where the transaction occurs (patient's home/ surrogate's home/hotel), the impact upon minor children of the surrogate and their status as a parent are all exceptionally "sticky" ethical issues. *Time* (June 17, 1974, p 90) asked this question: "Trick or Treatment?" Ten years later the question is still unanswered. The comparison is valid.

Questions about outcome, subsequent sex symptom reversal with the spouse, or carryover of the sexual skill into a valued relationship must be asked. How many times must the surrogate contact be made by the patient? What privacy (confidentiality) and protection is there for the patient and for the surrogate: from exposure, from personal, legal, or psychological harm, and from venereal disease?

The practice may be destructive, especially when there is a desparate misplaced focus on intercourse. What will a surrogate do with a man who says: "If I can't make it with you I'll kill myself?" Do long term social and sexual relationships develop between surrogate and patients? Is this a positive or negative outcome of surrogate "therapy"? What if a licensed therapist designates himself or herself as a surrogate?

For centuries, from the formulation of the Hippocratic Oath, reverence for the priviledge of the healing hand has warned against sexual misuse of vulnerable patients.[18,20,21]

Into whatever houses I shall enter I will go for benefit of the sick, holding aloof from all voluntary wrong and corruption, including venereal (sexual) acts upon the bodies of females and males whether free or slaves.

On this complex issue of surrogates, two arguments are given: First, within controlled settings for isolated sexually dysfunctional persons who need some sexual success and practice to build the confidence required to date and to marry. These patients, however, may buy the time and services of a surrogate. They cannot buy friendship, kindness, loyalty, concern, committment, or trust. These ingredients for closeness that build intimacy, take *time* and *testing* over months and years to gather. The second pro-surrogate argument is for patients with organic sexual problems; for example, paraplegia, etc. The same concern regarding purchase of a transient "sexual service" remains. It affirms regarding another person as a sex function or sex object.

There are serious additional reservations about the use of sexual surrogates in sex therapy. When the sex problems are not due to organic causes, emotional factors, such as internal conflicts or inhibitions within the person or interpersonal problems with the chosen partner are usually present. These will not dissolve with use of a sexual surrogate. Psychotherapy will be essential to assist resolution of the internal or interpersonal conflicts. One or two sucessful penetrations may not carry over into another relationship, expecially a conflictual one. No control group of solo men was researched at the St. Louis Foundation to see whether such variables as sex education, pressure for action in the form of masturbation (with permission and even prescription from authority) for the two weeks might have translated on follow-up to similar success. Such programs exist and report good results.[15,19]

Encouragement to build a social relationship first by learning over time to trust and then go on to sexual expression with a partner of his or her own careful choice has been done with shy, sexually inhibited women and men. If there are still sex problems, a committed partner may then be available to share what further sex therapy is needed. This comprises safe conservative practice, of lasting benefit to the patient.

EROTIC THERAPIST-PATIENT CONTACT

On a practical level, most professionals who serve their peers on an Ethics Committee will confirm that at least half of the complaints are regarding therapist-patient sexual exploitation. All other categories such as excess fees, fraudulent billing, patient abandonment, issues of informed consent, and clinical mismanagement together comprise the rest of the agenda. Censure, loss of membership, loss of licensure (through a later lawsuit), and loss of hospital privileges are all possible consequences for the professional who is considered to have behaved unethically, sexually or otherwise.

In some cases the physician or nonphysician therapist has argued that the Hippocratic Oath is antiquated, and that *touch* of the patient is healing and not harmful, stating there has been much emphasis in the last decade on the value of touching from infancy into the senium. While touch is essential in childrearing and also for satisfying human relationships, there are cultural sanctions regarding who may touch whom, when, how, and for how long. Touch hunger may occur at all ages, in singles and couples, in therapists and in patients, in pastors and in members of their flock.[22] Sustained and prolonged touch is a healing technique deliberately used for sexual arousal in sex therapy with a couple. However, between those who are unequal (minister/pastor/lawyer/physician/counsellor/therapist/nurse/teacher and parishioner/client/child/student/patient) the highly unequal relationship of a formal helper and a vulnerable "helpee" mandate great care in the type and duration of the touch exchanged because of the potential sexual arousal. Some accusations of patient-therapist sex may be misinterpretation of reassuring touch as romantic or sexual. Others may be malicious or part of a delusional system. As much care is devoted, therefore, during Ethics Committee hearings as in a court of law to sort out all the details because a professional career is at stake. At no time may a sex therapist meet his or her own touch or sexual needs through a patient even one who is over 21 and consenting or seductive. There is no clear delineation of when a patient ceases to be a patient in the eyes of medicine or the law.

Procedures for handling complaints of unethical conduct are formalized for almost all organizations whose members are licensed to provide services to the community. Membership and state licensure to practice provide for a vulnerable public some quality and ethical conduct assurance. There is less guidance and redress for the community when practitioners of a public service are self designated, unlicensed, and do not behave ethically.

To limit frivolous or malicious accusations complaints must be: (1) made in writing; (2) signed by the complainant; and (3) include supporting data regarding the charged member's unethical conduct.

The range of those who may make a charge is wide: colleagues, students, patients, their family, spouse, or guardian. Procedures within an organization may be complex and include national and local branches of Ethics Committees who will investigate, obtain additional materials, and set up hearings for the accused member (with or without legal counsel) and for the complainant. These may be at separate times on the same day or (rarely) both facing each other at the same hearing, which may take several hours. Deliberation will continue in committee and a vote finally taken regarding whether or not the accused member violated the avowed Code of Ethics.

The chairperson and members of ethics committees most certainly deserve special recognition. Their work requires long hours of unremunerated time, often on a weekend, and it is usually quite nerve-racking to assume the unfamiliar, informal yet highly responsible role of investigator, prosecutor, juror, and judge. To say it is emotionally depleting is not an over-statement. Concern for the patient is juxtaposed with concern for a colleague, who is often known and respected. It is a cognitive and emotional tightrope to walk between being an ethics committee member evaluating "facts, facts, facts" and attempting to understand the underlying psychodynamics of the accuser and of the alleged unethical behavior.

The options for committee members are to drop charges as unfounded or unproven or to find the charges well founded. If founded, then depending on the severity of the charges, the accused member may be:

1. Admonished not to repeat the behavior.
2. Reprimanded.
3. Suspended (temporarily) from membership.
4. Dismissed from membership with option to reapply.
5. Expelled without the option to reapply.

The Chairman of the Ethics Committee must then, in writing, inform the President of the organization, the charged member, the person bringing charges, and in some areas, also the State Licensing Board. It is a long, time-consuming, serious process for everyone involved. Civil damage charges against the charged member may have preceded or may follow the Ethics Committees hearings.

A sex educator must realize that a trainee or student has the same vulnerability and inequality in a teacher-student relationship as does the helper-patient. The same regard and respect must be accorded and the same code of ethical behavior prevails. It is totally inappropriate for a sex educator to demand a personal sex history, nudity, or sexual contact from a student. Although difficult to do in the dependency of a grading period or a thesis approval, the same procedures for unethical conduct may be launched by the student whose trust has been betrayed. This decision to bring charges has an additional burden of role reversal: a student admonishing a teacher responsible for providing an exemplary model for the would-be emerging professional.

In conclusion it is worth reflection that while absolute and infallible principles are beyond human attainment, nonetheless the quest for values and ethical excellence in clinical practice continues.[23] So too in the new subspecialty of sex therapy aimed at the best interests of patients who seek assistance with their sexual problems from caregivers in varying professional disciplines. Sexual expression is inextricably bound by each individual's emotions, education, moral values, and cultural customs. All are to be considered theoretically and clinically, also those changes that occur with age, knowledge, and evolving values clarification for therapist and patient alike.

REFERENCES

1. Masters W (1977). *Ethical Issues in Sex Therapy and Research.* Boston:Little, Brown & Company
2. Masters WH & Johnson VE (1970). *Human Sexual Inadequacy.* Boston:Little, Brown & Company
3. Dominian J (1977). *Proposals for a New Sexual Ethic.* London:Darton, Longman & Todd
4. Masters W (1980). *Ethical Issues in Sex Therapy and Research.* Boston:Little, Brown & Company
5. AASECT Code of Ethics, Washington, D.C., 1980
6. Uustal D (1978). Values clarification in nursing: application to practice. *American Journal of Nursing, 78,* 2058-2063

7. Fagothey A (1976). *Right and Reason*. St. Louis:Mosby Company
8. Raths R, Simon S, & Merrill H (1966). *Values and Teaching*. Columbus, Ohio:Charles E. Merrill Books
9. Simon B (1972). *Values Clarification: A Handbook of Practical Strategies for Teachers and Students*. New York:Hart Publishing Co.
10. Barry V (1982). *Moral Aspects of Health Care*. Belmont, California:Wadsworth
11. Lief H (1981). Sex and the Physician. In *Sexual Problems in Medical Practice*. Chicago:American Medical Association
12. Gadow S (1983). Basis for nursing ethics: Paternalism, consumerism, or advocacy? *Hospital Progress, 64*, 62-78
13. Englehardt T (1980). Value, Imperialism and Exploitation in Sex Therapy. In W. Masters (Ed), *Ethical Issues in Sex Therapy and Research, vol 2*. Boston:Little, Brown & Co.
14. Fried C (1980). Problems of consent in sex research: legal and ethical considerations. In W. Masters (Ed), *Ethical Issues in Sex Therapy and Research, vol. 2*. Boston:Little, Brown & Company
15. Renshaw DC (1978). Sexual surrogates. *Sexual Medicine Today, 2*, 39
16. Reiser SJ, Dyck AJ, & Curran WJ (Eds) (1977). *Ethics in Medicine*. Cambridge, Massachussets:MIT Press
17. Cole M (1984). Sex therapy -- A critical reappraisal. *British Journal of Sexual Medicine, 11*, 18-25
18. Knight JA (1979). Human values and sexual medicine. *Current Concepts in Psychiatry, 5*, 2-7
19. Zilbergeld B (1977). *Male Sexuality*. Boston:Little, Brown & Company
20. Renshaw DC (1978b). Sex and values. *Journal of Clinical Psychiatry, 39*, 716-719
21. Slovenko R (1979). The law: sex in the office. *Sexual Medicine Today, 3*, 16-17
22. Renshaw DC (1984). Touch hunger -- a common marital problem. *Medical Aspects of Human Sexuality, 18*, 63-70
23. Eccles JC (1980). *The Human Psyche*. Longon:Springer International

DISCUSSION QUESTIONS

1.   Discuss the steps in the evolution and development of a Code of Ethics for Sexual Therapist from the practice of Masters and Johnson to the AASECT Code. Compare this code to the codes contained in the Appendix. What are the similarities and differences?

2.   What is a "values-neutral" sex therapist or therapy?

3.   What is "values clarification?" Discuss the steps one takes in the process of "valuing."

4.   Twelve professional values that can be reflected in a policy statement of a sex therapy program are presented.   Discuss why one would include these values

and exclude others. Why should a sex therapy program have policies, philosophies, or goal statements?

5. A client seen in conjoint sex therapy at some risk tells you he is having an affair and does not want to have sex with his wife. The wife requested sex therapy because her spouse has lost his "sex drive." How would you proceed? Consider issues of confidentiality, honesty, deception, autonomy, and coercion.

6. What life styles or sexual activities are likely to maximize general happiness? Describe the life styles in terms of ethical positions, i.e., pleasure principal, self-actualization, etc. (see Chapter 2).

7. The client you are evaluating for sex therapy announces she has hired a surrogate sex partner at some trouble and expense. The client wishes to commence therapy as quickly as possible to hold down her expenses and because the surrogate's time is limited. What would you do? Use ethical terms and the decision-making model (described in Chapter 1) to formulate your answer.

8. Your client tells you his or her former sex therapist had the client masturbate while touching the therapist. The client asks if you think that was wrong or if the former therapist should be reported. Discuss the ethical issues invlolved. What action would you take?

9. If your training institution has an Ethics Committee, discuss what it does, how complaints are filed, and, if heard, what decision it can make and how it enforces its decision?

10. You notice an ad on the student bulletin board for research subjects. You apply and learn if you agree to be a sexual research subject you will be paid. You need the money. Discuss the ethical issues involved in your decision to participate in the research. What would you need to know about the program?

9

Jeffrey M. Brandsma
E. Mansell Pattison
James L. Muyskens

Roles, Contracts, and Covenants: An Analysis of Religious Components in Psychotherapy

Jeffrey M. Brandsma, Ph.D., is Professor of Psychology and Training Director of the Psychology Internship, Department of Psychiatry and Health Behavior, Medical College of Georgia. He received his B.A. from Central College and Ph.D. from the Pennsylvania State University. Author of more than 30 articles, his three co-authored books include: *Provocative Therapy*, *Therapy for Couples*, and *Outpatient Treatment for Alcoholism*.

E. Mansell Pattison, M.D., is Professor and Chairman, Department of Psychiatry and Health Behavior, Medical College of Georgia. He received a B.A. from Reed College, an M.D. from the University of Oregon, and trained in psychiatry at the University of Cincinnati. In 1969 he was Man of the Month in Pastoral Psychology, and in 1977 received an APA Significant Program Achievement Award. Author of over 400 publications, his books include: *Clinical Psychiatry and Religion*, *The Experience of Dying*, *Pastor and Parish--A Systems Approach*, and *The Encyclopedic Handbook of Alcoholism*.

James L. Muyskens, M.Div., Ph.D., received a M.Div. from Princeton Theological Seminary in 1967 and an M.A. and Ph.D. in Philosophy from the University of Michigan in 1971. He has written numerous scholarly articles in both the philosophy of religion and ethics and is the author of two books: *The Sufficiency of Hope: The Conceptual Foundation of Religion* (1979) and *Moral Problems in Nursing: A Philosophical Investigation* (1982). A National Endowment for the Humanities Fellow at the Hastings Center in 1983-1984, Muyskens

ETHICS IN MENTAL HEALTH PRACTICE
ISBN 0-8089-1738-2

153

is currently Professor of Philosophy and Associate Provost at Hunter College, The City University of New York.

The authors of this chapter discuss the context in which psychotherapeutic relationships occur. They carefully explore what "Christian psychotherapy" is and what the role of the Christian psychotherapist includes. Role changing relationships are viewed by the authors as reciprocal and complementary. These relationships are summarized in a table and are used as a basis of their discussion. Specifically, the authors present the use of a convenantal relationship in psychotherapy that is based on the absolutist ethical principles of Christian theology.

The dance between psychiatry and religion, psychotherapeutics and philosophy, continues apace in our pluralistic society. The partners in many ways were "made for each other," but have undergone many "spats" and rifts as the complexity of the modern world weighs upon them. Pattison[1] has iterated the cultural and historical reasons for their separation and estrangement, and also some of the directions taken toward attempted integration. In a true historical process of thesis-antithesis-synthesis, many distinctions and divergences could not hold, at base because the human creature strives to integrate the multiple aspects of his or her living into a whole cloth.

Historically, both the priest and the physician roles grew out of that of the shaman, the one who in a primitive society encompassed both roles. Today in a very complicated society the psychotherapist, "a non-disciplinary professional"[2] has at times reunited in himself or herself the schism between existential human beings and their ontology. This unification is, however, unstable at a social level. Today society is too complex and the various knowledge bases too large to allow a return to the shaman role. Separatism is unavoidable, practical, necessary -- but also often dysfunctional for the individual sufferer.

> Priests and physicians grew too far apart. It left a large bulk of suffering persons with no adequate healers, for the priest must retain some nonspecific medical functions, and the physician must retain some nonspecific spiritual functions.
>
> This need was met by the emergence of the psychotherapeutic healer, holding to universalistic and non-normative moral stances, while offering a non-particularistic covert religious ideology. While this offers a general solution for a pluralistic society..., it is also an unstable solution as people seek a more particularistic venue for healing. A clear resolution of this problem is not readily evident. But I suspect that we will see the development of both universalistic...and particularistic oriented mental health services which will serve different segments of our pluralistic society.[1]

Pattison's suspicion has become a prediction with much truth value. In American culture today many seeking help of a psychological nature (from a bewildering array of techniques, philosophies, and cults on the psychological side) have thought it legitimate to ask for psychotherapists who are identified with a particular religious tradition or at least a Christian affirmation. Currently in the 1980s the terms "Christian psychotherapy" and "Christian psychotherapist" have gained currency, but are begging definition, while raising fundamental questions about the psychotherapeutic enterprise.

Many psychotherapists scoff at these labels because they do not refer to differences in technique, in currently popular psychological theory, or in research. They feel the labels do not draw meaningful distinctions.[3] In many ways this is so, but it is not the whole story. In contrast, we are convinced that psychotherapy involves much more than the theoretical, the objective, and the technical. The enterprise is based on more than technique and psychological theory. Therapeutic relationships occur in the context of general philosophical and moral commitments, particular cultural traditions, and varying social and political roles and understandings. These set the boundaries for the therapeutic relationship. Thus, a psychotherapeutic relationship based on the popular, Western, secular ideal of individual self-sufficiency and freedom from the demands of others[4] is likely to be quite different from, for example, a psychotherapeutic relationship embedded in a religious conception of self as interdependent and, as first and foremost, a member of a community. The techniques used in treatment and even the psychological theory behind them may be identical, but the relationship and its goals are likely to be quite different.

With this as introduction we wish to explore the implications of a Christian orientation for the therapeutic relationship and the practice of psychotherapy. In what ways, if any, do the roles and moral obligations of the Christian who engages in psychotherapy differ from those of the nonChristian? In order to address this issue, it may be helpful to begin by considering the following fundamental questions:

1. How, if at all, is Christian psychotherapy different from non-Christian psychotherapy?
2. What are the dangers of mixing religion and therapy?
3. What, if any, are the advantages of Christian oriented therapy?
4. What is the ethical foundation of Christian psychotherapy?
5. Under what conditions, if any, may or should a psychotherapist express his or her religious views?
6. What standards must a Christian psychotherapist and a pastor/counselor meet and what credentials are necessary?

We will utilize role theory and a table of role relationships to formulate and guide our analysis toward an answering of these questions. This will lead to discussions of professionalization, ethical principles, and convenantal psychotherapy.

ROLE THEORY

All humans in a society, whether they are aware of it or not, are involved in a vast panoply of role exchanges throughout their lives. We live in groups and communities that maintain a degree of organization through the consistent patternings of behavior, that is, through the taking of roles.[5] Typically an individual has a variety of roles (e.g., police officer, parent, child, brother or sister, uncle or aunt, church member, homeowner, citizen, and so on). None of these roles is played in a vacuum. The responsibilities and expectations of any particular role can be clear or confused. One can succeed or fail in carrying out a role. A person's multiple roles compete with each other; some roles are incompatible with others; some take priority over others.

When one's role relationships are in disarray in any of these ways, or when they are not fitting for the individual or just are not working, specialized role transactions such as counseling or psychotherapy are provided. Their function is to change attitudes or behaviors so that a person can re-order those roles that are in disarray and attend to the multiple psychological and social consequences of this. "Change agent" roles have the right, obligation, and responsibility to impact on others. Change in behavior or attitude is produced by these roles because of certain characteristics they obtain and employ. Psychotherapy is just one of many behavior changing roles, and as we shall see, not the most important; it is artificially delimited and enabled by various levels of social contract.

Out of the vast panoply of roles, Table 9-1 attempts to iterate and organize behavior changing relationships in terms of combinations of two reciprocal, positively complimentary roles, e.g., parent-child, spouse-spouse, pastoral counselor-client, etc. These roles are not defined by the label given, but by the rules governing them, and the values and functions that underlie them. First we shall make some general comments about these role relationships and then discuss in brief the nature of the dyads in the table.

The relationships in Table 9-1 differ from one another in a variety of ways as iterated in the table, e.g., they differ in the degree of emotional investment, in the range of strategies available to effect changes, in their purposes, etc. Many other dimensions could be iterated such as commitment to role, social potency, specificity of outcome, etc. The numbers in the table ranging from 1-10 are our estimates of the degree of strength and importance of the various categories for the range of reciprocal roles under study. The values are assigned from 1-10, with 10 being highest, and these values being representative for the modal enactment of the role. Whether the same relative values we have assigned are those that others or empirical research would also assign is not critical; the assignments are made to illustrate how various roles can be compared or contrasted -- and to clearly indicate that they are, indeed, different. Later comparison of several of these roles will make this clearer.

1. Value Community

Table 9-1 makes explicit the limits or boundaries of the community of values that undergrid the therapeutic enterprise. The community is narrowly defined at the top of the table and widens out at the bottom, with the service provider having no defining community *per se* except perhaps the economic one. Likewise and related is the potency of roles, with the more potent generally at the top of the table and less at the bottom.

2. Role Strain

These roles are clear and well-defined in our society, but problems arise when the boundaries of these roles are not clear, thus creating a subjective and objective state that can be termed "role strain." For example, a *father* of a delinquent son who is also a *principal* of a high school where the delinquency occurred may have to act in one role differently than he would prefer to act in the other. There are individually and socially imposed constraints on these roles, as for example, when a Roman Catholic *priest* considers becoming a *spouse* through marriage. Likewise, there are extrinsic as well as intrinsic constraints, as when a *surgeon*(spouse) considers operating on his or her spouse.

MAINTENANCE/CHANGE

Another very important constraint operating in these relationships is whether the function of the role is to induce *change* or supply *maintenance*. All relationships have a differing balance of these two, but as a rule the more maintenance involved (i.e., nurturance functions, shared values, lifestyle, and ways of being), the less change capacity exists in a role. Changes must be attempted within the parameters of what one is committed to maintain. Too much change results in a loss of personal identity; too little in arrested development. Too much change will violate not only an optimal level of maintenance in one's life, but also have impact on the overall values to which one ascribes.

In turning to the explication of Table 9-1, we note in overview that the role of the parent is the most potent and provides the real transference or generalization basis for all the others. Anchoring the opposite end of the table is the so called "service provider." These are people such as tax accountants, specialized lawyers, or various kinds of experts. Their services are contractual, completely voluntary, and emotional involvement is usually slight. Between these extremes is the role of pastor. Since it is a complex role it is broken down into four categories in Table 9-1. In the *pastor* role he or she "shepherds the flock," counsels, comforts, engages in the liturgy, and deals in moral distinctions and obligations. This role is often more community oriented and liturgy based. The *preacher* role is more narrow in time and place, but can be a very potent role; it involves aspects of being a teacher, an expositor, or a persuader. A *teacher* role has greater flexibility in strategies to be employed than the preacher and has greater opportunity for reciprocal interaction, but not as much potency. Yet, the clergyman-teacher functions within the bounds of a specific denominational and theological understanding and world view. The denominational counselor role is the pastor who provides counseling services to parishioners, usually voluntarily negotiated and involving no fee.

The term *therapist* in the Table 9-1 is meant to denote a fully professionalized role definition based on training and credentialing, usually with fees involved. This is a delimited role of a socially defined healer of persons in the sick role. This person "gives help," does not "deliver services." The social role model of a therapist used here is one taken from dynamically oriented psychotherapy, not a behavioral technician. Both, however, consistently orient themselves to the healing task, i.e., self-exploration or behavior change as one's ideology may indicate.

The role of a friend or witness is added to the table to heighten its contrast with the others. It should be engaged in with awareness, and not in the professional context without strategic intent. Its potency and its range of variability are exceedingly large, and thus it does not fit easily into the table; nor does discussion of the complex issues that friendships raise fit into the scope of this essay.

With this brief overview to orient we turn to explicate in more depth the implications of some of the more critical of these roles for our purposes. We shall look at the parent role and various therapist roles.

As stated, the parent role is the most potent, having developmental survival value and "real" transference operating all the time. A parent will tend to be more

Table 9-1. Behavior Changing Relationships

Reciprocal Role Labels	Community of Values or Experience Base Informing Behavior	Voluntaryness	Range of Content Areas of Mutual Concern
Parent-Child	Idiosyncratic single family tradition	1	10
Spouse-Spouse	Multiple family traditions; idiosyncratic ethnic and social interpersonal experiences	3	9
Kin-Kin	Multiple family traditions	1	1-7
Friend (Witness) -Friend	Idiosyncratic personal experience	10	1-7
Clergyman- Member			
-Pastor	Parish tradition	2	8
-Preacher	Denominational theology and tradition	4	7
-Teacher	Denominational theology and tradition	6	7
-Denominational Counselor-Client	Parish tradition; idiosyncratic interpersonal experience	7	9
Pastoral Psychotherapist-Patient	Theology and tradition of Christendom psychotherapeutic tradition	8	4
Christian Psychotherapist -Patient	Psychotherapeutic tradition; theology and tradition of Christendom	9	3
Secular Psycho- therapist -Patient	Universalistic human value of the world community	9	3
Service Provider- Client	None in particular; benefit to both parties	10	1

Range of Strategies Used for Change	Degrees of Emotional Investment	Emotional Reciprocity	Range of Outcome	Purpose
10	10-1	10	10	Continues family tradition; mold offspring
9	10	9	9	Meet personal and family needs
1-5	Variable	Variable		Uphold family values
1-5	Variable	Variable	5	Sharing, support
3	8	8	7	Strengthen local congregation:
2	7	5	5	-ideology -boundaries
2	5	6	4	-spiritual health
2	6	7	7	
4	5	7	2	Enhance growth of whole person; identification with larger Christian community
3	4	7	3	Therapeutic work; integration of conflict
3	4	7	4	Therapeutic work; integration of conflict
2	1-3	0	1	Mutual benefit

coercive in his or her teachings of the values of the family, and the parent controls potent rewards in that regard. Parents often use techniques of shame, guilt, seduction, and positive and negative reinforcement in intense ways -- and not always with negative outcomes because of other intensive and extensive qualifying aspects to their relationship. In contrast, therapists are constrained from using such techniques for moral reasons (to be discussed below) as well as pragmatic ones because they do not want to deal with the complications. Simply, a therapist does not have the potency, ongoingness, or extensivity of relationship to work out such complications.

The pastor generally has a different role and point of view from the parent as well as from the psychotherapist. This one appeals directly to a religious tradition and experience, and uses their theological training and church credentials to back them. Because of this, he or she has authority and credibility when making proclamations in the name of the highest authority: "Thus saith the Lord..." or "It is written in the Holy Word..." The pastor is in a position of considerable power to enjoin parishioners to meet the obligations and ideals that their sub-community of belief and practice espouse. One implication is that the pastor usually feels and acts as if he or she is more responsible for the patient's moral behavior than the therapist would. If successful in counseling and preaching (unfortunately at times those who identify themselves as pastors fail to keep those roles distinct), one will enable individuals to function well within the religious community and to support the work of the congregation.

The danger of abuse of this role is readily evident. When one accepts the role of speaking for the Lord, is empowered to issue moral injunctions, and is supported in these activities by an entrenched and venerated tradition of beliefs and practice, the temptation to use the power of the role "for another's good" or for self-aggrandizement is great. In contrast, the Christian psychotherapist does not perform these multiple roles and is not clothed in the symbols of the religious community. As a result, the Christian psychotherapist works with more institutional safeguards, ones that are *not* present for the pastoral counselor.

The psychotherapist's role has greater latitude than the pastor's. Its only constraints are the bounds of the widest range of values of the social community and the constraints that the community puts on the role itself. If an outcome of therapy is socially and personally tolerable (even if not personally desirable), a therapist can work with a person and affirm the process. The therapist must only fit into the widest framework of human values to do his or her work. Despite the great leeway, of course, this role too has certain limits. Thus for example, a therapist *qua* therapist cannot participate in helping one to murder or to disenfranchise another in some way. Yet the latitude of the role allows for one to work quite easily with sexual perversions and peripheral, socially deviant people who affirm no subcommunity of tradition or values. By the same token, a therapist in general can accept a wider range of verbal process and behavioral outcomes than the pastor or pastoral psychotherapist.

Perhaps paradoxically, although the therapist functions within the widest range of values, his or her role (which is determined by the therapeutic task) is the most disciplined behaviorally. Consistently, the therapist must orient to the task of self-exploration, and will not alter the role (except in extreme cases of patient dangerousness) in a way that will do violence to the usual therapeutic task. The therapist will likely use the technique of silence most assiduously, not use the injunctive mode as much, and will likely, if responsive to his or her training, have a wider range of techniques to choose from, but always be oriented toward the strategic goal.

An important part of the discipline of being a good therapist is *to be willing to be in a less potent position* than a parent or pastor, unless, of course, seduced by counter-transference or desires for illegitimate potency. Most critically, it is perhaps clearest with the therapist's role that if one changes it without being explicit, one does violence to the implicit understandings of the relationship and to the usual therapeutic task in the future sequences of the relationship.

The pastoral psychotherapist and the Christian psychotherapist are closely related, with the former being more identified with the pastoral tradition, the latter more with the psychotherapeutic tradition. The pastoral psychotherapist often has a different content area to deal with in addition to how things are going at home, school, work, etc. Most secular counselors would willingly discuss the patient's "outlook on life," but the pastoral psychotherapist implicitly or explicitly takes a stand on important aspects stemming from their religious tradition. They will actively help patients to "find their way" in the Bible or their prayer life. Problems of suffering, loss, and pain are more likely to be put in a religious context of understanding. Both the secular and sacred traditions could look at beliefs and values critically, but in the sacred tradition the insights of a certain religious tradition will be applied as a "yardstick" or as alternatives. Concepts such as acceptance, forgiveness, and hope would be dealt with openly, perhaps more frequently, and in certain ways that are not available to secular counselors (for example, to suggest prayer for the person that needs to be forgiven). Other concepts that are usually not dealt with in secular psychotherapy such as sin, salvation, and sanctification would be explained or invoked. Subjects such as anger resolution and confession would have a different slant in this type of therapy, with more of an emphasis on the goals: specifically that one should go beyond anger resolution to bring in the "fruits of the Spirit" -- love, joy, and peace -- and that confession would be to relieve real ontological or existential guilt, not just inner conflict. Many therapists prescribe meditation. The pastoral psychotherapist would recommend considering the person of Jesus rather than a meaningless sound mantra, or a number, or an aspect of the universe (for example, stars, space, or trees). In contrast, the Christian psychotherapist would not explicitly or at least not as readily make references to theological concepts, since he or she functions much like a secular psychotherapist while identifying himself or herself as a Christian. More will be said of this later.

We have compared and contrasted a variety of reciprocal, behavior changing relationships. We have seen how each role has reference to a more or less broad community of values. These roles are undergirded in their expression by cultural and moral traditions. In many contexts the boundaries between roles are not clearly defined. In fact, at times where one role ends and another begins may be indistinguishable. Yet we have seen the importance of drawing these lines and clarifying boundaries where possible. And we have seen that in addition to such clear differences as function or technique or underlying psychological theory, a variety of subtle factors can distinguish one role from another. For example, verbal behavior in two distinct roles may be identical. Yet other features of the relationship (as examples, the range of shared background value commitments, the degree of emotional reciprocity, goals) may be different. Any one of these differences may mark the difference between one role and another.

As an example, consider the following contrast: the goal or intent of a therapist is to consistently explore the psychological meanings of a problem or communication in light of overall personality functioning, perhaps at times to question beliefs, whereas the primary goal of the pastor beside questioning a belief would be to correct the content of a belief in a particular way. Thus, we must look at the sequence, organization, and intention of overall role behavior in order to be clear about the similarities and differences of the various roles, and their appropriate and ethical enactment.

As mentioned in the text but not iterated in the table, the maintenance-change balance in a relationship is critical in viewing these roles, especially those that are related to *emotional* change and maintenance as contrasted with *instrumental* change or maintenance. A service provider as consultant can ask or direct one to make a small instrumental change in behavior, but usually will do very little with regard to maintenance or emotionally involving issues; he or she is low on both maintenance and change. In contrast the parent of a young child will be responsible for high levels of emotional and instrumental change and maintenance, and spouses will be moderate on all levels in an ongoing relationship. Pastors are usually high on maintenance, but low on change. In contrast, secular therapists are in a role that is high on change and low on maintenance because of their circumscribed relationship, less directive stance, and commitment to a wider community of values. In a word, the secular therapist is more willing to "let the chips fall where they may." We shall return to this at several points.

4. Unethical Role Enactment

Given this understanding of roles, there are several ways to be unethical in their enactment.[6] First of all, where there is role conflict (even when we have eliminated forbidden relationships where there is inherent role conflict), one can exhibit *inappropriate role performance*. For a stark example, when the high school principal mentioned earlier is called upon to discipline his student-son, he instead invites him into his office to play a game of "horsey" (which, at this level of inappropriateness, would be seen as a sign of personality decompensation). In the religious sphere, inappropriate role performance occurs when a suffering parishioner comes to visit a pastor for succorance and instead gets a 20-minute sermon from the preacher. Thus in certain contexts, certain simultaneous roles are in conflict. Even if the principal or pastor mentioned above were to enact his role appropriately, he would probably feel subjective anxiety or discomfort, that is, "role strain," since the multiple roles and one's organization of identity would tend to pull in different directions. Similar tensions have frequently been felt by Christians participating in abortion, using birth control, undergoing a divorce, or supporting pacifism; coming to terms with these issues often involves role conflict. Role strain is often subtly experienced by Christians when engaged in psychotherapy, for here, too, roles can come into conflict (for example, the role of witness and the role of therapist). As we have implied, however, when roles are mixed, the integrity of the relationship can be destroyed and the purpose of the therapeutic role can be undermined.

A fundamental moral requirement of the therapist is to keep his or her roles and role boundaries straight. Not all roles can be integrated smoothly. These conflicts must be recognized and addressed. A therapist must develop a philosophy and procedures for dealing with these conflicts. If this is not done, it is very likely that the role he or she is enacting will be ethically invalidated. The therapist will have slipped into another that does not fall within the social-contractual relation. Concomitantly and reciprocally, he or she will have forced patients to change their role as well. If the therapist persists in this, the patient -- who has less power in the relationship -- is faced with two bitter choices: either to go along and compromise his or her own integrity or the efficacy of the therapy, or to abandon the relationship and lose the possibility of getting the help that is being sought through the relationship.

A second, perhaps more obvious, moral criticism that can be leveled against a therapeutic relationship is that of *inadequate role performance.* The inadequacy may result from charlatanism at the one extreme to personal inadequacy and incompetence on the other. At the far end of the spectrum is the psychopathic, self-proclaimed "minister" who sets himself or herself up as a therapist-counselor to entrap the gullible. More commonly we encounter (especially among the least affluent) well-meaning, but ill-trained and ill-equipped ministers engaged in psychological as well as spiritual counseling. In these cases one's criticism must often be tempered by the fact that these ministers may see that indeed, they are the only help available to these people, and the clergy have historically had many roles thrust upon them.[7] At a higher socio-economic level, we see people who are well trained and professionalized in helping roles, but because of counter-transference or personal inadequacy (i.e., narcissism) are unable to refer patients when they cannot handle their problems. This leads to a different level of inquiry: the professionalization of roles, "credentialing," and "policing" of practitioners.

PROFESSIONALIZATION

Professionalizing the role of helper or "change agent" has several functional benefits: it protects the public from unqualified practitioners and it gives the professional the status and leeway to do their job properly. For example, physicians must have ready access to other people's bodies in order to conduct thorough examinations required for accurate diagnosis and treatment; thus over the centuries society has set up explicit and implicit contracts with them on when, where, and how this can be done. These contracts protect the practitioners from lawsuits charging assault and provide clients with procedures that minimize anxiety.[8] Ethical questions concerning the propriety of a professional's behavior must be answered in reference to the tradition of long-standing practices that define the roles and relationship between professional and client.

While training is not totally correlated to how one operates in a social role (much unneeded knowledge abounds in all professional training), it is definitely not irrelevant. An important part of professional training is to become immersed in the values and understandings of the profession. When one calls oneself a therapist, one has both explicitly and implicitly accepted as one's own a socially defined, professional role. In return for the privilege of wearing the professional label and making one's livelihood by providing these services, society requires proper training, credentials, and a commitment to use one's skills for the benefit of the client. Society reserves the right to bar from practice those who fail to satisfy these requirements.

As society has grown more complex, more "professional" roles have been created, particularly in the area of mental health services. The community mental health movement accelerated a role blurring between a large variety of professional, almost professional, and evolving, aspiring professional disciplines. It has highlighted again the stages of evolution of a profession as delineated by various sociologists.[9-11] Let us iterate these briefly.

Professions are defined around universal social concerns, i.e., life and death, health, or concerns that are widely experienced (i.e., the search for meaning). In contrast with an occupation, professions will have all of the following in greater or lesser degree:

1. A defined body of knowledge and theory that is (usually) implied by a requirement of an educational degree from an accredited university.
2. A training period of substantial length and specialization that deals with symbols, not things, and develops an important subculture.
3. A highly developed sense of community and service orientation. All services are based on universal humanitarian norms and public access (not self-interest).
4. Autonomy, i.e., the professional proceeds by his or her own judgment or authority without supervision.
5. The professional has an enduring commitment to his or her profession as an identity, a calling. The profession has an enduring set of normative and behavioral expectations that the professional internalizes.
6. A highly developed code of ethics and a professional organization to maintain standards.
7. A system of symbolic awards or achievements in the profession.

Professionals hold power in societies because they claim useful and valued skills not commonly shared. Health care professionals are prepared to wage battle against death, disease, and discomfort with an armamentarium not available to the ordinary person. Professional power and effectiveness is tied to the confidence of the general public that these skills will be used for the patients' good. Professionals ask to be trusted to handle certain matters better than others would or could. Thus professionals are not hired, but rather are retained or engaged.[12]

Physicians acquired a role permeated with the religious quest for immortality, a magic manipulation of nonempirical forces, and imbued with technical-scientific-empirical skills. Thus, a physician can with relative impunity engage in socially taboo activities through his or her role. However, when acting in a professional role, he or she is not acting strictly as an individual, but as a part of a profession and part of a community. It is appropriate that physicians are looked to as the most salient profession, because this profession grew many centuries ago out of concerns over life and death, although any widely experienced, universal social concern can be the basis for other professions.

The fundamental moral question then is whether the professional warrants such trust. Does the professional have the moral right to hold this privileged position? The complimentary but fundamental social and political questions are: (1) how can a society protect itself from would-be professionals who do not warrant the trust they seek, and (2) how can it secure an adequate supply of worthy professionals? The first of these social-political questions is answered in part by the establishment of legal sanctions that can be applied to those professionals who fail to meet the minimal standard of customary care for the profession. Support for education of future professionals is one of the ways a society (or groups within a society) addresses the second question. Insisting on high educational standards, holdingprofessionals to stringent codes of ethics, and demanding that professionals have the ability to think critically and analytically are some of the traditional strategies for responding to the fundamental moral questions.

As can be seen from the traits of a profession listed above, at its core, *the notion of a profession is a moral one.* The professional is called apart from the masses (4, 7) to develop character traits (3, 5) and technical skills (1, 2) for the benefit of those to be served (6). Of course, as with any ideal it can be, and often is, distorted and twisted to achieve nonmoral or nonprofessional ends, for example, self-aggrandizement, riches, or individual or collective power. Yet the danger of distortion of professional ideals (no matter how real and pervasive) is less of a threat than is the danger of nonprofessional individuals (those not embued with the values and skills of the professional) assuming the role of he professional.

Some cardinal, "higher order" qualities of the three historic professions -- medicine, clergy, law (the most fully evolved professions) involve: (1) free access to these services when needed; (2) universalistic norms; and (3) the professional assumes responsibility for the person(s) in his or her care. Because a person is not often in the position to evaluate the competence of the professional, it must generally be assumed. The role of caretaker is implicitly always established, i.e., all transactions are duplex with an at least implied parent-child aspect, no matter how contractual are the explicit negotiations. The caretaker is expected to provide what people need in their best interest, not necessarily to profit the self, but in real measure to be there for the person. These aspects will later lead us to discuss the nature of the therapeutic covenant.

Seen in this light, many pastoral psychotherapists who "hang out a shingle" and charge fees are operating unethically; they do not have the training and credentials that provide the protection from fraudulent practice or the level of competency that society has a right to expect. Clergy who have had a smattering of mental health training may fall victim to the same moral fault. Yet there is a difference: they do not charge fees and, as we saw earlier, they have multiple roles thrust upon them by the parish. Their relationship to the client is different. Clergy who do counseling and wish to function in a morally appropriate manner must be able to ascertain when a case should be referred to someone with greater training in psychotherapy.

The converse is also as true. A professionally trained psychiatrist who has not had formal training in theology but teaches a theology in his therapy has crossed over to a role for which he or she is not qualified or certified. Unfortunately, there are fewer than 1000 fully trained pastoral psychotherapist professionals in America -- those who have the requisite training and credentialing in both psychotherapy and pastoral theology. A strengthened pastoral psychotherapy profession in numbers and credentials is needed if "Christian psychotherapy" is to avoid these pitfalls.

Descriptively the fully professionalized pastoral psychotherapist is anchored in the broad theology and tradition of Christendom, aware of its extreme diversity and variability, but affirming its oneness of spirit and the centrality of its underlying theology. A pastoral psychotherapist's intent in therapy is usually not to present a subcommunity or a denomination, but to offer the abstract values of the larger Christian community. The commitment is to enhance persons no matter what their problem or philosophy, but ultimately to steer them into a lifestyle that could be called Christian, at least in its broad themes.

From our vantage point there are some others who are not fully professionalized, yet who could (arguably) do pastoral psychotherapy; but most are quite unaware of the very demanding requirements of enacting this role well and professionally. There are two basic forms of incompetence in this role: (1) pastorally trained people who set themselves up as counselors, and (2) people trained in the clinical sciences (at various levels) who affirm their brand of Christianity in their counseling. We have labeled these perversions "denominational psychotherapy" in Table 9-1 because it is not true pastoral psychotherapy or secular psychotherapy.

ETHICAL PRINCIPLES UNDERLYING
CHRISTIAN PSYCHOTHERAPY

A third intersecting component that must be examined when looking at the legitimacy of the role of Christian psychotherapy is ethical principles. All roles have rules and expectations, customary norms, and legal elements, but they can be superseded by ethical principles and obligations. As has been discussed, specific roles are embedded in a larger context of social and cultural values. Underlying these values and traditions are fundamental moral principles. It is helpful to picture these as arising from a basic social contract that all humans agree to adhere to when they live in groups -- agreements not to harm others, to be truthful, to keep just agreements and promises, to be loyal. A citizen cannot claim exemptions from the duty to adhere to these principles.

Of course, in certain contexts the principles come into conflict, as when one cannot both keep a particular agreement and be truthful. For example, in the case of a young woman in Holland during the Nazi occupation, she has agreed not to tell anyone that her neighbor is hiding a Jewish family. An acquaintance, who may be a Nazi sympathizer or a member of the Underground, has some reason to suspect that the neighbor is offering sanctuary to the family and questions her. Her quandry is this: If she tells the truth or even hints that she knows, she breaks her solemn agreement; if she says without hesitation that she does not know, she keeps her word but fails to tell the truth.

Ethical theories are proposed as suggestions for resolving these sorts of conflicts of principles by providing ways to order them. To examine these here would take us far afield. Suffice it to say that the only way an individual is released from the requirement to adhere to duties such as truth-telling and keeping promises is to be in a situation in which one duty is in direct conflict with another, and a case can be made that one of the conflicting duties rightfully takes precedence over the other(s).

From a moral point of view, the institution of professionalized roles defines and specifies how for certain relationships certain sorts of conflicts between principles are to be resolved. For example, in the spouse-spouse relationship loyalty and confidentiality are given additional weight, and hence (barring other more stringent obligations, e.g., to save a life) they outweigh an obligation to tell the truth about one's spouse to an inquiring official of the department of social services. Similarly the lawyer-client, doctor-patient, and pastor-parishioner relationships are designed with special premiums on confidentiality. In these relationships, the duty to maintain confidentiality is specified somewhat differently and more precisely than in general relationships. Far fewer other duties will have the strength to outweigh this duty within such a relationship than outside. In this way, the role partially determines the proper ordering of conflicting duties.

In addition to the basic social contract for all citizens it is useful to see the institution of roles as a contract that society makes with professional groups in order to make certain that valued social tasks are performed (for example, the sick with health care professionals). Once the contracts are (historically) "drawn up" and various practices are instituted within the society, it is an individual who performs the role. At this point we have a third level of contract in which individual professionals make arrangements with individual clients or patients to perform the activities appropriate to the role. Just as the roles that a society contracts for must be compatible with the original social contract, so too must the individual arrangements be compatible with the agreed upon professional role. The individual contracts are thus embedded in two other levels; but just as different institutional patterns are compatible with the original social contract, so also are there variations and special stipulations between individual professionals and clients that can be entered in.

There are two basic ways in which both the activities of professions and of individual professionals can be criticized morally. One is to show that the implicit and explicit contracts under which they practice are incompatible with or no longer advance the fundamental commitments of the society. The second form of moral criticism is to show that actual practice falls far short of what has been agreed to.

WHAT IS CHRISTIAN PSYCHOTHERAPY?

The distinction just made between professional role considered as a collective (e.g., the generic psychotherapy role) and as individually enacted (e.g., a psychotherapist's role) has two different underlying conceptualizations of Christian psychotherapy. On the one hand, we may see Christian psychotherapy as a distinct professional role with its own particular professional standards. On this view, we would look for differences between it and other forms of psychotherapy and expect it to engage in all the activity that goes along with developing a new discipline or specialty. On the other hand, we may see Christian psychotherapy as a label for the special and unusual variations in therapy practiced by individual psychotherapists with particular skills and commitments. On this view, our main concern would be that these special arrangements not undermine the psychotherapeutic relationship.That is, we would want to work out the moral and professional parameters within which the therapist who is a Christian can function.

To determine which of these views is preferable, we turn again to the goal or aims of psychotherapy, to be followed by consideration of those of Christian psychotherapy. In general, the goal of psychotherapy is to remove hindrances and to enhance a person's autonomy (ability to be self-legislating) and the ability to engage in satisfying interpersonal relationships. The aim is to liberate the patient from the control of unconscious drives and unacknowledged forces. A patient is seen as in need of a therapist's help when inadequately acknowledged forces within prevent him or her from achieving the independence and strength required to shoulder the ordinary roles and responsibilities of everyday life. The therapist's fundamental moral duties arise both from the general professional commitment to work toward the goals outlined, as well as the more particular duties arising from the agreement(s) made with the patient.

The general aims and concomitant duties of the psychotherapist apply equally to the Christian psychotherapist. If there is a difference on the most basic level between a psychotherapist who is secular, Christian, Jewish, or whatever, it has to do with how *content* is given to key concepts of the definition of common aims: autonomy, independence, satisfying personal relationships, liberation from unacknowledged forces. For the Christian, the understanding and interpretation of these concepts would likely be informed by a picture of the ideal life (being a citizen in the Kingdom of God) that derives from scripture, tradition, and a community. But the *process* of psychotherapy would be the *same.*

The Christian picture of the ideal life for humans has as its focal point a God who intends that human beings be as fully human as they can be within the measure of their limitations. This God enters into a relationship with human beings to enable them to develop a richer, deeper, more fulfilling and satisfying life than would be possible without this divine initiative (an initiative based on God's goodness and mercy, and not on an individual's merit or worthiness). The fitting response for recipients of God's favor is to express gratitude through loving, caring, forgiving relationships with others. The truly autonomous life is one of consciousness of God. True human freedom will always be limited, but its essence resides in making the choice of who shall be one's master, and for the Christian that person is Jesus Christ. The relationship here is not as a slave but a steward, one of both appropriate subservience and participation. Among the unacknowledged forces and unconscious drives that restrict the abundant life from this perspective are the sins of self-centeredness, avarice, pride, vindictiveness, power seeking, etc.

In sum, in our view the general aim of the psychotherapist at the level of the second contract is the same whether Christian or not. Hence, *the duties deriving from the professional role are identical.* They share the fundamental professional duty to do the best one can for one's patients by assisting them in their efforts to liberate themselves in order to become more mature and responsible persons.

What may differentiate at the third level the Christian psychotherapist from the non-Christian is the framework within which the therapeutic relationship can take place.There can be a different ordering of values and a divergence in the conception of the good or the ideal life. (Since our culture is so permeated with Christian values, this may not be a great contrast.) These differences may include an understanding of the nature of illness and health, and in what would be appropriate treatment. A Christian therapist's understanding will in more or less complicated ways be integrated with concepts such as sin, salvation, faith, and forgiveness. Treatment may reflect this in techniques that include exploration of religious consciousness, whereas the secular therapist might place far greater emphasis on physiological or developmental etiology of illness, and tend to base therapy more narrowly on these considerations.

Perhaps due to Freud's views of religion as much as anything,[13] religion has seemed out of place in the psychotherapeutic relationship. If psychoanalysis is given the status of a world view, (with its own doctrines, ethics, community and cult) rather than a method, it appears to be and is in several ways antithetical to other religions.[14] Other religions for doctrinaire psychoanalysts are seen as part of a universal neurosis, a substitute for rationality, responsibility, and emotional maturity, a longing for a father's protection from childish helplessness in face of the harsh world. If this is true, religion will not be a help, but rather a hindrance in achieving the goal of personal autonomy and the ability to engage in mature, responsible relationships and projects.

The Christian psychotherapist, however, need not be an adherant of the life-denying form of Christianity criticized by Freud. On the contrary, we have tried to show that a Christian perspective can be life-affirming and self-expanding.The therapist who holds the life-offering understanding of Christianity outlined here holds a view that is very much in line with major, contemporary understandings of the goals of psychotherapy. If Christianity and psychotherapy are incompatible, it is not because they are inconsistent in aim or different in their generic emphasis on autonomy and accepting responsibility.

In large areas of the country where the vast majority of people identify themselves as religious, the cultural gap between nonreligious and antireligious psychotherapists and their typical patients can be detrimental to successful treatment. In these areas the Christian psychotherapist is likely to have a more sympathetic understanding and appreciation for the nuances of meaning in the language of a Christian patient. Christian therapists are more likely to be sensitive to the difference between the use of religious language and practice as a disguise for neurotic conflicts versus occasions when patients are struggling with genuine moral and spiritual issues.

If our discussion of the aims of psychotherapy is correct, it is evident that *the psychotherapist cannot achieve these goals by imposing a set of beliefs* as values upon a patient. One cannot be coerced into autonomy and maturity. Autonomy entails developing one's own beliefs and values without undue internal and external constraint. Maturity entails living by these values and accepting responsibility for the choices one makes.

A therapeutic encounter involving a Christian therapist and Christian patient begins with a large number of shared beliefs and values. The therapist is in an ideal situation to work with the patient from within the patient's belief and value system. The great moral danger, however, of all therapeutic relationships is that the greater power of the professional in the unequal professional-patient relationship is misused. Paternalistic beneficence can replace or be used as a shortcut to autonomy and love. At some point the patient is not treated as an end in one's self, but as an object to be manipulated, albeit for good consequences. Motivated by concern for the patient's best interest, both well-meaning or manipulative therapists may impose on the patient, whether willingly or through countertransference, values or beliefs that arise from their own belief framework, and not that of the patient In order to obtain the relief sought, the patient may have no recourse but to attempt to reorder his or her life around these alien values or beliefs. *If so, the patient has not been treated with proper moral regard.* A large set of fundamental values and beliefs held in common by the therapist and patient may provide some protection for the patient who is vulnerable, but is certainly not a guarantee.

Parenthetically, one discredited way to try to avoid the problems of imposed values was to aim to be "value neutral" in the therapeutic relationship. If the therapist could keep his or her moral values and religious convictions out of sight and prevent them from finding their way into the relationship, it was thought it would be immaterial what they were. The problem with this strategy, as many critics have noted, is that no therapist can avoid imparting personal values and beliefs to patients. The relationship involves the therapist as a person-participant, not merely as a diagnostician or a listener. Of all the professions, psychotherapy especially requires involvement of the whole person. A therapist cannot be completely divorced from his or her values, beliefs, aspirations, hopes, etc.

Since the values and beliefs of the psychotherapist are not immaterial to the relationship, an ethical concern for honesty or integrity in human relationships suggest being as open about them as one can be, considering the role. Very often this will mean only that the therapist is honest with himself or herself, but when it involves choices for the patient, the therapist might be compelled to state his or her bias so that the patient is clear where the therapist stands. The patient who knows the orientation of a therapist is in a stronger position to maintain a healthy, critical stance. A therapist who is honest about his or her values and beliefs is more likely to be alert to their influence in the therapeutic relationship.

A therapist who truly understands the theology and also the community behind religious traditions is also in a far better position to understand the needs of patients in these sub-communities. Religious institutions and practices are notorious for rewarding the pious, the uncomplicated, the uncritical person while they censor the thoughtful, the perplexed, and the nonconformist. The dynamics of a religious sub-community that fits this description can cause or exacerbate personal problems that come to the attention of therapists. Offering help in these sorts of situations requires sensitivity to the social and religious dimensions of these persons' lives. It at times requires a willingness to help such people confront the implicit, stifling standards of behavior and assessment of the religious sub-community to which these patients belong, and requires responses on the part of the therapist that reflect his or her own religious and moral convictions. Since the aim of psychotherapy is to assist the patient in personal growth, therapists must be able to be critical of the values and practices of the religious community -- even the one he or she belongs to -- and encourage critical reflection on the part of his patients. The benefit of working from within the values of a patient's religious community cannot be overemphasized. It is often essential for effective therapy and in order to help the person maintain their position in that community and with their value commitments. *However, this does not presuppose an uncritical attitude.*

With a doctrinaire doctrinal orientation, it is quite possible to misuse the language and relationship of psychotherapy in much the same way that it is done in an ideological society such as Russia where dissidents are labelled "mentally ill." For those who wish to protect Orthodoxy as well as the *status quo* or their own favorite position, categorizing the heterodox as "sick" or "possessed" or "in need of treatment" is a perhaps convenient, but insidious technique. This is one of the greatest moral dangers that can arise when inadequately trained pastors or Christian laymen engage in psychotherapy. Not only do they not have the skills of trained professional psychotherapists, they also do not share the psychotherapeutic and moral aims or goals of personal growth and autonomy. Instead, their primary concern may be evangelism, doctrinal purity, or social control within their church. This kind of behavior must be condemned in the strongest possible terms; it violates the most basic principles of ethics and fails as psychotherapy. Role confusion and nonsophistication can easily lead to unethical practice.

COVENANTAL PSYCHOTHERAPY

Western society and particularly American culture, have in our opinion overemphasized the individuality and rationality in human nature. In contrast to the East, where interdependence and deference for the whole underlie cultural expression, in the West we see independence of the individual, self-assertion, and an insistence on rights.[4] This has resulted in a Western cultural philosophy of social organization and relationship that resorts to legal and contractual modes. Hence we see a burgeoning need for legal services, litigation, and an increase in malpractice suits.

The consumer-oriented and contractual society has produced an erosion of professional roles. Many have the intuitive feeling that there is something basically inadequate in conceiving of certain professional relationships purely in terms of contractual arrangements.[15] Concepts of code and contract do not allow for the potency of the relationship or provide an adequate ethical underpinning for difficult treatment decisions. The major problem in understanding professionalism in our society exists because of an increasing tendency to put human care services in the same category as commodity transactions. This has led to much role and contractual confusion, and an nadequate basis for professional ethics.

In contractual framework, two parties calculate their own best advantage by agreeing in symmetry and mutuality to contractual obligations. Collaboration is encouraged, rights and duties are clear, and it can be legally enforced if necessary. There are, however, several problems with this orientation when applied to professional relationships: (1) it suppresses acknowledgment of the underlying relationship; (2) it encourages a minimum, concrete response when the process is basically unpredictable; (3) trust level is minimal and limited; (4) it tends to provoke defensive reactions that are not in the best interest of the client, but rather the treator; and (5) under certain conditions (for example, emergencies), and for certain rights of patients, it cannot apply. That is to say, at times a helper must act without consent and a patient should not ever, even in principle, be able to waive certain basic rights.

The problem with an ethic that eschews paternalism and demands respect for the patient's autonomy presupposes a negotiated contract between equals in sophistication, something that only rarely occurs in the areas of psychology or theology. The contract may not be possible to be explicit because a patient does not know what he or she needs, wants, or how to achieve these desires. Sophisticated, conscious negotiation before treatment is not often possible or even desirable. Thus, we wish to look into the convenantal relationship of psychotherapy as a basis where ethical principles are informed by Christian theology.

The most profound understanding of a convenantal underpinning comes from the historical experience of the Hebrews in their relationship to their God, Yahweh. This relationship was based on historical events that formed a tradition; it was an exchange of experiences that led to an internal commitment. From these experiences, three elements were inculcated into the Hebrew culture for all covenants: (1) gifts were exchanged; (2) promises were made based on the exchange; and (3) the subsequent lives of both parties were shaped by the commitment. Fidelity in the covenantal relationships exceeded specification; it was a lifetime loyalty no matter what the specific or general circumstances. Over time the relationship grew, and was expected to -- it was not limited, and was often called upon to bring to bear deeper resources in the committed partners. From Yahweh's side there was always surplus obligation, which, despite His anger at times, was spent on behalf of His people; the same could not be said from the side of the Hebrews.

Ethics based on this kind of model covenant are responsive, not gratuitous or contractual, and go well beyond self-interest. It is most fully understood in a context of transcending grace where one realizes that one is inexhaustibly the object of a great gifting from God, i.e., as one example, life itself. One is in an ongoing state of neediness and indebtedness to God, and one's gifts to others are only symbols of or responses to God's gifting. A transcendent reference provides a total ontological context for understanding professionalism and prescribes normative ethical standards for both parties in therapist-patient transactions.

The context of grace goes beyond ethical social principles. In I Corinthians 6:1-11, Paul places the principle of love above that of justice and, by implication, all others -- at least in the community of the church. He differentiates between the person's *status* before God (saved, redeemed), and his *state* on earth (misguided, sinful). Thus Christian love as understood from the Bible would be exhibited in covenantal psychotherapy as consistent, tolerant, personal, nonself interested, and oriented toward the growth or development of the other within their resources and appropriate bounds of autonomy and responsibility.

A covenantal relationship is not as restrictively personal as that of a parent or friendship, but it is not so professional or exclusive that it dims larger responsibilities. In this context, certain limits are put on a patient's dependency. The limitations occur from the patient's own obligations to others and society, and in the therapists' obligations to others, the profession, and to act in the patient's best, long-term interest. The covenantal relationship should not dim considerations of competent techniques on the therapist's side, and the patient is still viewed as and encouraged to be an active participant in the business of bringing about "health or disease."

Contracts are subordinate to covenants, that is to say, they can be made or changed within this relationship, but the relationship itself goes on and becomes internalized. But in those cases of practical human affairs the therapist cannot be unlimited in surplus covenantal obligation. Even as the word of Yahweh at times became rare in Old Testament experience, so the therapist must at times withdraw from destructive relationships. An example would be the repeated attempts by a client to seduce the therapist sexually wherein the therapist finds he or she cannot maintain the therapeutic role and appropriate distance. The covenant might not be broken, but the therapy might terminate at this time by referral or a hiatus.

We have tried to lay the groundwork for iterating how the roles of the pastoral and Christian psychotherapist can be carried out ethically and professionally, and to this issue we now turn more specifically. It can be seen that the roles of the secular psychotherapist and the pastoral psychotherapist can be clearly distinguished, and some appropriate differentiation made at the level of content as previously iterated. In this regard, it seems clear that a pastoral psychotherapist can engage in Christian psychotherapy rather explicitly with clients.

More problematic is the role of a Christian who is also a professional psychotherapist. As stated implicitly above, in terms of content, technique, and social roles, there is relatively little difference from the secular psychotherapist. With a secular client the difference can be conceived as occurring at the ontological level, i.e., in how the Christian psychotherapist sees his or her role and enacts it. Here the quality of the relationship between them is at least conceived (and hopefully, enacted) within the constraints of a covenantal understanding. The Christian psychotherapist sees his or her role as a calling in a different, richer sense than a secular counterpart, i.e., the call is from God to be a type of Christ, and goes beyond having an internal sense of vocation or professional allegiance alone. Thus, the therapeutic relationship is enriched by being conceived as a type of covenant (as iterated previously) with all the meanings and constraints that apply.

Ethically speaking, the Christian psychotherapist would be very careful to specify personal opinion and to respect the autonomy of the client within the covenantal relationship. Despite the fact that one believes that Christianity is the most robust world view, and that it would be good for the client (the paternalistic principle of beneficence), one realizes that the principles of *honesty* (about opinions and one's professional status), *keeping promises* (concerning one's social role), and *autonomy* (respect for the client's freedom and potential) *supercede that of beneficence.* Thus, a therapist would be very careful in discussing theological matters explicitly, and do so only in very rare circumstances. Above all ethical principles, he or she would try to temper the relationship and understanding of these principles by that of Christian love to be exercised with this person, a fellow sinner and potential brother or sister in Christ. This is the essence of an implicit covenantal relationship, one that we would hope that secular therapists would engage in as well, at least on the behavioral level. It would even be hoped that secular therapists could be adept at using a patient's spiritual beliefs to resolve problems, relieve suffering, and be sensitive to their integration.

Another situation may present itself when a Christian client explicitly or implicitly asks a psychotherapist who is a Christian to provide an explicitly Christian psychotherapy. The situation is that presumably the client would know that the therapist is a Christian and assume without much thought that it is appropriate to talk of such things. When this occurs, several things seem essential:

1. The therapist should make the client aware and understand that one is changing the nature of the social contract perhaps in ways that one really would not prefer if he or she understood clearly.
2. The therapist should make the client aware that the therapist is not fully professionalized in the area of pastoral theology.
3. This particular therapist and client could enter into a contract of Christian psychotherapy, if the therapist has theological training and personal experience enough and is willing to identify what is being affirmed as being personal opinion.
4. The therapist believes he or she could attempt this content, (and it is not a defense for the client), but succeed at remaining true to the psychotherapist role and avoid that of the pastor or denominational psychotherapist.
5. The therapist would enter into this contract with a great spirit of humility and an awareness of the many possible problems here.

All these caveats are stated to make clear that this is a tall order and a very difficult role, but precisely the one that may be necessary for the client to integrate and resolve problematic thinking or behavior. Although replete with many pitfalls, if entered with awareness and humility, it can be very rewarding for both the therapist and client. What is called for at times is the very difficult task of *role transcendence* wherein the therapist does not violate the norms of the role *qua* therapist but is able to go beyond its requirements into a coalesence of roles that does not undermine the professional role. The more intense *and* covenantal (in the sense iterated above) the relationship, the more there is commitment to the person, the more self-involvement of the therapist, and thus the more possible multiple roles that inhere in the relationship. When the context demands or the needs are great, the therapist feels the obligation to offer a response, and may do so outside of the usual professional role. But he or she will not let this occasion redefine the relationship inappropriately and will be *very* careful to keep track of countertransference and limits as a person-therapist. It is our humbly offered opinion that for most cases it is better not to attempt role transcendence (especially the young professional), and even when attempted, it probably transpires well only rarely. It is better to sequence roles with awareness, and that infrequently, and with a commitment to one's professional role to which the client came for help.

CONCLUSION

The dance goes on. Hopefully we have clarified our questions and given some answers. We believe that Christian psychotherapy does go on in many forms, conceived of in many ways. We would hope that this essay clarifies how it can be done ethically. All the roles mentioned can be ethically enacted (with the exception of the "denominational psychotherapist" who does not acknowledge his or her orientation), but not simultaneously. Legitimate role boundaries must be maintained for ethical enactment. Likewise therapists must openly define their roles and be aware of these boundaries, wrestling in individual cases with their own philosophy of helping, role, and role transcendence. We opt for role clarity, increasedprofessionalization, and covenantal relationships to insure ethical enactment.

In this final section, we wish to collect the major points of our analysis into a set of propositions:

Proposition one. Religion and healing have always been historically and functionally intertwined, originally within the role of the Shaman. Although the roles of Priest/Pastor and psychotherapist are more distinct now than in the past, imposing a separation of spirituality from psychological suffering, it is artificially simplistic and historically dysynchronous with psychotherapeutic practice. The attempt to ignore the religious components of patients' lives is often clinically inappropriate, and impossible to achieve unless pathological denial is employed by therapist and patient alike.

Proposition two. The professional task of psychotherapy is conceptually a moral task, from which morals, values, and ethics cannot be divorced.

Proposition three. There are many social relationships and many social roles that involve "changing the psychological functioning" of a person. Psychotherapy is only one such "change relationship" and the psychotherapist role is only one of several social roles of "change agent."

Proposition four. There is considerable behavioral overlap between all social roles of "change agents." For example, a father or mother, a pastor, and a psychotherapist, may all engage in many of the *same* interactions.

Proposition five. The major distinctions in social roles of "change agents" are the role definitions and role boundaries, their context, and the value community to which they belong.

Proposition six. Each social role of "change agent" has its inherent assets and liabilities, but effectiveness is critically related to enactment within accepted role boundaries. For example, a child psychiatrist who plays the role of child psychotherapist with his or her own children will fail to fill the role of actual parent miserably. By the same token, the child psychiatrist will fail as a psychotherapist if he or she plays the role of parent with children in treatment at the child guidance clinic.

Proposition seven. The current proliferation of "religious therapies" in American culture is a cultural reaction to the inappropriate lack of attention to religious issues in psychotherapy, and the fallacious attempt to construct a "value-free" model of psychotherapy.

Proposition eight. The current state of confused "religious therapies" reflects role boundary confusion and ill-conceived role diffusion, which vitiates a robust definition of both professionalized pastoral roles and professionalized psychotherapist roles.

Proposition nine. We object to pastoral services that are "unprofessionalized" psychotherapeutic tasks; and we object to psychotherapeutic services that are "unprofessionalized" pastoral tasks. We believe that this role confusion is a distortion of the professional structure of both professions. We do not support the practice of "denominational psychotherapy," by which we mean the *covert* transformation of pastoral relations into a therapeutic relationship, or the *covert* transformation of a psychotherapy relationship into a pastoral relationship.

Proposition ten. We support the appropriate tasks of pastoral counseling conducted by a pastor "within a pastoral role."

Proposition eleven. We support the task of religious exploration and expli- cation as an appropriate task to be undertaken in a technically and ethically competent manner, by any psychotherapist "within the psychotherapeutic role."

Proposition twelve. We suggest that there is an appropriate social role model, which we called pastoral psychotherapist, for the professionally trained and pro- fessionally defined person who explicitly combines the pastoral and psycho- therapist roles, based on professional training and competency in both roles; *and* who proffers professional services explicitly based on such mutual role com- petency and is publicly identified as competent in both roles.

And finally, we believe that a convenantal understanding of the underpinning of professional roles is critical for their appropriate and ethical enactment, with role transcendence being an (infrequent) possibility within this framework.

REFERENCES

1. Pattison EM (Fall 1978). Psychiatry and religion circa 1978: analysis of a decade, part I. *Pastoral Psychology, 27,* 8-25
2. Henry WE, Sims JH, & Spray SL (1971). *The Fifth Profession.* San Francisco:Jossey-Bass
3. Greaves GB (Summer 1980). Are you a christian therapist? Religiosity and religious issues in psychotherapy. *Pilgrimage, 8,* 118-125
4. Chang SC (January 1982). The self: a nodal issue in culture and psyche -- an eastern perspective. *American Journal of Psychotherapy, 36,* 67-81
5. Bertrand AL (1972). *Social Organization: A General Systems and Role Theory Perspective.* Philadelphia:F.A. Davis Co.
6. Bowie AL (February 1982). Role as a moral concept in health care. *The Journal of Medicine & Philosophy, 7,* 57-64
7. Gustafson JM (Fall 1963). The clergy in the United States. *Daedalus: Journal of American Academy of Arts and Sciences, 92,* 724-744
8. Means JH (Fall 1963). Homo Medicus Americanus. *Daedalus: Journal of American Academy of Arts and Sciences, 92,* 701-723
9. Barber B (Fall 1963). Some problems in the sociology of the professions. *Daedalus: Journal of American Academy of Arts and Sciences, 92,* 669-688
10. Moore WE (1970). *The Professions: Roles and Rules.* New York:Russell Sage Foundation
11. Pavalko RM (1971). *Sociology of Occupations and Professions.* Itasca, Illinois:FE Peacock
12. Hughes EC (Fall 1963). Professions. *Daedalus: Journal of American Academy of Arts and Sciences, 92,* 655-668
13. Wallace ER (1983). Freud and religion: a history and reappraisal. In LB Boyer, W Muensterburger, & S Grolnick (Eds): *The Psychoanalytic Study of Society, Vol X.* Hillsdale, New Jersey:The Analyst Press
14. Wallace ER (1963). Reflection on the relationship between psychoanalysis and christianity. *Pastoral Psychology, 31,* 215-243
15. May WF (1975). Code, covenant, contract or philanthropy. *The Hastings Center Report, 5(6),* 29-38

DISCUSSION QUESTIONS

1.   You are doing a mental health evaluation on a client who informs you he is Jewish. You are a Christian psychotherapist. Discuss your ethical responsibilities to the client. Can you be an effective "change agent'?

2.   You are a psychiatrist, a Hindu, and a vegetarian. Your client is Roman Catholic, a patient in an isolated small state mental hospital. Your client believes you are an agent of Satan. Discuss the ethical dilemmas evoked by the relationship between you as therapist and your client.

3.   A client is seen by you for a severe depression. She is a minister's wife and was seen by a psychotherapist whom she was referred to by her church. She tells you the "Christian" psychotherapist held her and caressed her during the sessions because he felt she needed "love and touch" not given her by her parents. While seeing the therapist she felt strongly attracted to him. He encouraged her to reject her parents and trust him. She asked to see the therapist after hours. He met her alone in his car and held her. She announced to him four days later that she was divorcing her husband and wanted to marry him. He told her that therapy was over and that he would no longer see her. What do you do? Discuss the role conflicts illustrated by this case. What are the ethical issues?

4.   What are ethical issues that might arise when a Christian psychotherapist works with a team of mental health workers, some of whom are not Christians?

5.   Compare and contrast how Christian psychotherapy differs from other types of psychotherapy.

6.   Discuss when it is ethical to impose or discuss one's own values or religious viewpoints with a client.

7.   Compare and contrast absolutist and relativist ethical theories. (See Chapters 1 and 2).

8.   How might one go about becoming qualified to be a "Christian psychotherapist"? What are the professional standards of a "Christian psychotherapist"?

9.   Discuss whether the cultural gap between religious and anti-religious psychotherapists and clients may be detrimental to successful treatment.

10.   Discuss values Christian psychotherapists might hold beginning with those that would supersede all others.

10

Richard Sherlock

My Brother's Keeper?
Mental Health Policy
and the New Psychiatry

Dr. Richard Sherlock, Ph.D., received his B.A. from the University of Utah and his M.T.S. and Ph.D. from Harvard University. He is an associate professor of philosophy at Utah State University. Most recently he was a Senior Research Scholar, Center for Bioethics, Clinical Research Institute of Montreal and member, Department of Humanities and Social Services in Medicine, Faculty of Medicine, McGill University. Dr. Sherlock has held previous teaching positions at Northeastern University, The University of Tennessee Medical School, and Fordham University. While in Tennessee he developed a program in ethics and psychiatry and taught a seminar in ethics that was required for all psychiatric residents. His current interest includes work on problems of competency and consent in psychiatry.

In this chapter, Dr. Sherlock discusses the issue of involuntary psychiatric hospitalization and treatment. He reviews the two great changes in psychiatry, deinstitutionalization and the biological basis of mental illness. He traces the progression of the skepticism of paternalistic interventions of psychiatrists and hospitals and the emphasis on autonomy and patient rights that led to public policy revision. The chapter concludes with a critical review of the assumption that mental illness was a phenomenon of labeling resulting in commitment laws that shifted the reason for hospitalization from treatment of an illness to protecting the public from dangerousness. He advocates a return to a value of being "our brother's keeper."

ETHICS IN MENTAL HEALTH PRACTICE
ISBN 0-8089-1738-2

Mental health policy in the United States stands in a state of ferment, if not chaos. The verities that have guided policy makers in many states in the past generation are under increasing assault from public and professional skepticism, scientific developments, and ruthless budgetary pressures. In many states established policies are under attack from patient advocates, ex-patient groups, professionals, legislators, and even blue-ribbon study commissions. In Massachusetts, for example, a commission recently recommended closing all of the state's residential hospitals for the mentally ill. Those who are criminally violent would be transferred to the jurisdiction of the department of corrections under this plan, while the rest of the patient population would be discharged to the care of community based programs and clinics.[1]

This is one example of the radical criticism of the past now being seriously entertained by mental health professionals and policymakers in the state of ferment in which they now find themselves. In the next decade critiques such as this are certain to mount as policy at every level is scrutinized by those both inside and outside of public service wrestling with the formation of new mental health policies adapted to an era of new knowledge and decreased fiscal support.

At this point the shape of a new policy consensus is unknown. One observation may be made with certainty, however. Whatever new policies emerge in the coming years will reflect a set of pre-understandings of mental illness and the means of diagnosing and treating those afflicted with such illness, as well as a set of moral assumptions that will exercise a powerful influence on the shape of any new policies that emerge from the confusing array of alternatives that exist at present.

The crisis in mental health policy that we now face is the result of the congruence of two powerful but distinct revolutions that have enveloped American psychiatric practice in the last generation. This chapter will discuss the nature of these two revolutions, their background, the beliefs that animated them, and their implications for therapy and policy regarding the mentally ill. This is a necessary prelude to developing new policies for the next generation. It is especially important to see the permanent truths embedded in each of these revolutions, truths that we can all afford to neglect. The last section of this chapter will say something of what these two transformations suggest for the care and treatment of the mentally ill in the future and what kind of public policy best fits what we now know about mental illness.

The material covered here is so enormous and the implications so rich and varied that we cannot do anything more than the barest sketch of what is needed for a full study. Recognizing the limitations of space we nevertheless can make a reasonable attempt to sketch the main lines of the argument and cite as much evidence in its behalf as possible in the footnotes. Hopefully, this essay will stimulate others to work along these same lines or at least on these same problems and we hope such work will ultimately be of benefit to practitioners and patients.

The two revolutions that have engulfed American psychiatry, especially public psychiatry in the last two decades, are on the one hand a revolution in public policy and on the other hand a revolution in psychiatric practice. The policy revolution is perhaps the most visible and obvious, at least to the public. Though the most visible event in this revolution has been the deinstitutionalization of large numbers of mental patients, deinstitutionalization itself is only part of a more fundamental policy transformation -- toward a much greater emphasis on the autonomy and rights of the patient and a much greater skepticism regarding the paternalistic interventions of psychiatrists and hospitals. As such, this transformation involves changes in commitment laws, retention policies of institutions, and an increased attention to and expansion of the rights of psychiatric patients, including most notably the right to refuse treatment even while committed by the state for care and treatment.*

Alongside of this policy revolution that stresses the freedom and rights of the patient has come a second transformation in psychiatric theory and practice that may be summed up in two words: biological psychiatry. A generation ago American psychiatric practice was largely rooted in a psychodynamic paradigm for the understanding of serious mental disorder, a paradigm primarily derived from psychoanalytic sources and rooted in psychotherapeutic modes of treatment. Over the last two decades an impressive body of data has emerged that demonstrates unquestionably that the most serious forms of mental illness, those about which public policy must be concerned, are based in biological malfunctioning of the affected individual. In some cases where psychotherapy has proven to be completely ineffective, e.g., agoraphobia, the proper medication, in this case antidepressant drugs, may return the patient the full functioning in the same manner as antibiotics cure pneumonia.[3-8]

The convergence of these two revolutions has, I believe, brought us to the crisis we now face in mental health policy and practice. On the one hand we are more sensitive than ever to the claims patients make for their autonomy vis-a-vis the psychiatrist and the hospital, while at the same time our understanding of the biological roots of their illness may afford us powerful new tools with which to treat them even in the absence of their consent. Even where such tools are absent the biological understanding of mental disease orients us to the way in that serious mental disorder incapacitates the person against his or her will and may require care and custody even in the absence of cure. But before we can properly assess the convergence of these two revolutions we should examine them in some depth.

THE POLICY REVOLUTION

The policy revolution in mental health that has passed under the name deinstitutionalization involved three connected but distinct changes: (1) tighter commitment laws and admission policies of institutions; (2) the release of thousands of chronic patients into the community; and (3) a renewed emphasis on the autonomy and rights of those in the institution. In short it has become much harder to get someone in a mental hospital, much more difficult to stay for an extended period, and more difficult to treat an institionalized patient who does not want to be treated.

---

*The policy revolution of the last generation is actually another part of a cyclical form of mental health policy optimism. In the progressive era at the turn of the century a great optimism surrounded the idea of the "mental hospital" as a place of treatment that was different from the "assylum," which had turned into a warehouse. The new hospital was supposed to utilize the latest means to treat mental illness, especially the new finding of Freud, Krapelin, Blueler Adler, Sullivan, etc. Soon however the "hospital" became simply another warehouse and the treatment function vanished. By the end of the 1950s both the profession and society were ready for something new to replace the failed policies of the past. Deinstitutionalization and outpatient care met this need precisely.[2]

Over the last 20 years commitment laws have been fundamentally altered in a number of ways in a large majority of states.[9-19] Though diverse, these changes reduce themselves to one fundamental change: a serious tightening of the criteria under which an individual can be involuntarily committed to a psychiatric facility for care or treatment.[20,21] However, it is worded this change almost invariably entails dropping the notion that the state may commit those who are simply in need of "care and treatment" for mental illness. The newer, tougher standards invariably limit the possibility of commitment to those patients who are dangerous either to themselves or others or, in some cases, to those patients who are so gravely disabled by their illness that they cannot provide for their own basic needs for food or shelter.[†,22] This difference is well captured in two state commitment laws.

In Rhode Island the patient may be involuntarily committed if either of two conditions is met: (1) the person is "dangerous to the peace and safety of the people of the state" or (2) "Restraint and treatment is necessary for his own welfare."[23]

In California under the new (1967) Lanterman-Petris-Short act a person can only be involuntarily committed in two ways:

1. if he is "imminently dangerous...(defined as) "Threatened attempted or actually inflicted physical harm upon the person of another ... and ... presents an imminent threat of substantial physical harm to others." or
2. if he is "gravely disabled ... A condition in which a person, as a result of mental disorder is unable to provide for his basic personal needs for food clothing and shelter."[24]

This tightening of commitment laws was patently moral in character, reflecting a widespread attachment to the dictum that the only rationale for interference with individual liberty was that others would be harmed without such intervention. If the person were mentally ill and disposed to be dangerous to others then he or she could be prevented from doing harmful deeds.[25-30] If not, what the individual wishes to do is his or her business. Ultimately the logic of these changes in commitment laws leads to the question of whether the state may intervene when the only harm is to that person (i.e., suicide) and to the conclusions reached by the Massachusetts Commission. If the state may only exercise its commitment powers to prevent dangerous behavior then it is simply subterfuge to use a psychiatric justification as a cover for what is in fact a preventive detention program.[31]

Even in its usually more modest form this change resulted from a general apprehension of what many authors called the "therapeutic state" in which government undertook to "perfect" citizens, not merely "protect" them. In general these changes in commitment laws represented this commitment to the libertarian view, tempered by the knowledge that a few individuals are, at some times, so mentally disabled that without social intervention they will starve or freeze as a result of their own improvidence.[25,32-34] But the clear thrust was, as seen in California, to limit commitment to the fewest cases with the most compelling justifications possible. Invariably these were in the vast majority of cases, persons who might be dangerous and who were mentally ill, not just criminally disposed.

---

†One of the earliest versions of this move is seen in the District of Columbia Hospitalization of the Mentally Ill Act (1964), which eliminated "need for treatment" altogether as a basis for intervention or commitment and substituted strict criteria of dangerousness. D.C. Code 21--501.

Alongside of this tightening of commitment laws and stemming from the same moral commitments the policy revolution also included the practice of deinstitutionalization by which it has come to be characterized in the public mind.[35-37] The figures alone suggest the change that has been wrought in the retention policies of state institutions. In 1955 the population of state hospitals peaked at close to 560 thousand persons. By the middle of the 1970s that population had dropped to about 193 thousand, a decline of better than 60 percent.[38]

This policy of releasing hundreds of thousands of mental patients into the hands of community care rested at the outset on revulsion, hope, and moral conviction, not on hard data. The "facts" that everyone knew were the dismal, subhuman conditions of public mental hospitals in almost every state. Chronic underfunding and public indifference had conspired with a lack of effective therapies to create the dismal warehouses that were the target of the critics of the last two decades. Ill clothed, ill fed, ill washed patients, in institutions staffed by at best indifferent or at worst incompetent caretakers were so obviously badly treated that most serious professionals knew it had to be ended.[§,39] This revulsion combined with hope and conviction to produce deinstitutionalization as we know it.[#] It must be underlined, however, that at the outset there was no body of data that anyone could point to that would have suggested that these patients could be adequately cared for in the community. Such data simply did not exist and in fact only a small and uneven amount of it exists now, even after two decades of the experiment.[¶,42,43] Hope and conviction took the place of facts. The hope was that patients could be maintained in their communities if only adequate support facilities were created. Facilities that were believed to be less costly than hospital care. These hopes combined with the first real introduction of anti-depressant and anti-psychotic medications into psychiatric practice, drugs that had been noted to have significant therapeutic effects on patients in the hospital.[44] The reasoning at this

---

§The most trenchant indictment of the system may have been offered by Dr. Harry Solomon in his 1958 presidential address to the Americal Psychiatric Association when he wrote: "I do not see how any reasonably objective view of our mental hospitals today can fail to conclude that they are bankrupt beyond remedy. I believe therefore, that our large mental hospitals should be liquidated as rapidly as can be done in an orderly and progressive fashion."[40]

#This optimism was seen best in President Kennedy's 1963 message to Congress relative to the establishment of community mental health programs for the effective treatment of mental illness. Said the President: "Many such hospitals and homes have been shamefully understaffed, overcrowded, unpleasant institutions from which death too often provides the only firm hope of release... I propose a national mental health program to assist in the inauguration of a wholly new emphasis and approach to the care of the mentally ill. This approach relies primarily upon the new knowledge and new drugs acquired and developed in recent years which make it possible for most of the mentally ill to be successfully and quickly treated."[41] Also see the work of Gerald Caplan and Leopold Bellak cited below.

¶Aside from limited data many of the studies are methodically inadequate. Often the experimental groups exclude high risk patients such as those who are severely disturbed or alcoholic. In this manner the results achieved may show success but not of the kind that can be relevant to policymaking for those excluded, also various studies differ at the point of experimental intervention e.g., does it come before admission as an alternative, as a modification of traditional hospitalization (typically a very short as opposed to long stay) or as an alternative to long term hospitalization.

point was obvious: if we could just provide access to these medications and perhaps group or individual psychotherapy as necessary we could treat and even cure these people in their own communities.

Moreover, deinstitutionalization followed from the same libertarian attachments as did tighter commitment standards. If it was wrong to commit people who weren't dangerous it was wrong to keep them hospitalized for any other reason. Given the hope for community care and the dismal state of public institutions, deinstitutionalization as a national policy followed.

Over time this act of libertarian faith has given away to the sober realization that, if measured by the claims of its early enthusiasts, deinstitutionalization hasn't worked very well. Anyone who studies the data objectively must come to the conclusion that when 30-40 percent of the residents of bowery welfare hotels in New York City are ex-mental patients with no where else to go, something has gone wrong.[45,46] That reality does not reflect hope is due to a number of factors, including budgetary pressures that have only mounted under the realization that adequate outpatient care for severely mentally ill people may be more expensive than comparable hospital care. Furthermore, a careful examination of the data from properly run outpatient programs shows that even in expensive, experimental programs the level of patient functioning does not appear to be any better than the level of functioning achieved by hospital care.[**,47-49] Moreover, in a number of studies that have shown improvement in functioning as a result of outpatient care, the results may be illusory. In one study improvement in psychosocial functioning occurred only in the context of intensive on-going intervention in the activities of daily living on the part of the patient. But this improvement dropped markedly when the intervention ceased.[50,51]

It seems clear, therefore, that a continued commitment to deinstitutionalization, as seen in the Massachusetts study, cannot be based on a demonstrated capacity of community care to further patient welfare. This is especially true at present when the reality of deinstitutionalization is in many states at least as squalid as the institutions from which these patients may have come and far more dismal than the meager results achieved by the experimental programs noted above.[38] Commitment to outpatient care for these sorts of persons must thus rest on the libertarian moral convictions to which we have called attention throughout.

These same moral convictions lie behind the third part of the policy revolution

---

[**]"Improvement in community functioning, as reported in the introduction, has been an enigma to even the best of in-hospital programs. In view of wide spread hopes that community treatment might offer a clear solution to this problem, the results reported in this paper might appear disappointing. That is, many of the studies revealed no difference in psychosocial functioning between in-hospital and community programs, with the level of functioning usually reported as quite low."[42] Two points can be made with regard to data on the cost effectiveness. First, most studies have found that quality outpatient care, i.e., care that leads to as much psychosocial functioning as in the hospital will be as expensive as or more expensive than care in the hospital. The cost effectiveness of out-patient care only appears when the increased earnings of those cared for in the community are added into the analysis. While this is important it should be noted that for policymakers the crucial fact will be that the direct program costs assocated with outpatient care will very likely be higher than hospital care. Also, once the patient is discharged he can be abandoned to his fate more easily with hidden consequences than is possible in public institutions.

in mental health: the increasing attention to and respect for the rights of patients in the hospital, especially the right to refuse treatment.[52-57] In the last several years this concern for the rights of psychiatric patients has centered around a series of cases in which courts have held that involuntarily committed patients have a right to refuse any treatment even though, being committed, they cannot be discharged as other noncooperative patients can.[58-61] While the resolutions reached in the various cases differ in the strenuousness with which they uphold this right and the conditions for its being overridden, the general tenor of all the cases is to press to whatever limit the court views as reasonable the right to refuse therapy.[††] The extent to which this right is being pressed in the courts is best seen in the description by the court of one of these patients.

> Throughout this period plaintiff was inconsistent in his attitude toward various medications, refusing at times and cooperating at others. One of the main causes of his repeated discharges and readmissions is his failure to continue taking medications. Plaintiffs twelfth and present admission to Ancora began on August 10, 1976, pursuant to an involuntary commitment. Although committed he has never been declared incompetent. The admitting diagnosis was manic depressive psychosis, circular type. He was placed on Lithium and on suicidal and homicidal precautions. Later psychotropic drugs were added. Again at various times medication was refused. In December 1976 the Public Advocate's office became involved in Mr. Rennie's case. After conversation with ... it was agreed that medication would not be forced against the patient's will. Following an injection of prolixin decanoate on January 5th plaintiff became extremely psychotic and threatened suicide. During 1977 plaintiff was shifted between a number of medications, including thorazine, prolixin, etrafon, haldol, elavil, and lithium. Frequent incidents of fights with other patients and attendants were also reported. Sucidal and delusional periods were also reported.[62]

In cases such as these it is apparent that the assertion of the right of the patient to refuse therapy must rest on a belief in the overriding importance of autonomy as distinct from any assessment of what might be in the best interest of the patient. It seems clear that in these sorts of cases the patient's interests are best served by taking medication and since the medication may be effective in a given patient without his or her consent; his or her interest might be served by giving medication whether consent is granted or not.

This policy revolution in mental health was, as we have seen, rooted in moral considerations, not clinical data. No one knew whether these policy changes would further patient welfare. What they "knew" was a moral conviction that favored liberty or autonomy as a very great good that took precedence over almost every other possible human good. It was this conviction that generated policy and supported the hope that these policies would be of benefit to the patients.

In liberal theory this commitment to individual autonomy was given its most trenchant presentation in Mill's *On Liberty*. Essentially Mill held that individuals have a primary right to live as they wish, a right that cannot be overridden by

---

[††]In all of these cases the limiting factor to the exercise of a right to refuse medication is the patient's dangerousness to self or others. The cases differ in the extent to which they require the danger to be imminent or merely likely. In some cases courts have held that only the immediate violent behavior of the patient will justify the use of medication the patient has refused.

claims of what might be best for them or what morality requires of them. Society cannot act as a parent or enforcer of "proper" behavior. Rather society's only interest must be with behavior that is demonstrably harmful to specific other human beings. We may restrain a person who shoots guns in a public place but we have no right to prevent someone who wishes to go for long walks in zero degree weather without a coat. If one prefers this sort of behavior it is his or her business not ours.

> The object of this essay is to assert one very simple principle ... that principle is that the sole end for which mankind are warranted, individually or collectively in interfering with the liberty of action of any of their number is self protection. That the only purpose for which power can be rightfully exercised over any member of a civilized community, against his will is to prevent harm to others. His own good, either physical or moral is not a sufficient warrant. He cannot rightfully be compelled to do or forbear because it will be better for him to do so, because it will make him happier, because in the opinions of others to do so would be wise or even right. These are good reasons for demonstrating with him or reasoning with him or persuading him or entreating him but not for compelling him.[63]

This principle lay behind much of the policy revolution in mental health that we have just observed, especially the strenuous critiques of civil commitment and institutional care that dot the literature of the last two decades. Since mental illness was largely conceived to be just abnormal behavior, society had no proper role in treating or confining it, especially in a coercive fashion. It is the individual's right to decide how he or she wishes to live life and if one chooses to behave differently than others, that is his or her business, no one else's.

Almost immediately, however, Mill modifies the simplistic principle with which he starts. It is, he says, applicable "only to human beings in the maturity of their faculties." Children are the obvious class excluded here, a point that Mill makes explicit. But Mill also clearly intends his exception to be taken more broadly when he notes:

> Those who are still in a state to require being taken care of by others must be protected against their own actions as well as against external injury. For the same reason we may leave out of consideration those backward states of society in which the race itself may be considered in its nonage. The early difficulties in the way of spontaneous progress are so great and there is seldom any choice of means for overcoming them; a ruler full of the spirit of improvement is warranted in the use of any expedients that will attain an end, perhaps otherwise unattainable. Despotism is a legitimate mode of government in dealing with barbarians, provided the end be their improvement and the means justified by actually effecting that end.[§§,63]

The central issue of the mental health policy revolution is thus posed even from within Mill's defense of liberty. If mental illness is illusory or its effects mild, then Mill's primary principle clearly enjoins respect for liberty, even one that includes abnormal or stupid choices. On the other hand, if mental illness reduces the

---

§§Kant also explicitly excluded children and the "insane" from his concept of respecting the choices and "valuations" of others.[64]

capacities of the person for choice and reason to a state similar to children or what Mill calls "barbarians" then he, at least, would not preclude coercive intervention aimed at their good. Paternalism is, in this instance justified, on behalf of the best interests of the patient that he or she is now incapable of judging or pursuing.

Though Mill is unclear just why we should permit paternalism in these cases we might venture an interpretation not unlike the position taken in favor of this sort of paternalism by a number of recent writers.[65] In Mill's discussion, the importance of liberty clearly seems to presuppose the notion of individuals examining a number of different courses of action and adopting those that they find preferable, advantageous, or required of them on some antecedent grounds. In other words, we must be free to "frame the plan of our life to suit our character."[63] Mill clearly has in mind here such examples as persons choosing between various religious beliefs, moral principles, political activities, or careers. The various examples with which he explicates his meaning reflect precisely these sorts of choices. In such instances individuals gather the relevant information and weigh the various courses of action open to them, selecting the one that best fits personal goals, cohers with prior beliefs, in personally pleasing, and fulfills a moral obligation that they believe they have, etc.

In the case of those "lacking in maturity," however, the very capacity to choose a life plan, pursue a course of action, or adhere to a religious dogma is lacking. Thus as Mill would say, their capacity for "free voluntary undeceived consent and participation" is compromised or absent.[63] This is, as he says, a prequesite to the exercise of the "rightful liberty" espoused by the primary principle. In other words, only when we can say that the person has actually chosen the plan of life he or she now pursues need we respect what he or she does under its banner. Responses to coercive pressures or biological drives, as in the young child, do not count, nor do actions engendered by the deceptions of others.

But where then does mental illness fit, where the coercion or "deception" (if any exists) lies within the psyche of the individual. Take the following sort of case as an example.

Mr. K was a 53-year-old man brought to the psychiatric service by his family. He appeared disheveled and was uncommunicative. The family said that he had lost 20 lbs. over the last month and that he had trouble sleeping. They also reported that he had frequent crying spells. On interview the man was uncommunicative and lethargic. In response to many questions he was silent at other times he simply said "I don't know" or "I don't care" in a low slurred voice. When pressed he seemed to know the answer to many questions but he also didn't really care what the answer was.

On the face of it Mr. K seems to be severely disabled by his depressive illness in ways that substantially limit his capacity for autonomous choice and action. Most of the ways in which other persons exercise their autonomy and for which they cherish it seem not be open to him. Viewed in this light Mr. K seems to be the archtype of Mill's "child" where the libertarian principle may be set aside. If so then it would seem absurd to claim that hospitalization and treatment of Mr. K, even absent his consent, is an onerous assault of his autonomy. On this account Mr. K's depression is another form of coercion, as powerful as that of any tyrant and as such paternalistic interventions aimed at freeing the individual are clearly justified even in Mill's terms.[66,67]

But Mill's justification of paternalism and not his primary principle of liberty only applies if we regard the condition of Mr. K as an involuntary affliction, not a conscious choice. Someone who prefers to be lethargic and uncommunicative may be making an unwise choice, but he or she is making a choice, not merely responding to coercive social or biological forces. If it is Mr. K's choice to be as he is, Mill's principles at least would enjoin respect for this choice, no matter how unwise or improvident we believe Mr. K to be.

It was precisely the former view of mental illness as a condition that "defeated" the liberty principle that justified the paternalism of the older mental health policy. Hence, before the liberty principle could plausibly ground policy either or both of two conclusions had to be reached. First it might be concluded that mental illness was illusory or so mild that it did not plausibly bring into play Mill's justification for paternalism. Alternatively one might conclude that irrespective of theoretical claims regarding mental illness no one knew how to reliably diagnose or treat it and as such civil intervention was likely to be so disastrously broad, imprecise, or ineffective that it would be unjustified even if the cogency of some forms of paternalism or some cases of mental illness be granted. In fact both of these claims about the nature of mental illness and the nature of psychiatric practice and hospital care are central in the critical literature of the last two decades. These assumptions made the libertarian transformation of mental health policy seem increasingly plausible, if not mandatory.

The most significant of these assumptions were those concerning the reality of mental illness as a disease entity. During the two decades from 1960 to 1980 a number of radical critiques emerged that challenged the very basis of psychiatric practice, namely, the reality of the entity it is supposed to treat. These radical critiques differed in method and substance but they aimed at the same end, the claim that mental illness as a disease did not exist.[68]

One version of the critique developed in terms of labelling theory, which held that "mental illness" was simply a socially constructed label for abnormal behavior.[69-73] This label then caused others to respond to the labeled individual as if she or he were "sick" or "crazy." Since the self in this view is itself inherently social, the individual soon comes to internalize these perceptions and the cycle is complete as he or she now believes himself or herself to be crazy and acts in abnormal ways. But mental illness itself is nothing more than the label. Behind it is nothing more than a group of people who prefer to act differently than the rest of us.

This view of mental illness as a social label is basic to the various radical critiques of psychiatric practice. In Szaz's famous account, the label hides the reality that the patient is involved in an elaborate game, through which she or he seeks to master the world. The only problem is that she or he is playing a different game, with different ends and different rules than most of us play everyday. The patient is not sick, she or he is different. Abnormal she or he may be in a strict sense of that term but abnormality itself is not a disease.[74]

Szaz's prime example was hysteria, a particularly apt case for making his view seem plausible. He claimed, however, a broader relevance for his position, one encompassing all of the categories of mental illness, even psychosis.[75] It remained for others to work out such a transactional view of schizophrenia and depression, the two most severe forms of "mental illness." Based on the work of Dewey and Mead, Becker's theoretical structure supposed mind to be completely a social construct, emerging out of the interaction of organism and society. Schizophrenia and depression are abnormal ways of engaging in this interaction that are caused at the earliest stages of the growth of mind, i.e., in early childhood. The schizophrenic person for example experiences a loss of meaning and a failure in "empowerment" that incapacitates him or her in life. This diminishment of the power to act is rooted in a sense of the absence of power and meaning at the beginning of the mind's development, and in Becker's discussion maternal deprivation plays a large role.[76]

It remained for the British theorist R.D. Laing to complete the critique of standard psychiatric theory begun by Szaz and Becker with his contention that the schizophrenic "break" that is usually seen in early adulthood is, in reality, a rather reasonable, i.e., sane, break with an otherwise intolerable situation. Out of his early work on the families of schizophrenics Laing concluded that many of them come from "pathological" family situations; from this he argued that the schizophrenic's troubles are rooted in his family dynamics and that his "break" represents a sort of existentialist "leap" from an intolerable situation to one of freedom.[##,77-80]

Whatever the sources of these radical critiques of standard psychiatric theory they have exercised a substantial influence on the transformation of mental health policy in the last two decades.[¶¶] While many policymakers were not quite ready to go all the way with Szaz and Laing, the labelling theory did strike a responsive chord in many. If mental illness were only a label or at least was r ɔted in the social dialectic of self and other that underlay labelling theory, then the "medical model" of mental illness and its attendant language, practice, and policy must be fundamentally mistaken.

Furthermore this sort of pervasive skepticism regarding the reality of mental illness itsel has been reinforced by skepticism regarding the reliability of psychiatric diagnosis and the effectiveness of treatment. In one widely cited study initially published in a prestigious journal, a researcher had individuals appear at a psychiatric emergency service claiming auditory hallucinations. They were all admitted to the hospitals involved, and despite normal behavior as an inpatient and claiming no more hallucinations they were not discharged rapidly.[82] This study and others like it were repeatedly cited as evidence of the unreliable nature of psychiatric diagnoses and the powerful influence of the label "mentally ill" in shaping institutional responses.

These and other studies noted above influenced a number of policy writers and mental health law experts by calling into question the applicability of the one relevant exception to Mill's liberty principle: the mental disorder of the patient. In the language of medical ethics these sorts of critiques have the effect of transforming what were *prima facie* cases of weak paternalism into cases of strong paternalism, which is much more difficult to justify.[83] In the relevant literature strongly worded titles like "Flipping Coins in the Courtroom" or "Into the Abyss" abound. [84-89] Most of these very radical critiques of psychiatric practice and ability are based on the work of radical critics like Szaz. For example, in a book

---

[##]Laing's debt to existentialist sources is patent. In fact his description of the "ontologically insecure and schizod person "bears a striking resemblance to the manner in which man authetically exists in the world, especially in Sartre's thought. In some ways then the schizophrenic break is a break from inauthentic to authentic existence. This view of the essential rationality of the people who are labelled mentally ill is also found in the work of Braginsky and Ring.[80]

[¶¶]The influence of labelling theory is especially pervasive and no amount of simple citations can adequately do justice to the way in which the assumptions of labelling theory pervade the relevant policy oriented literature. Its influence can be seen in most the literature cited in this paper. Especially pronounced is its influence in the substantial study by the Harvard Law Review. [81]

significantly entitled *Prisoners of Psychiatry* one of the most strenuous legal and policy critics of the 1970s used a Szazian view of mental illness to launch a full scale assault on mental hospitalization, either voluntary or involuntary.[90] More temperate critics simply claimed that no one knew very much about the etiology and diagnosis of mental illness at that, in large measure, labelling theory was correct in its understanding of the nature of mental illness. In a recent extensive treatment of mental health law this skepticism of professional competence appeared in less lured but still similar tones:

> Although the terms "mental disorder" or "mental illness" connote that some-thing more than abnormal behavior is wrong with the person it must be emphasized that a diagnosis or label, of mental disorder means primarily that a person behaves differently. "Mental disorder" does not imply any necessary, scientifically proven findings about recognized underlying causative abnor-malities of the person's brain, nervous system, heredity, diet, hormonal balance, past history, sexual conflicts, social environment or other vari-ables.... Mental disorder is thus diagnosed by observing the person's behavior. There are no physical tests for the presence of mental disorder. Statements about underlying disease processes, whether based upon interviews, psychological tests (which are simply more or less structured behavior samples) or other observations are theoretical speculations.[30]

A decade earlier the authors of a widely cited and influential article had written in the same spirit;

> One need only glance at the diagnostic manual of the American Psychiatric Association to learn what an elastic concept mental illness is. It ranges from the massive functional inhibition characteristic of one form of catatonic schizo-phrenia to those seemingly slight aberations associated with an emotionally unstable personality ... obviously the definition of mental illness is left largely to the user and is dependent upon the norms of adjustment that he employs. Usually the use of the phrase "mental illness" effectively masks the actual norms being applied. And, because of the unavoidably ambiguous generalities in which the American Psychiatric Association describes its diagnostic categories, the diagnostician has the ability to shoehorn in to the mentally diseased class almost any person he wishes, for whatever reason to put there.[91]

These sorts of criticisms of psychiatric practice are not merely academic. They influence both directly and indirectly the way in which both courts and policy-makers shape mental health policy. For example, in a recent case involving the right of a committed patient to refuse treatment the court described the state of medical knowledge thusly, citing as authority one of the most strenuous non-medical critiques of current policy.

> K.K.B. is suffering from schizophrenia, the etiology of which is unknown. There are no physical symptoms and no physical basis for schizophrenia. However, almost half of the patients comprising the population of our public mental health facilities suffer from this psychosis. It is the most likely disorder to be treated with psychotropic drugs but the precise nature of the benefits of these drugs is as yet uncertain and the dangers the drugs seek to avoid are usually not great.[92]

This passage of course, does not display the same skepticism borne of labelling theory that the other passages do but it does reflect a skepticism regarding psychiatric knowledge in general and therapeutic knowledge in particular that is clearly connected to the other kinds of skepticism already noted.

Ironically the adoption of a framework for mental health policy along Mill's lines only furthered the skepticism regarding the reliability of psychiatric judgment. In adopting Mill's view without considering the exceptions to it, it became clear that the only justification for civil commitment was the liklihood of dangerous behavior on the part of the patient.***,[93] Since the criminal justice system existed to handle actual violent behavior, the mental health system was reduced to committing those predicted to be dangerous unless held and treated. Thus the crucial judgment for commitment purposes became a prediction of dangerousness.

Unfortunately, no one, least of all psychiatrists, seems to be particularly good at predicting violence on the part of specific patients. The data in this regard is uniformly disappointing, especially for policy purposes; the means of reliably predicting violent behavior simply don't exist and in every study the margin of error in overpredicting dangerousness was so broad that it could not be the basis of any reasonable policy.[94-97] The difference in prediction scores among psychiatrists in these cases stand in marked contrast to the recent studies of diagnostic reliability per se. This sort of data only served to cast further doubt on the very idea of civil commitment, especially if dangerousness was the crucial criterion, which it must be if the libertarian position is to be maintained.

This skepticism regarding psychiatric practice, whether of the radical or the milder sort, was a necessary part of the libertarian critique and transformation of mental health policy. It was, as we have noted, precisely this sort of general skepticism that rendered Mill's dictum powerful in shaping policy. This skepticism also forced courts and policymakers to see the psychiatric hospital in a new light in keeping with the essence of Mill's position and in turn this new view of the hospital served to buttress the policy revolution that made it more difficult to admit, commit, and keep a patient. Since either mental illness itself was a fiction or the label applied to any particular person was likely to be fictitious, the idea of a "mental hospital" must also be fictitious. A hospital is a place where disease is treated and if these propositions regarding the disease be granted then the "hospital" was simply mislabelled. Rather the hospital became a sort of preventive detention center and hospitalization, especially involuntary hospitalization came to be increasingly described as incarceration.[25,26,32,73,98,99] Once the premises are granted, the logic of this conclusion is flawless. If we assume that individual liberty or autonomy are at stake, then hospitalization surely restricts one's liberty just as incarceration does. Once the intervening variable of mental disease and the limits it places on autonomy is removed, then the language of incarceration becomes the only truthful language available.

This view of hospitalization as incarceration is a recurring image in the critical and policy literature of the last two decades, finding its way into numerous court decisions, including several of major importance. Books and articles like Ennis' *Prisoners of Psychiatry* and Kittre's *The Right to Be Different* repeated the view with regularity and precision. The language itself often betrays the image that animates the argument as in a widely cited article in which the authors argue that

---

***For a trenchant presentation of this position see Bartol. Bartol simply assumes that labelling theory is a proven fact regarding mental illness and proceeds from that point.[93]

involuntary commitment of the mentally ill is wrong:

> If in the criminal law it is better that ten guilty men go free than that one innocent man suffer, how can we say in the civil commitment area that it is better that fifty four harmless people be incarcerated lest one dangerous man be free.[100]

Even where the language remains that of the hospital the argument often betrays the image. In Kittre's book *The Right to Be Different* the discussion of mental illness and mental health policy retains the language of hospitalization while transforming the content into that of the criminal law model of incarceration. This change is seen best in how he argues that the entire apparatus of criminal adjudication, including trial by jury, should be adopted in mental health law.[25]

The language and content of the incarceration/jail model of mental hospitalization was not the province solely of radical critics and legal scholars. Though utilized by these writers, it found its way into numerous court decisions, culminating in its use by the supreme court in its landmark decision in the case of *Donaldson v. O'Connor* and in *Lessard v. Schmidt* a case from the Federal district court in Wisconsin. In *Donaldson* the Supreme Court concluded in dicta:

> A finding of mental illness alone cannot justify a state's locking a person up against his will and keeping him indefinately in simple custodial confinement ... Moreover the state may arguably confine a person to save him from harm, incarceration is rarely if ever a necessary condition for raising the living standards of those capable of surviving in freedom.[101]

Two years before this the Federal district court in Wisconsin had reached the only logical conclusion for policy once the jail model is granted: require all of the procedural and substantive standards of the criminal law in the civil commitment process. This holding in *Lessard* was widely criticized by professionals but it makes perfectly good sense if we grant the incarceration model of hospitalization and the skepticism on which it is based.[102]

This view of the hospital as a jail seems deeply embedded in and reinforced by the policy transformation discussed above. In fact, the essential core of the change in commitment standards can be described in legal terminology as a change from a *parens patrie* justification to a *police power* justification for civil commitment. In the former the state's power to intervene is like that of a parent protecting an individual from the vicissitudes of life and the improvidence of his or her own behavior. In the latter the state aims at preventing demonstrable harm to other persons.[†††] The policy revolution we have been examining represents the dominance of police power justifications for hospitalization, which then become a means of preventive confinement of the potentially dangerous. But if, as the critics of the last generation have argued, this is the only possible justification for civil commitment then the hospital is, in fact, little more than a jail.

Furthermore, by moving the justification for intervention from paternalism to prevention it moved the relevant psychiatric evaluation from the diagnosis of mental disorder to the "predicted" dangerousness of the individual. Under the police power doctrine mental illness or the lack of it was, at best, a secondary

---

[†††]For a discussion of this distinction see Stone.[9]

consideration. To be sure the person had to be mentally ill before he or she could be committed, but the *sine quo non* for commitment was not illness but dangerousness. In this sense the most crucial judgment was a prediction that this person would be dangerous to others if left to do as he or she pleased.

By shifting the argument from disease to dangerousness, however, the skepticism of psychiatric expertise was only increased. The capacity of the psychiatrist to predict dangerousness is easily shown to be extremely limited, a fact not lost on the radical critics of recent years. In this regard the very use of the police power model for civil commitment dialectically carries with it the seeds of its own negation. Since dangerousness is now the critical prediction, inability to predict it accurately calls into question the very enterprise of civil commitment itself.

THE REVOLUTION IN PSYCHIATRIC PRACTICE

As we have so far seen the policy revolution of the last generation was rooted fundamentally in a moral outlook that was made relevant by a set of assumptions about the nature of mental disease and the capacities of the psychiatrist to diagnose and treat it. The second of the two revolutions that have engulfed American psychiatric practice in the last generation concerns precisely these assumptions about mental illness and its potential for treatment that shaped the policy consensus of the last two decades.

The critical literature of the 1960s referred often to a number of supposed facts concerning "mental illness," facts that justified the position taken. Two large categories of supposed facts were mainly in evidence in this literature. First, the critical literature often referred to the confusing array of conditions defined as mental illness in standard psychiatric thought. Since the category was so broad as to encompass such completely dissimilar things as schizophrenia and hysteria, then its usefulness is seriously compromised. The label covers so much that it cannot denote anything specific. To say that the person is mentally ill and in need of treatment is therefore no more helpful than to say that he or she is physically ill. In both cases the terms are so vague and the referrent so imprecise as to render the claim virtually meaningless.§§§

Furthermore, the very breadth of the term, especially in the area of personality disorders or what used to be termed neurosis ensures that almost everyone can be diagnosed as mentally ill in some fashion. As some psychoanalysts were fond of pointing out, everyone has some neurotic segments to their personality. It is simply a matter of which ones and how severe they become. But this result constitutes

---

§§§This breadth can be seen in any number of psychoanalytic works but is most influentially found in the work of Dr. William Menninger the Chief Psychiatrist of the Army in World War II. Using his broad categories Menninger had a very much higher rate of rejection for psychiatric reasons than did the British who experienced no higher rate of mental disturbance in those actually inducted than in those rejected. However, after the war Menninger concluded that based on his work with draftees about 40 million adult Americans needed mental health care, almost half of the adult population.[103]

perhaps a reduction of the category of mental illness. For the notion of illness itself seems to presuppose a differentiation between illness and health, between those who are sick and those who are not. But when the category itself is so broad as to include all or almost all instances of both sickness and health then it cannot be said to provide the necessary differentiation among cases required by its meaning.###

These general observations about the imprecision in the term mental illness were buttressed with a number of other supposed facts about psychiatric practice. What is striking about the critical literature, however, is how often its view of mental illness is shaped by psychoanalytic or psychodynamic modes of thinking about mental illness. As a result, the generation of mental illness was seen in various intra-psychic processes and conflicts (e.g., the object relations/object loss theory of the etiology of depression) or in interpersonal conflicts (e.g., the game theory of hysteria advanced by Szaz).[107] From this sort of understanding of the etiology of mental illness flowed the importance of psychotherapy as an essential mode of treatment. Whatever else might be tried the older psychiatric paradigm saw psychotherapy as a therapeutic *sine quo non*. This is not to deny the very substantial disagreements among various schools about what the therapist ought to do and what he or she ought to aim at in the patient. These battles, often fierce and unremitting scar the landscape of psychiatry throughout the twentieth century. But despite these differences, an essential commonality remained: mental illness was a psychic phenomenon requiring a psychotherapeutic mode of treatment.

One sees this sort of view of mental illness and treatment in a number of influential sources of the 1960s and 1970s. To be sure, the radical critics from Szaz to Laing saw mental illness in broadly psychodynamic terms. This, in fact, was the key to their attack on the mental illness notion as a medical term.¶¶¶,[108] More to the point, many of the more moderate critics pointed to confusions in diagnosis and treatment in what were usually called neuroses. But these sorts of "characterological" or "personality" disorders were precisely those rooted in psycho-dynamic processes, requiring psychotherapeuticforms of treatment. That is, in pointing out confusing and contradictory diagnostic claims in these sorts of cases they articulate an understanding of illness and treatment that is plainly derived from what the psychiatric mainstream was a generation ago.

This view also profoundly influenced the early enthusiasts for deinstitutionalization. In their view mental illness was largely a matter of "difficulties in living" that could only be effectively treated outside of institutions with psychotherapeutic and counseling services. To be sure, some few people would need the assistance of what was then new pharmacological means of treatment, such as anti-depressant drugs. For the most part, however, outpatient intervention and therapy for those too ill-situated or too psychologically weak to withstand the vissicitudes of life was the preferred mode of treatment. As the best case in point here one can cite Gerald Caplan's 1964 pean to optimism, *Principles of Preventive*

###The literature on the concepts of disease and illness in growing. The point made in the text seems to me to be a *sine quo non* of any useful concept disease or illness.[104-106]

¶¶¶All of these writers, Szaz especially, are explicit in their desire to reestablish the capacity of those labelled "mentally ill" for voluntary "willed" choices. In other words, these persons remain subject to Mill's primary principle, not the exception.

Psychiatry in which psychodynamically oriented intervention in the lives of people and institutions is the key to successful "preventive psychiatry," a form of "emotional innoculation" that he saw as the psychiatric equivalent of sanitation or vaccination.****,[109]

This view of mental illness rooted in psychodynamic models of etiology and psychotherapeutic modes of treatment was extremely influential in shaping the policy consensus of the last generation. This observation is especially true in the negative sense. For, granting the view just noted, the observation of an early enthusiast for deinstitutionalization that "hospitalization as such is an important cause of disability" is not far wrong.[111] At least if mental illness is reduced to "problems in living" then the hospital is at best a useless appendage. Furthermore, the sqalid warehouses of the 1950s and 1960s are what one would expect if this paradigm of psychiatric practice is granted. Even assuming that these facilities were as poorly equipped and understaffed as their critics claimed, it is not clear that any staffing ratio would have done what everyone wanted: cure these patients of their disease. The fact is that psychotherapy has never been shown to be very effective with seriously disabled patients. Psychotherapy done according to the tenets of whatever school of thought requires both substantial motivation and cognitive capacities that are at best marginal in deeply disturbed patients. A schizophrenic patient who hears voices or who believes that "red" people are after him or her is simply not in a position to benefit from psychotherapy. This fact has been noted repeatedly in the number of studies of psychotherapy in schizophrenic patients.[112-115] In severe unipolar or bi-polar depression the situation changes very little. Severe depression produces both motivational and cognitive capacities that markedly hinder the prospects for psychotherapy. In milder forms of depression (e.g., cyclothymia and dysthmia) psychotherapy has been tried with uncertain success.

The point of these observations is that precisely in those forms of mental illness with which public policy and law need to be concerned, the psychoanalytic or psychodynamic view of mental illness does not fare very well. Its view of etiology does not seem to bear up under analysis and its methods of treatment largely turn out to be unsuccessful. Moreover the psychodynamic paradigm focuses attention on a broad sweep of problems, including behavioral and personality disorders as well as overt psychosis. The breadth of its concern is reflected especially in the first and second editions of the American Psychiatric Association's *Diagnostic and Statistical Manual* in which a number of unconnected diagnostic categories were grouped as mental illness with the only seeming justification for such a grouping

****Leopold Bellak, a New York Psychiatrist and very influential leader in the community mental health movement, advocated "legislative psychotherapy" and coercive psychodynamically oriented interventions of many different sorts.[110]

The importance of psychodynamic modes of thinking is seen in a preliminary review I have made of the two leading American Journals: *American Journal of Psychiatry* (AJP) and *Archives of General Psychiatry* (AGP). Taking based years of 1955 for AJP and 1960 for AGP and 1980 for both, I examined all articles dealing with diagnosis or treatment. In earlier years the journals contained a very high number of articles reflecting the older paradigm or evidencing a first step away from it, i.e., use of the new drugs such as Thorazine in order to enable a patient to get into psychotherapy. In the latter year the journals were very much filled with articles reflecting the biological paradigm.

being that the conditions were (1) distressing, and (2) have no physical etiology. Many of these personality disorders do respond to psychotherapy in motivated individuals and this fact only reinforced the psychodynamic paradigm.[116]

Ironically, however, this connection between psychotherapeutic success and psychoanalytic understanding of mental disorder served to include as mental illness precisely the broad categories that fed the critical work of the 1960s and 1970s. One needs only examine the range of "mental disorder," especially personality disorder in the second edition (1968) of the manual to see what the critics were charging. These critics were, in a measure, correct when they charged that in these imprecise terms almost anyone could be found "mentally ill and in need of treatment." Furthermore, given the imprecision and confusion in diagnostic categories there would be a high rate of missed and inaccurate diagnosis, with no two clinicians agreeing on diagnosis or even on the fact of mental illness. In a number of studies from the 1950s and 1960s these claims of diagnostic imprecision were born out with interrater reliability coefficients that hovered around five. This means that almost half of the time two psychiatrists presented with the same patient will make a different diagnosis.[117-119]

For the older *parens patrie* model of civil commitment these conclusions from studies of the psychodynamic paradigm of mental illness are very important. What they meant was that in nearly half of the cases the threshold finding of mental illness could not be reliably met; and though one may need "treatment" of some kind it was unlikely that he or she would be cared for properly in this regard by the use of treatment models then available and professionally approved. In other words the older psychiatric paradigm led to a broadening and confusion of diagnostic categories and the employment of doubtfully successful means of therapy that undercut the very *parens patrie* basis for the older mental health policy. Thus the necessity and desirability of the policy revolution of the recent past seemed assured.

At the very time that this older paradigm was, in a sense, giving rise to the radical critiques of the past and impetus to the policy revolution, its very cogency was fundamentally challenged to the point that it can no longer be asserted as a correct manner in which to view serious mental disease.

We cannot here go into the detail necessary to fully describe the new biological psychiatry. Such has been done elsewhere much better, especially for the non-specialist. Only the barest essentials can be noted here. It is almost certainly the case that the most severe forms of mental illness (schizophrenia and manic depressive illness) are genetically based and biologically rooted. Twin studies of both diseases show clearly the genetic connections of these disorders. This is not to say that genetics determines the presence of the illness in every case. Such a conclusion is too strong. What genetic background does do is predispose the individual to the disease, either strongly or weakly. For example, schizophrenia in an uncle would be less strongly predispositive than schizophrenia in a mother.[120-122] Moreover it seems certain, given current knowledge, that both of these disorders involve biological malfunctioning of various centers in the brain. We are not sure exactly which sites control which forms of thought, mood, and behavior and are therefore casually linked to which forms of mental disease. We are, however, reasonably certain that we know something of what must be involved, especially as a result of studies of the site and mechanism of action of various drugs that control the manifestations of mental illness. For example, we are relatively certain that dopamine receptor sites play a role in the etiology of schizophrenia and that one of the actions of anti-psychotic drugs is to block these receptors. However, we also know that our knowledge of the precise biological mechanism at work here is very imprecise and our conclusion must be tentative. The same may be said of our knowledge of the etiology of depressive illness and the role of biogenic amines such as norepinepherine.

More to the point for ethics and policy, the biological paradigm gave rise to three interconnected developments that are of serious import for the shaping of policy. First, was a substantially greater degree of diagnostic precision and reliability, especially for cases of serious mental illness. Secondly, it provided new and far more effective means of treating mental illness and either controlling the symptoms of the disease or actually curing the patient, even in the absence of consent. Thirdly, biological psychiatry focussed attention on the fact that mental illness was not the result of choice or will on the part of the patient, even an unconscious choice. As such, in those forms that are currently untreatable, e.g., disorganized schizophrenia, the patient is likely to remain sick and even get worse as the disease progresses, no matter what he or she might wish. Each of these points deserves a brief comment.

In the first instance biological psychiatry has quite properly focussed attention on serious forms of mental disease for which the evidence of biological basis was strong. By focussing on these severe forms and adhering to rigorous standards for inclusion and exclusion, precision in diagnosis has been improved markedly. In the interrater reliability studies done with the final draft of DSM III the interrater reliability for the major disorders (schizophrenia and depressive illness) was better than .8.[123] This is a very substantial increase from the .5 and .6 typically found in studies in the 1960s. Furthermore, biological psychiatry offers some hope that various biological measures may aid in diagnostic precision and reliability. Presently this is possible in two ways. First are the new tests for "biological markers" of certain forms of mental illness, e.g., the dexamethasone suppression test for depression.[124] Secondly, it is known that some drugs only are effective with certain forms of mental illness; so if a patient responds to one of these drugs we may have evidence to confirm a diagnosis. Lithium, for example, is only effective in depressive or manic depressive illness. As a result, if a person in a florid psychotic state responds to lithium we may be reasonably sure that he or she is manic and not schizophrenic.[125]

Secondly, and at the heart of the biological paradigm is the emergence of pharmacological and other biological therapies for severe mental disorder. The importance of these therapeutic developments cannot be underestimated. Since the late 1950s they have transformed the clinical practice of psychiatry, controlled or cured the disease process in hundreds of thousands of patients, and lent serious credence to the biological model of mental illness itself. For our purposes the importance of these developments lies in the capacity of such therapies to work, at least initially, independently of the "desires" of seriously disturbed persons. Perhaps this point can best be seen in two cases drawn from my own experience in a clinical setting.

Mr. AW was a 56-year-old man admitted to the psychiatric service with a diagnosis of severe unipolar depression. On admission he was markedly depressed on all clinical indicators (anhedonia, anorexia, sleep disturbance). He appeared disheveled, distressed and often tearful. He reported that over the last several months he was increasingly weak and unable to perform tasks that he formerly could do with ease. His wife reported depressed mood and lack of pleasure with things that used to give him pleasure. The patient was initially placed on tricyclic anti-depressant medication and suicide precautions (he had talked of suicide but had made no real plans). Due to severe side effects, however, he could not tolerate a therapeutic dose of drugs and they had to be discontinued. He was then presented with the option of ECT, which had a high likelihood of therapeutic success. However Mr. AW was terrified of the procedure and believed that it would make him go blind. He was repeatedly convinced to accept it and just as often he would refuse again just before beginning a course of treatment. In two cases he started a course of treatments but refused to complete them because of his fear of the treatment and his belief that they would make him go blind. He continued to speak of suicide and he eventually began refusing some of his food because "it was poisoned." Finally he was told that if he did not consent to ECT he would involuntarily be committed and treated anyway. He did, then, complete a course of ECT treatments and experienced a complete lifting of his depression. He was able to return to his home, resume his former activities, and take up new leisure activities.

Mr. C was a 30-year-old man who had been hospitalized 4 times in the last 6 years, each time with a diagnosis of chronic schizophrenia, disorganized type. For the past several months he had been noncompliant with prescribed medication and his family had been unable to force him to take it. As a result his condition deteriorated, with reduced ability for self care, increased delusional thinking (e.g.,"the space people can see me all the time"), and pronounced auditory hallucinations. Much of the time his thought is markedly incoherent and his affect in completely inappropriate. On admission to the hospital he is placed on antipsychotic medication and the most bizarre of his symptoms subside. After a few weeks he becomes more manageable and the family can take him home again, and this time they hope to be able to make him stay on his medication with the help of the hospital staff where he will return for outpatient visits.

Mr. AW was a very sick man, completely dependent on the hospital for whatever was done on his behalf. The fact that he could not tolerate tricyclics made our choice easier. ECT was in fact more likely to produce a favorable outcome with fewer side effects than tricyclics.[126] As such, except for the frightening connotations in the mind of the patient, it would be the treatment of choice. Mr. AW's inability to tolerate the drugs made that choice moot. But though he did not want ECT he was treated with it and cured of his disease. Not all cases turn out this way. In the case of Mr. C cure is not possible. The most that can be expected is that he will stay on his medication so that his family can manage to care for him. In enough cases various biological therapies do have a therapeutic effect such that the tip of a very large iceberg with enormous moral and policy implications can be seen. We know, for example, that in the case of agoraphobia, for which psychotherapy and behavior modification are ineffective, anti-depressant medication cures the disease. But this cure can be effected independently of any choice on the part of the patient.

The third implication of biological psychiatry for mental health policy may be the most important of all, namely, the fact that some of the most severely disabling forms of the disorder are involuntary and untreatable. No one who has actually encountered a person with chronic disorganized schizophrenia, like Mr. C, could suppose that someone wished to be in this condition. Even the notion of unconscious wishes or desires such as in Sullivan's conception of schizophrenia as a defense mechanism, seems not to fit the fact that the usual means of treating such unconscious wishes, i.e., psychoanalytic psychotherapy, has been a dismal failure in such patients. But even with newer pharmacological methods of treatment, the actual functioning of the patient will not improve very much, if at all. Hallucinations may stop and behavior may be more tolerable but the capacity for independent, unsupervised living will remain, at the very best, extremely marginal.[3,4]

In other words the person will remain afflicted with an involuntary disorder that renders him or her incapable of living without supervision and assistance on a continuing basis. Moreover the patient's often chronically disorganized thought process will entail very substantial limitations on any capacity for autonomous choice or action. Such a patient may not be able to buy food, pay bills, or even get into the clinic for medication without assistance, or go some distance from a place of residence without supervision. In the most serious cases such as disorganized schizophrenia, e.g., Mr C, it will be impossible for the person to live without the kind of care and supervision that a family or a hospital can provide. When the family cannot or will not provide care then we can either abandon the patient to the street or provide necessary care in an institutional setting of some sort. Further, even where the patient can be cared for in a group home or "halfway house" the actual restrictiveness of the setting may be as great as that in an inpatient ward.[††††] Given the nature of the disorder these sorts of choices most often must be made by the clinician at the clinical level and by society at the policy level. Thus the biological revolution in psychiatry has deepened our understanding of the chronic disabling character of some forms of mental disorder and thus forced upon us policy choices regarding permanent care for those who manifestly do not have just "difficulties in living."

The implications of the biological paradigm extend in numerous ways many of which are not germaine to our study. Fundamentally, the emergence of the biological paradigm undercuts the foundation of the critiques of psychiatric practice so common over the last two decades, and the policy to which these critiques have given rise. It will be recalled that at the core of the critiques was a pervasive skepticism regarding the existence of mental illness, or at least its diagnosis and treatment by psychiatric medicine. It was this skepticism that brought into play the powerful libertarian argument against the *parens patrie* basis of the older mental health law and policy. But it is precisely this skepticism that is increasingly called into question by the biological paradigm and its proper focus on serious mental disorder. The cases presented above are isolated only in the sense that most patients offer what passes for consent. Steadfast refusal as in the case of Mr. AW is not common.[129] What is important in these cases is the way in which diagnosis and treatment proceded in a patently paternalistic manner.

In this manner the biological paradigm for serious mental illness seems to call into play the very paternalistic exception clause from Mill's doctrine that the critics sought to over come as the basis of policy. On the one hand, for some disorders it offers a basis for hope that the autonomy of the patient can be fostered through what may appear as coercive intervention and, on the other hand, it demonstrates that in some cases the person is involuntarily in an incompetent state and as such needs care and attention even when cure is not possible.

At this juncture then, two paths appear for mental health policy in the future. One is to attempt to reconstruct the libertarian mental health policy of the recent past on new grounds. The other is to search for a new policy framework that

---

††††In the literature on deinstitutionalization this point is often ignored but it must be given more attention.[127,128]

would renew the older emphasis on illness and treatment while restricting its range of application from the broad and vague categories of personality disorder that plagued it in the past. In my view only the latter of these alternatives is a plausible, humane basis for policy but adopting it will require substantial rethinking of a number of key concepts, concepts that are themselves complicated and difficult.

The first move, however, is to try to reconstruct the argument for the new mental health policy of the recent past. The most interesting of these attempts is to bypass issues of diagnosis and potentially effective treatment and to admit that some people are demonstrably mentally ill but that given the physical facilities, staffing ratios and budget cuts, these people simply will not get proper care even if they are hospitalized by the state. This move grants in principle the relevance of the transformation of psychiatric practice to which we have called attention but asserts that the results of this transformation that can be seen in private practice or in academic centers simply will not be duplicated with any degree of regularity in typical state facilities.[130]

The squalid record of institutional care, even in the very recent past, is something no one wishes to continue. In our haste to refashion institutional care we are apt to forget that barbaric conditions and ill trained, poorly motivated staff have been a repeated feature of institutional care, even in the recent past. The record of some institutions, especially as uncovered in right to treatment litigation in the 1970s makes very depressing reading.[131,132] Any recommendations for actual policy changes must take cognizance of the propensity of institutional care to regress to inhumane conditions with little care and no treatment present. Budget pressures, institutional locations, patient populations, and public indifference will continually conspire to depress the effectiveness of any policy of institutional care.

Nevertheless, while we must remain cognizant of these practical realities, they ultimately cannot be decisive in the shaping of policy. This is true for several reasons. In the first place this sort of argument does not, like its predecessor, deny the reality of mental disease and its seriously debilitating effects on its victims, such as in the cases of Mr. C and Mr. AW. Neither does it deny the capacity of professionals to diagnose and treat it. Thus this argument does not deny that there are people who suffer through no fault of their own and who are in need of the help that professionals can give; its quarrel is with the manner and location in which this help is likely to be offered. But if the argument is for the superiority of outpatient care then all of the pragmatic difficulties to which they point reappear in a new setting. In fact all of the squalid conditions of institutional care can be matched point for point with barbaric conditions in which a very substantial percentage of ex-mental patients live, sleeping under bridges or fighting for space in welfare hotels and shelters. Furthermore, given the fact that proper outpatient care is at least as expensive as hospital care this situation is not likely to change very much in the short term.[38,133]

Secondly, we note that this line of defense of recent policy and attack on institutional care is fundamentally pragmatic. As such it cannot reach principled conclusions about what the basis of policy must be, especially about which principles and goals ought to guide policy. Suppose for example that the institutions in a given state did not fit the image of squalid warehouses so represented in the recent literature. Would coercive institutional care then be acceptible? If so, for which patients, on what principles? Would dangerousness be the best threshold or should we return to the "need for treatment" standard? The pragmatic critique of civil commitment answers none of these central questions and as such cannot really be of use to those fashioning the new mental health policies of the future, except in a cautionary sense.

If this sort of pragmatic defense of the anti-institutionalization ethos of recent policy is inadequate then the alternative is to refashion a policy of institutional and outpatient care on a foundation different than that which has guided the policy revolution of the recent past. At present the most important proposal along these lines has been that advanced by several authors to combine assessments of mental disease with assessments of competency as the crucial variables in the decision to intervene paternalistically in the form of hospitalization or even coercive outpatient care.[9,134,135] Essentially the argument is that while mental illness is a disease, patients should be free to refuse preferred care just as they are in other forms of disease. In the case of mental illness this simple policy is complicated by the effects of the disease on the capacity of the patient to deliberate about treatment and choose the course of action he or she prefers. For example, a manic patient whose delusions include the psychiatrist as an agent of the world conspiracy may not be able to decide in any rational manner concerning the therapy offered by the psychiatrist. In such cases the patient's incompetency to choose for himself or herself makes it necessary for someone else to make these choices for him or her. Since the psychiatrist is in the best position to know what is in the best interest of the patient, the psychiatrist's judgment ought to be crucial. The presumption is that patients would want their best interests served and would do so were they able.

This policy is frankly paternalistic but in the best and proper sense of the word. It presumes that those subject to commitment or other forms of coercive intervention will be those who lack what Mill calls "maturity" and are therefore like children in need of care and attention lest they unwittingly harm themselves as a result of their mental incapacities. This conclusion surely seems more humane and just than does the alternative of presuming a capacity for informed choice that does not exist in a given person, especially when that presumption leads to suffering and harms for these persons.

Consider someone like Mr. C noted above. Do we really wish to say that we should let Mr. C fend for himself when he is too disorganized in his thinking to be able to provide the barest necessities such as food or shelter.[§§§§] Suppose such a person is too disabled to seek proper medical care for a serious, easily treatable disease such as an acute infectious process. Should we let the disease get worse simply because such a person does not or cannot consent to treatment? There will, of course be cases that are more difficult to resolve such as those like Mr. AW, who may not starve or freeze but who are extremely disabled and unable to consent to effective therapy. Even in these cases I submit that adherence to whatever they say regarding treatment may be another form of abandonment, abandoning the person to his "rights." Furthermore, even in cases like that of Mr. AW, it seems that respect for his refusal of treatment cannot be based on a true concern for his autonomy. Mr AW's illness now severely limits his autonomy, preventing him from living at home, carrying on his job, getting pleasure from simple pursuits that used to give him pleasure, etc. How can it plausibly be maintained that we respect his autonomy by leaving him so disabled by his disease?[137,138]

---

§§§§In my view Brock's position that involuntary hospitalization is only justified by three conditions: (1) mental illness, (2) incompetency, and (3) treatability, is much too narrow. Disorganized schizophrenia is, at present, untreatable and in cases like Mr. C his incompetency means that we cannot describe any hospitalization of such patients as voluntary. If so then his view apprently is that we cannot hospitalize Mr. C. But this view seems clearly counterintuitive given Mr. C's incapacity to survive on his own.[136]

In this respect this policy better fits the most primitive principle of justice, *suum cuique*, than does the alternative. For this policy recognizes what is patent to every clinician, namely the varying capacities for informed choice among persons suffering from mental disorder.#### Such differences are obviously important in how we should respond to their wishes or their silence regarding treatment. To ignore these differences, i.e., to presume a capacity that does not exist in a given case is unjust in the most basic sense and the alternative under examination is therefore more just than the alternatives. Though morally and clinically sound in these ways this alternative does raise a number of crucial issues of its own. Primarily these have to do with its fundamental threshold for paternalistic intervention, competency. There are no universally agreed upon tests for competency and the extant clinical guidelines for making competency assessments are often vague and contradictory, factors which could easily produce unacceptable disparities of treatment.[140,141] Whether such problems develop and persist in such a policy as this will depend upon how we resolve the problem of competency and its assessment; a problem that is much disputed at present. While space prevents a full discussion of these matters here, some of the essential problems involved can be noted.

First, the requisite assessment of competency will require but cannot be limited to an evaluation of whether the patient knows the nature of his or her situation and the therapy proposed for it. This is the most commonly employed competency assessment in clinical use at present. Its relevance is obvious. Persons who do not know what they are doing or who cannot appreciate the nature of the choices they face cannot plausibly be held to be competent regarding their medical care. Attention should be called to the fact that any assessment along these lines must include more than an evaluation of how much of what he or she has been told the patient can remember and repeat to the evaluator. In the case of mentally ill persons this observation is of crucial importance. Patients may be able to repeat what they have been told but their illness itself may prevent them from actually appreciating their situation. Their delusions or ideas of reference and control may make it impossible for them to believe what they have been told or to trust their physician in any real manner. In some cases the inclusion of the psychiatrist in patients' delusional systems will preclude their appreciating anything that they are told from that source. In other cases, such as mania, patients may feel that they are not ill and may refuse all professional advice that conflicts with this assessment of their situation.[142,143]

While it is therefore important to assess whether individuals truly understand the nature of their medical situation, this assessment is essentially only a variation of widely employed competency tests in current use. It may be, however, that in order to take account of some important sorts of cases where we intuitively very much want to intervene, we need a broader and reshaped concept of competency. Consider for example this sort of case:

####Even in the case of voluntarily committed patients whose mental state is probably better than those who are committed, competency is very limited in a very high percentage of cases.[139]

Mr. N was a 34-year-old man who was admitted to the psychiatric service with a diagnosis of depression. On all clinical indicators he was severly depressed and actively suicidal. This was his third admission for treatment of depression in 4 years and each time he had responded to treatment and had returned to live with his 60-year-old mother. This time, however, she made it clear to the hospital staff that she would not take him back. She claimed that she had "had enough" of trying to care for Mr. N and his recurrent depressive episodes. At the end of the second full week in the hospital Mr. N was sent home for the weekend. Since he could not go to his mother's house he went to stay at his sister and brother-in-law's house. They were willing to have him come for the weekend but they have made it clear that they will not provide care on a long-term basis. During the weekend his sister is unexpectedly called to work and he goes to spend the rest of the time at his mother's house. At the end of the weekend he does not want to return to the hospital. At that point his mother calls the local sheriff. The sheriff puts Mr. N in handcuffs and returns him to the hospital. The next morning Mr. N feels utterly hopeless about his situation. He feels that everyone has rejected him and that he has no friends and lacks any love or concern from any source. He asks one of the nurses to drive him to the bridge so he can jump off and he even says that he will write a note so that she will not get into trouble. When she says she can't leave the hospital he then asks her to tell him which bus to take to reach the bridge.

Intuitively, we want to intervene with Mr. N. At the very least we want to prevent him from jumping off of a bridge. Such a conclusion, which might justify committing this patient, does not however, seem to follow from an assessment concerning how much the person understands of his current situation. In fact Mr. N has a fairly realistic view of his current situation. He has no friends and his family has rejected him in a violent manner. He undoubtedly lacks a feeling of love or care from any source. But it seems odd and perhaps dangerous to conclude that he is incompetent for this reason. Perhaps the only way in which the policy I am advocating can take account of these cases is by concluding that the depressive illness renders the person unable to appreciate the possibilities for change in his or her currently bleak situation. Their disease makes them mistake a bleak present for a bleak prognosis for the future. They confuse a lack of happiness now with a lack of any possibility for happiness in the future. In this sense they fail to appreciate their situation just as much as the patient who believes that she or he is going to die when in fact the prognosis is excellent. In this manner we might account for these sorts of intuitively appealing cases without going too far beyond the typical cognitive criterion for competency.

As currently formulated by Stone and Stromberg, this policy framework for civil commitment seems to rely heavily on this sort of cognitive understanding of competency.[¶¶¶¶,144] That is, the crucial judgment is the assessment that the patient does not "understand the nature and effects of treatment" or cannot engage in a "rational decision making process" about treatment. Nevertheless, we must develop a policy of humane care, often institutional care, for these persons, recognizing that such care may need to be relatively permanent, or long term.

¶¶¶¶This statute has been endorsed by the American Psychiatric Association.

CONCLUSIONS

These are just some of the difficult policy implications that seem to be raised by the revolution in psychiatric medicine in which we now find ourselves in the mental health field. I have no illusions that psychiatric medicine will remain static in its knowledge or that the kind of policy response sketched here is perfect. There will be difficult choices in any number of individual cases, choices about which reasonable clinicians, ethicists, or laymen may disagree and in which the agony of doubt and uncertainty will remain. Can this patient live at home? Can he live in a group home? Can the patient survive independently in a "day treatment" center? Such choices and decisions will always plague clinicians and other professionals and policymakers will wrestle with the choices presented by various treatment alternative and the resources needed to fully fund each alternative. Nevertheless, I remain convinced that some such policy as I have sketched here, including involuntary hospitalization where necessary, is the most just response to the problems of serious mental disorder, especially given what we now know of its etiology, therapy, and prognosis.

It is tempting to believe the claims of radical psychiatry, especially if one has actually encountered hysterical or malingering patients whose problems are obviously inter or intrapersonal. Giving in to such temptations relieves one of the burden of policy choices that are difficult and disputed. It has done so for the radical psychiatrist and the policy writers who follow their lead. But the seductiveness of this position should not be confused with correctness or justice. Serious mental illness will always afflict a certain percentage of the population. For every hysterical patient or obsessive-compulsive personality with bothersome behavior there will be Mr. AW's or Mr. C's whose disease brings them suffering, limits their autonomy, and severly impairs their capacities for independent living. It is for these sorts of persons, just as for the severely retarded or the severely demented, that we may legitimately ask: "Am I my brother's keeper?" In my view the only humane and morally just answer must be -- yes.

REFERENCES

1. *Mental Health Crossroads* (1982). Boston:Massachusetts
2. Rothman D (1978). Conscience and convenience: the assylum and its alternatives. In *Progressive America*. Boston:Little Brown
3. Klein D & Wender P (1982). *Mood and Medicine*. New York:Farrar, Straus
4. Snyder S (1974). *Madness and the Brain*. New York:McGraw-Hill
5. Klein D (1980). *Diagnosis and Drug Treatment of Psychiatric Disorders*. Baltimore:Williams and Wilkins
6. Freedman D (1975). *Biology of the Major Psychoses*. New York:Raven Press

7. Akiskal H & Webb W (1978). *Psychiatric Diagnosis: Exploration of Biological Predictors.* New York:Spectrum

8. Nicoli A (1977). *Harvard Guide to Modern Psychiatry.* Cambridge: Harvard University Press, pp 81-102

9. Stone A (1976). *Mental Health and the Law: A System in Transition.* New York:Jason Aronson

10. Wexler D (1981). *Mental Health Law: Major Issues.* New York:Plenum Press

11. McGarry AL & Kaplan HA (1973). Current trends in mental health law. *American Journal of Psychiatry, 130,* 621-630

12. Walker O (1973). Mental health law reform in Massachusetts. *Boston University Law Review, 53,* 986-1017

13. McGarry AL (1974). Massachusetts new mental health act. In FJ Ayd (Ed): *Medical Moral and Legal Issues in Mental Health Care.* Baltimore: Williams and Wilkens, pp. 179-194

14. Wexler D & Scovile S (1971). The administration of psychiatric justice: theory and practice in Arizona. *Arizona Law Review, 13,* 1-60

15. Wexler D, Sadmen H, & Shapiro R (1971). Arizona mental health services act: overview and analysis of proposed amendments. *Arizona Law Review, 19,* 313-378

16. Comment (1969). Civil commitment of the mentally ill in California: 1969 style. *Santa Clara Lawyer, 10,* 74-98

17. Bezanson RP (1975). Involuntary treatment of the mentally ill in Iowa. *Iowa Law Review, 6,* 261-396

18. Contemporary Studies Project (1979). Involuntary hospitalization of the mentally ill in Iowa. *Iowa Law Review, 64 ,* 1284-1378

19. Comment (1968). Civil commitment of the mentally ill in Nebraska. *Nebraska Law Review, 48,* 255-271

20. American Bar Foundation (1961,1971). *The Mentally Disabled and the Law.* Chicago:University of Chicago Press

21. Mental Health Law Project (1977). Suggested statute on civil commitment. *Mentally Disability and the Law Reporter, 2,* 127-155

22. Schwitzgabel RK (1978). A survey of state commitment statutes. In AL McGarry (Ed): *Civil Commitment and Social Policy.* Cambridge: Harvard Medical School

23. R.I. Gen. Laws 26-2-3

24. Calif. Welf. and Inst. Code sec 5034

25. Kittre N (1971). *The Right to be Different.* Baltimore:Johns Hopkins University Press

26. Miller K (1976). *Managing Madness.* New York:Free Press

27. Wexler D (1972). Therapeutic justice. *Minnassota Law Review, 57,* 289-361

28. Chambers DL (1972). Alternatives to the civil commitment of the mentally ill: practical guides and constitutional imperative. *Michigan Law Review, 70,* 1108-1200

29. Note. Overt dangerous behavior as a constitutional requirement for civil commitment. *University of Chicago Law Review, 44,* 562-595

30. Morse S (1978). Crazy behavior, morals and science: an analysis of mental health law. *Southern California Law Review, 51,* 521-624

31. Friedman JR & Daly RW (1973). Civil commitment and the doctrine of balance: a critical analysis. *Santa Clara Lawyer, 13*, 503-517
32. Ennis B & Emery R (198?). *The Rights of Mental Patients.* New York:Avon Books, p 198
33. Halleck SL (1971). *The Politics of Therapy.* New York:Science House
34. Greenberg D (1974). Involuntary psychiatric commitments to prevent suicide. *New York University Law Review, 49*, 227-269
35. Borus JF (1981). Deinstitutionalization of the chronically mentally ill. *New England Journal of Medicine, 305*, 339-342
36. Bassuk E & Gerson S (1978). Deinstitutionalization and mental health services. *Scientific American, 288*, 45-53
37. Bachrach L (1977). *Deinstitutionalization: An Amalytical Review and Sociological Perspective.* Rockville, MD:National Institutes of Mental Health
38. General Accounting Office (1977). *The Mentally Ill in the Community.* Washington D.C.:Government Printing Office
39. Joint Commission on Mental Health and Illness (1961). *Action for Mental Health.* New York:Basic Books
40. Solomon HC (1958). The American Psychiatric Association in relation to American psychiatry. *American Journal of Psychiatry, 115*, 1-9
41. *Message from the President of the United States.* February 5, 1963, 88th Congress First Session, Doc. #58
42. Test MA & Stein LI (1978). Community treatment of the chronic patient: research overview. *Schizophrenia Bulletin, 4*, 350-364
43. Braun P, Kochansky G, & Shapiro R (1981). Overview: deinstitution-alization of psychiatripatients, a critical review of outcome studies. *American Journal of Psychiatry, 138*, 736-749
44. Deniker P (1970). The introduction of neuroleptic chemotherapy into psychiatry. In FJ Ayd & P Blackwell (Eds): *Discoveries in Biological Psychiatry.* Philadelphia:J.B. Lippencott, pp. 155-164
45. New York Times, November 18, 1979 pp. 18ff
46. Scull AT (1977). *Decarceration Community and the Deviant.* Englewood Cliffs:Prentice Hall
47. Weisbrod BA & Stein M (1980). Alternatives to mental hospital treatment II: cost benefit analysis. *Archives of General Psychiatry, 37*, 400-405
48. Murphy JG & Datel W (1976). A cost benefit analysis of community vs institutional living. *Hospital and Community Psychiatry, 27*, 165-170
49. May PR (1971). Cost efficiency of treatment for the schizophrenic patient. *American Journal of Psychiatry, 127*, 1382-1385
50. Test MA & Stein LI (1978). Training in community living: research design and results. In MI Test & LI Stein (Eds): *Alternatives to Mental Hospital Treatment.* New York:Plenum, pp. 57-74
51. Fairweather GW (1969). *Community Life for the Mentally Ill.* Chicago: Aldine
52. Stone A (1981). The right to refuse treatment. *Archives of General Psychiatry, 38*, 358-362
53. Brooks AD (1981). The constitutional right to refuse anti-psychotic medications. *Bulletin of the American Academy of Psychiatry and Law, 8*, 179-221

54. Mills MJ (1981). The rights of involuntary patients to refuse pharmco-therapy: what is reasonable. *Bulletin of the American Acadamey of Psychiatry and Law, 8,* 313-333
55. Doudera E & Swazey J (Eds) (1982). *Refusing Treatment in Mental Health Institutions.* Ann Arbor:AUPHA Press
56. Rhoden N (1980). The right to refuse psychotropic drugs. *Harvard Civil-Rights Liberties Law Review, 15,* 363-413
57. Mills MJ, Yesavage J, & Gutheil T (1983). Continuing case law development: the right to refuse treatment. *American Journal of Psychiatry, 140,* 715-719
58. *Rogers v. Okin* 478 F. Supp. 1342 (1980), 634 F. 2d. 650 (1981)
59. *Rennie v. Klein* 462 F. Supp. 1131 (1978), 476 F. Supp. 1294 (1979), 653 F. 2d 836 (1981)
60. *In re K.K.B.* 609 P. 2d. 747 (Kansas, 1981)
61. *In re Guardianship of Richard Roe* 421 N.E. 2d. 40 (Mass. 1982)
62. *Rennie v. Klein* 462 F. Supp. 1131 at 1135.
63. Mill JS (1939). On liberty. In EA Burtt (Ed). *The English Philosophers from Bacon to Mill.* New York:Random House, p. 955-956
64. Kant (1964). *The Doctrine of Virtue* (trans. M. Gregor). New York: Harper, p 122
65. Childress J (1982). *Who Should Decide: Paternalism in Health Care.* New York:Oxford University Press
66. Krapelin E (1921). *Manic Depressive Insanity and Paranoia* (Trans. M. Barclay). Edinburgh:E. and G. Livingstone
67. Cohen RM, Smalberg S, & Weingarther A (1982). Effort and cognition in depression. *Archives of General Psychiatry, 39,* 593-597
68. Moore M (1975). Some myths about mental illness. *Archives of General Psychiatry, 32,* 1483-1497
69. Goffman E (1961). *Asylums.* Garden City:Doubleday
70. Scheff T (1966). *Being Mentally Ill.* Chicago:Aldine
71. Scheff T (1974). The labelling theory of mental illness. *Amererican Sociology Review, 39,* 444-452
72. Gove W (1975). Labelling and mental illness. In W Gove (Ed): *The Labelling of Deviance.* New York:Wiley and Sons, pp. 35-81
73. Schrag P (1978). *Mind Control.* New York:Pantheon Books
74. Szaz T (1974). *The Myth of Mental Illness.* New York:Harper and Row, 2nd. ed
75. Szaz T (1976):*Schizophrenia: Sacred Symbol of Psychiatry.* New York: Basic Books
76. Becker E (1964). *Revolution in Psychiatry.* New York:The Free Press
77. Laing RD (1960). *The Divided Self.* London:Tavistock
78. Laing RD (1964). *Sanity, Madness and the Family.* London:Tavistock
79. Collier A & Laing RD (1977). *The Philosophy and Politics of Psychotherapy.* New York:Pantheon Books
80. Braginsky BM, Braginsky DD, & Ring K (1969). *Methods of Madness: The Mental Hospital as a Last Resort.* New York:Hold, Reinhart and Winston
81. Comments (1974). Developments in the law of civil commitment. *Harvard Law Review, 87,* 1190-1406

82. Rosehan DN (1973). On being sane in insane places. *Science, 179,* 250-258
83. Feinberg J (1974). Legal paternalism. *Canadian Journal of Philosophy, l,* 113-116
84. Roth R & Dayley M (1973). Into the abyss: psychiatry reliability and emergency commitment statutes. *Santa Clara Lawyer, 13,* 400-446
85. Ennis B & Litwack L (1974). Psychiatry and the presumption of expertise: flipping coins in the courtroom. *California Law Review, 64,* 693-752
86. Hardesty JH (1973). Mental illness: a legal fiction. *Washington Law Review, 48,* 732-766
87. Kaplan L (1969). Civil commitment: as you like it. *Boston University Law Review, 49,* 14-45
88. Note (1972). Conditioning and other technologies used to treat?, rehabilitate?, or demolish? prisoners and mental patients. *California Law Review, 45,* 616-658
89. Plotkin R (1977). Limiting the therapeutic orgy. *Northwestern Law Review, 72,* 461-503
90. Ennis B (1972). *Prisoners of Psychiatry.* New York:Harcourt, Brace and World
91. Livermore J, Malmquist C, & Meehl P (1968). On the justifications for civil commitment. *University of Pennsylvania Law Review, 117,* 80
92. *In re K.K.B.* 609 P 2d 747 at 748
93. Bartol C (1981). Parens patrie: poltergeist of mental health law. *Law and Policy Quarterly, 4,* 191-207
94. Dershowitz A (1970). The law of dangerousness: some fictions aboud predictions. *Journal of Legal Education, 23,* 24-56
95. Cocozza J & Steadman H (1976). The failure of psychiatric predictions of dangerousness. *Rutgers Law Review, 29,* 1048-1117
96. Monahan J (1981). *The Clinical Prediction of Violent Behavior.* Washington D.C.: Government Printing Office
97. Frederick C (Ed) (1978). *Dangerous Behavior: A Problem in Law and Mental Health.* Washington D.C.: Government Printing Office
98. Rothman D (1973). Decarcerating prisoners and patients. *Civil Liberty Review, 1,* 8-30
99. Schwartz BM (1974). In the name of treatment: autonomy, civil commitment and the right to refuse treatment. *Notre Dame Lawyer, 50,* 808-842
100. Sartorius R (1979). Paternalistic grounds for involuntary civil commitment: a utilitarian view. In T Englehardt & B Brody (Eds): *Mental Illness: Law and Public Policy.* Boston:D. Reidel, pp. 137-145
101. *Donaldson v. O'Connor* 422 U.S. 563 (1975)
102. *Lessard v. Schmidt* 349 F. Supp 1078
103. Menninger W (1948). *Psychiatry in a Troubled World.* New York: Macmillan
104. Charles Culver C & Gert B (1982). *Philosophy in Medicine.* New York Oxford University Press
105. Margolis J (1976). The concept of disease. *Journal of Medicine and Philosophy, 1,* 233-255
106. Boorse C (1975). On the distinction between disease and illness. *Philosophy and Public Affairs, 5,* 49-68
107. Mendlesson M (1979). *Psychoanalytic Concepts of Depression.* New York:Spectrum

108. Brown P (Ed) (1973). *Radical Psychology*. New York:Harper and Row
109. Caplan G (1964). *Principles of Preventive Psychiatry*. New York:Basic Books
110. Bellak L (1964). *Handbook of Community Psychiatry and Community Mental Health*. New York:Grune & Stratton
111. Hunt R (1959). Ingredients of a successful rehabilitation program. In *An Approach to the Prevention of Disability from Chronic Psychosis*. New York:Milbank Memorial Fund
112. Klein D (1980). Psychosocial treatment of chizophrenia or psychosocial help for people with schizophrenia. *Schizophrenia Bulletin, 6*, 122-130
113. Rogers CR, Gendlin E, & Keisler D (1967). *The Therapeutic Relationship and Its Impact: A study of Psychotherapy with Schizophrenics*. Madison: University of Wisconsin Press
114. Grinspoon LS, Ewalt J, & Schader R (1972). *Schizophrenia: Psychotherapy, Pharmacotherapy*. Baltimore:Williams and Wilkins
115. May PR (1968). *Treatment of Schizophrenia: A Comparative Study of Five Treatment Methods*. New York:Science House
116. American Psychiatric Association. *Diagnostic and Statistical Manual*. Washington, D.C. 1st ed. 1952, 2nd, ed. 1968
117. Beck A, Ward C, & Mendelsohn M (1962). Reliability of psychiatric diagnosis. *American Journal of Psychiatry, 49*, 351-355
118. Spitzer RL & Fleiss J (1974). A Re-analysis of the reliability of psychiatric diagnosis. *British Journal of Psychiatry, 125*, 341-347
119. Helzer JE, Clayton P, & Pambakian R (1977). Reliability of psychiatric diagnosis. *Archives of General Psychiatry, 34*, 136-141
120. Kety S, Wender P, & Rosenthal D (1971). Mental illness in the biological and adoptive families of schizophrenics. *American Journal of Psychiatry, 128*, 302-306
121. Wender P, Kety S, & Rosenthal D (1968). A psychiatric assessment of the parents of schizophrenics. In D Rosenthal & S Kety (Eds): *The Transmission of Schizophrenia*. Oxford:Pergammon Press
122. Mendlewicz J & Ranier JD (1977). Adoption study supporting genetic transmission in depressive illness. *Nature, 268*, 327-329
123. American Psychiatric Association (1980). *Diagnostic and Statistical Manual*. Wash. D.C., 3rd ed. pp. 467-472
124. Carroll BG, Greden J, & Feinberg M (1981). A specific lab test for the diagnosis of melancholia. *Archives of General Psychiatry, 38*, 15-22.
125. Baldessarini R (1977). *Chemotherapy in Psychiatry*. Cambridge:Harvard University Press
126. Kalinowsky L (1975). The convulsive therapies. In D Freeman, *et al.* (Eds): *Comprehensive Textbook of Psychiatry*. Baltimore:Williams and Wilkens
127. Scull A (1981). A new trade in lunacy: recommodification of the mental patient. *American Behavioral Scientist, 25*, 751-754
128. Reich W (1973). Care of the chronically mentally ill: a national disgrace. *American Journal of Psychiatry, 130*, 751-754
129. Applebaum PS & Gutheil TS (1980). Drug refusal: a study of psychiatric inpatients. *American Journal of Psychiatry, 137*, 340-346
130. Morse S (1982). A preference for liberty. In C Warren : *The Court of Last Resort*. Chicago:University of Chicago Press, pp. 69-109
131. *Wyatt v. Stickney* 344 F. Supp 373 (1973)
132. Talbott J (1978). *The Death of the Assylum*. New York:Grune & Stratton

133. Kirk S &Thierren ME (1975). Community health myths and the fate of former hospitalized patients. *Psychiatry, 38,* 209-217
134. Roth L (1979). A commitment law for patients, doctors and lawyers. *American Journal of Psychiatry, 136,* 1121-1127
135. Rachlin S, Pam A, & Milton J (1975). Civil liberties versus involuntary hospitalization. *American Journal of Psychiatry, 132,* 189-192
136. Brock D (1981). Involuntary civil commitment: the moral issues. In T Englehardt & B Brody (Eds): *Mental Illness: Law and Public Policy.* Boston:D. Reidel, pp. 147-173
137. Applebaum P & Gutheil T (1979). Rotting with their rights on: constitutional theory and clinical reality in drug refusal by psychiatric patients. *Bulletin of American Acadamy of Psychiatry and Law, 7,* 306-321
138. Chododoff P (1976). The case for involuntary hospitalization of the mentally ill. *American Journal of Psychiatry, 133,* 496-501
139. Applebaum P, *et al.* (1981). Empirical assessment of competency to consent to hospitalization. *American Journal of Psychiatry, 138,* 1170-1176
140. Roth L, Meisel A, & Lidz C (1977). Tests of competency to consent to treatment. *American Journal of Psychiatry, 134,* 180-185
141. Sherlock R (1983). Competency to consent to medical care.*General Hospital Psychiatry, 5,* 85-91
142. Roth L, Appelbaum P, & Sallee R (1982). The dilemma of denial in the assessment of competency to consent. *American Journal of Psychiatry, 139,* 910-913
143. Faden R (1977). False belief and the refusal of medical treatment. *Journal of Medical Ethics, 3,* 133-136
144. Stone A & Stromberg C (1983). A model state statue on civil commitment of the mentally ill. *Harvard Journal of Legis., 20,* 275-396

DISCUSSION QUESTIONS

1. What was deinstitutionalization and what assumptions was it based upon?

2. Discuss Thomas Szaz's assumptions about the nature of mental illness.

3. When did John Mill believe individuals do not have a primary right to live as they please?

4. What does the commitment law in your state establish as criteria for involuntary psychiatric treatment and hospitalization?

5. What is the effect of shifting the reason for commitment from mental illness to dangerousness?

6. Describe why absolute freedom may not be the greatest good for a chronically mentally ill person.

7. Discuss the issues involved in giving informed consent to take medications if your client is involuntarily hospitalized.

8. If a client is committed to your hospital for care, who are you responsible to for his or her care? What is the client-therapist relationship?

9. A relative calls you to tell you your client is behaving in a physically threatening manner. The relative is afraid and wants you to do something. Discuss your ethical responsibilities to the client and others.

10. Discuss the ethical considerations of being "my brother's keeper."

APPENDIX

A PATIENT'S BILL OF RIGHTS: AMERICAN HOSPITAL ASSOCIATION

The American Hospital Association presents a Patient's Bill of Rights with the expectation that observance of these rights will contribute to more effective patient care and greater satisfaction for the patient, his physician and the hospital organization. Further, the Association presents these rights in the expectation that they will be supported by the hospital on behalf of its patients, as an integral part of the healing process. It is recognized that a personal relationship between the physician and the patient is essential for the provision of proper medical care. The traditional physician-patient relationship takes on a new dimension when care is rendered within an organizational structure. Legal precedent has established that the institution itself also has a responsiblility to the patient. It is in recognition of these factors that these rights are affirmed.

1.   The patient has the right to considerate and respectful care.

2.   The patient has the right to obtain from his physician complete current information concerning his diagnosis, treatment, and prognosis in terms the patient can be reasonably expected to understand. When it is not medically advisable to give such information to the patient, the information should be made available to an appropriate person in his behalf. He has the right to know by name, the physician responsible for coordinating his care.

3.   The patient has the right to receive from his physician information necessary to give informed consent prior to the start of any procedure and/or treatment. Except in emergencies, such information for informed consent, should include but not necessarily be limited to the specific procedure and/or treatment, the medically significant risks involved, and the probable duration of incapacitation. Where medically significant alternatives for care or treatment exist, or when the patient requests information concerning medical alternatives, the patient has the right to such information. The patient also has the right to know the name of the person responsible for the procedures and/or treatment.

4.   The patient has the right to refuse treatment to the extent permitted by law, and to be informed of the medical consequences of his action.

5.   The patient has the right to every consideration of his privacy concerning his own medical care program. Case discussion, consultation, examination, and treatment are confidential and should be conducted discreetly. Those not directly involved in his care must have the permission of the patient to be present.

6.   The patient has the right to expect that all communications and records pertaining to his care should be treated as confidential.

7.   The patient has the right to expect that within its capacity a hospital must make reasonable response to the request of a patient for services. The hospital must provide evaluation, service, and/or referral as indicated by the urgency of the case. When medically permissible a patient may be transferred to another facility only after he has received complete information and explanation concerning the needs for and alternatives to such a transfer. The institution to which the patient is to be transferred must first have accepted the patient for transfer.

8. The patient has the right to obtain information as to any relationship of his hospital to other health care and educational institutions insofar as his care is concerned. The patient has the right to obtain information as to the existence of any professional relationships among individuals, by name, who are treating him.

9. The patient has the right to be advised if the hospital proposes to engage in or perform human experimentation affecting his care or treatment. The patient has the right to refuse to participate in such research projects.

10. The patient has the right to expect reasonable continuity of care. He has the right to know in advance what appointment times and physicians are available and where. The patient has the right to expect that the hospital will provide a mechanism whereby he is informed by his physician or a delegate of the physician of the patient's continuing health care requirements following discharge.

11. The patient has the right to examine and receive an explanation of his bill regardless of source of payment.

12. The patient has the right to know what hospital rules and regulations apply to his conduct as a patient.

No catalogue of rights can guarantee for the patient the kind of treatment he has a right to expect. A hospital has many functions to perform, including the prevention and treatment of disease, the education of both health professionals and patients, and the conduct of clinical research. All these activities must be conducted with an overriding concern for the patient, and, above all, the recognition of his dignity as a human being. Success in achieving this recognition assures success in the defense of the rights of the patient.

AMERICAN MEDICAL ASSOCIATION

PRINCIPLES OF
MEDICAL ETHICS

Preamble:

The medical profession has long subscribed to a body of ethical statements developed primarily for the benefit of the patient. As a member of this profession, a physician must recognize responsibility not only to patients, but also to society, to other health professionals, and to self. The following Principles adopted by the American Medical Association are not laws, but standards of conduct which define the essentials of honorable behavior for the physician.

I.   A physician shall be dedicated to providing competent medical service with compassion and respect for human dignity.

II.   A physician shall deal honestly with patients and colleagues, and strive to expose those physicians deficient in character or competence, or who engage in fraud or deception.

III.   A physician shall respect the law and also recognize a responsiblity to seek changes in those requirements which are contrary to the best interests of the patient.

IV.   A physician shall respect the rights of patients, of colleagues, and of other health professionals, and shall safeguard patient confidences within the constraints of the law.

V.   A physician shall continue to study, apply and advance scientific knowledge, make relevant information available to patients, colleagues, and the public, obtain consultation, and use the talents of other health professionals when indicated.

VI.   A physician shall, in the provision of appropriate patient care, except in emergencies, be free to choose whom to serve, with whom to associate, and the environment in which to provide medical services.

VII. A physician shall recognize a responsibility to participate in activities contributing to an improved community.

(Reprinted with the permission of the American Medical Association. Copyright 1980.)

The Principles of Medical Ethics
With Annotations Especially
Applicable to Psychiatry

Principles with Annotations

Following are each of the AMA Principles of Medical Ethics printed separately along with annotations especially applicable to psychiatry.

PREAMBLE

The medical profession has long subscribed to a body of ethical statements developed primarily for the benefit of the patient. As a member of this profession, a physician must recognize responsibility not only to patients, but also to society, to other health professionals, and to self. The following Principles, adopted by the American Medical Association, are not laws, but standards of conduct which define the essentials of honorable behavior for the physican.

SECTION 1

A physician shall be dedicated to providing competent medical service with compassion and respect for human dignity.

1. The patient may place his/her trust in his/her psychiatrist knowing that the psychiatrist's ethics and professional responsibilities preclude him/her gratifying his/her own needs by exploiting the patient. This becomes particularly important because of the essentially private, highly personal, and sometimes intensely emotional nature of the relationship established with the psychiatrist.

2. A psychiatrist should not be a party to any type of policy that excludes, segregates, or demeans the dignity of any patient because of ethnic origin, race, sex, creed, age, socioeconomic status, or sexual orientation.

3. In accord with the requirements of law and accepted medical practice, it is ethical for a physician to submit his/her work to peer review and to the ultimate authority of the medical staff executive body and the hospital administration and its governing body. In case of dispute, the ethical psychiatrist has the following steps available:

    a. Seek appeal from the medical staff decision to a joint conference committee, including members of the medical staff executive committee and the executive committee of the governing board. At this appeal, the ethical psychiatrist could request that outside opinions be considered.

    b. Appeal to the governing body itself.

    c. Appeal to state agencies regulating licensure of hospitals if, in the particular state, they concern themselves with matters of professional competency and quality of care.

d.   Attempt to educate colleagues through development of research projects and data and presentations at professional meetings and in professional journals.

e.   Seek redress in local courts, perhaps through an enjoining injuction against the governing body.

f.   Public education as carried out by an ethical psychiatrist would be presented in a professional way and without any potential exploitation of patients through testimonials.

4.   A psychiatrist should not be a participant in a legally authorized execution.

SECTION 2

A physician shall deal honestly with patients and colleagues, and strive to expose those physicians deficient in character or competence, or who engage in fraud or deception.

1.   The requirement that the physician conduct himself with propriety in his/her profession and in all the actions of his/her life is especially important in the case of the psychiatrist because the patient tends to model his/her behavior after that of his/her therapist by identification. Further, the necessary intensity of the therapeutic relationship may tend to activate sexual and other needs and fantasies on the part of both patient and therapist, while weakening the objectivity necessary for control. Sexual activity with a patient is unethical.

2.   The psychiatrist should diligently guard against exploiting information furnished by the patient and should not use the unique position of power afforded him/her by the psychotherapeutic situation to influence the patient in any way not directly relevant to the treatment goals.

3.   A psychiatrist who regularly practices outside his/her area of professional competence should be considered unethical. Determination of professional competence should be made by peer review boards or other appropriate bodies.

4.   Special consideration should be given to those psychiatrists who, because of mental illness, jeopardize the welfare of their patients and their own reputations and practices. It is ethical, even encouraged, for another psychiatrist to intercede in such situations.

5.   Psychiatric services, like all medical services, are dispensed in the context of a contractual arrangement between the patient and the treating physician. The provisions of the contractual arrangement, which are binding on the physician as well as the patient, should be explicitly established.

6.   It is ethical for the psychiatrist to make a charge for a missed appointment when this falls within the terms of the specific contractual agreement with the patient. Charging for a missed appointment or for one not cancelled 24 hours in advance need not, in itself, be considered unethical if a patient is fully advised that the physician will make such a charge. The practice, however, should be resorted to infrequently and always with the utmost consideration for the patient and his/her circumstances.

7.   An arrangement in which a psychiatrist provides supervision or administration to other physicians or nonmedical persons for a percentage of their fees or gross income is not acceptable; this would constitute fee-splitting. In a team of practitioners, or a multidisciplinary team, it is ethical for the psychiatrist to receive income for administration, research, education, or consultation. This should be based upon a mutually agreed upon and set fee or salary, open to renegotiation

when a change in the time demand occurs. (See also Section 5, Annotations 2, 3, and 4.)

8.   When a member has been found to have behaved unethically by the American Psychiatric Association or one of its constituent district branches, there should not be automatic reporting to the local authorities responsible for medical licensure, but the decision to report should be decided upon the merits of the case.

SECTION 3

A physician shall respect the law and also recognize a responsibility to seek changes in those requirements which are contrary to the best interests of the patient.

1.   It would seem self-evident that a psychiatrist who is a law-breaker might be ethically unsuited to practice his/her profession. When such illegal activities bear directly upon his/her practice, this would obviously be the case. However, in other instances, illegal activities such as those concerning the right to protest social injustices might not bear on either the image of the psychiatrist or the ability of the specific psychiatrist to treat his/her patient ethically and well. While no committee or board could offer prior assurance that any illegal activity would not be considered unethical, it is conceivable that an individual could violate a law without being guilty of professionally unethical behavior. Physicians lose no right of citizenship on entry into the profession of medicine.

2.   Where not specifically prohibited by local laws governing medical practice, the practice of acupuncture by a psychiatrist is not unethical per se. The psychiatrist should have professional competence in the use of acupuncture. Or, if he/she is supervising the use of acupuncture by nonmedical individuals, he/she should provide proper medical supervision. (See also Section 5, Annotations 3 and 4.)

SECTION 4

A physician shall respect the rights of patients, of colleagues, and of other health professionals, and shall safeguard patient confidences within the constraints of the law.

1.   Psychiatric records, including even the identification of a person as a patient, must be protected with extreme care. Confidentiality is essential to psychiatric treatment. This is based in part on the special nature of psychiatric therapy as well as on the traditional ethical relationship between physician and patient. Growing concern regarding the civil rights of patients and the possible adverse effects of computerization, duplication equipment, and data banks makes the dissemination of confidential information an increasing hazard. Because of the sensitive and private nature of the information with which the psychiatrist deals, he/she must be circumspect in the information that he/she chooses to disclose to others about a patient. The welfare of the patient must be a continuing consideration.

2.   A psychiatrist may release confidential information only with the authorization of the patient or under proper legal compulsion. The continuing duty of the psychiatrist to protect the patient includes fully apprising him/her of the con-

notations of waiving the privilege of privacy. This may become an issue when the patient is being investigated by a government agency, is applying for a position, or is involved in legal action. The same principles apply to the release of information concerning treatment to medical departments of government agencies, business organizations, labor unions, and insurance companies. Information gained in confidence about patients seen in student health services should not be released without the student's explicit permission.

3.   Clinical and other materials used in teaching and writing must be adequately disguised in order to preserve the anonymity of the individuals involved.

4.   The ethical responsibility of maintaining confidentiality holds equally for the consultations in which the patient may not have been present and in which the consultee was not a physician. In such instances, the physician consultant should alert the consultee to his/her duty of confidentiality.

5.   Ethically the psychiatrist may disclose only that information which is relevant to a given situation. He/she should avoid offering speculation as fact. Sensitive information such as an individual's sexual orientation or fantasy material is usually unnecessary.

6.   Psychiatrists are often asked to examine individuals for security purposes, to determine suitability for various jobs, and to determine legal competence. The psychiatrist must fully describe the nature and purpose and lack of confidentiality of the examination to the examinee at the beginning of the examination.

7.   Careful judgement must be exercised by the psychiatrist in order to include, when appropriate, the parents or guardian in the treatment of a minor. At the same time the psychiatrist must assure the minor proper confidentiality.

8.   Psychiatrists at times may find it necessary, in order to protect the patient or the community from imminent danger, to reveal confidential information disclosed by the patient.

9.   When the psychiatrist is ordered by the court to reveal the confidences entrusted to him/her by patients he/she may comply or he/she may ethically hold the right to dissent within the framework of the law. When the psychiatrist is in doubt, the right of the patient to confidentiality and, by extension, to unimpaired treatment, should be given priority. The psychiatrist should reserve the right to raise the question of adequate need for disclosure. In the event that the necessity for legal disclosure is demonstrated by the court, the psychiatrist may request the right to disclosure of only that information which is relevant to the legal question at hand.

10.   With regard for the person's dignity and privacy and with truly informed consent, it is ethical to present a patient to a scientific gathering, if the confidentiality of the presentation is understood and accepted by the audience.

11.   It is ethical to present a patient or former patient to a public gathering or to the news media only if the patient is fully informed of enduring loss of confidentiality, is competent, and consents in writing without coercion.

12.   When involved in funded research, the ethical psychiatrist will advise human subjects of the funding source, retain his/her freedom to reveal data and results, and follow all appropriate and current guidelines relative to human subject protection.

13.   Ethical considerations in medical practice preclude the psychiatric evaluation of any adult charged with criminal acts prior to access to, or availability of, legal counsel. The only exception is the rendering of care to the person for the sole purpose of medical treatment.

SECTION 5

A physician shall continue to study, apply, and advance scientific knowledge, make relevant information available to patients, colleagues, and the public, obtain consultation, and use the talents of other health professionals when indicated.

1.   Psychiatrists are responsible for their own continuing education and should be mindful of the fact that theirs must be a lifetime of learning.

2.   In the practice of his/her specialty, the psychiatrist consults, associates, collaborates, or integrates his/her work with that of many professional, including psychologists, psychometricians, social workers, alcoholism counselors, marriage counselors, public health nurses, etc. Furthermore, the nature of modern psychiatric practice extends his/her contacts to such people as teachers, juvenile and adult probation officers, attorneys, welfare workers, agency volunteers, and neighborhood aides. In referring patients for treatment, counseling, or rehabilitation to any of these practitioners, the psychiatrist should ensure that the allied professional or paraprofessional with whom he/she is dealing is a recognized member of his/her own discipline and is competent to carry out the therapeutic task required. The psychiatrist should have the same attitude toward members of the medical profession to whom he/she refers patients. Whenever he/she has reason to doubt the training, skill, or ethical qualifications of the allied professional, the psychiatrist should not refer cases to him/her.

3.   When the psychiatrist assumes a collaborative or supervisory role with another mental health worker, he/she must expend sufficient time to assure that proper care is given. It is contrary to the interests of the patient and to patient care if he/she allows himself/herself to be used as a figurehead.

4.   In relationships between psychiatrists and practicing licensed psychologists, the physician should not delegate to the psychologist or, in fact, to any nonmedical person any matter requiring the exercise of professional medical judgment.

5.   The psychiatrist should agree to the request of a patient for consultation or to such a request from the family of an incompetent or minor patient. The psychiatrist may suggest possible consultants, but the patient or family should be given free choice of the consultant. If the psychiatrist disapproves of the professional qualifications of the consultant or if there is a difference of opinion that the primary therapist cannot resolve, he/she may, after suitable notice, withdraw from the case. If this disagreement occurs within an institution or agency framework, the differences should be resolved by the mediation or arbitration of higher professional authority within the institution or agency.

SECTION 6

A physican shall, in the provision of appropriate patient care, except in emergencies, be free to choose whom to serve, with whom to associate, and the environment in which to provide medical services.

1.   Physicians generally agree that the doctor-patient relationship is such a vital factor in effective treatment of the patient that preservation of optimal conditions for development of a sound working relationship between a doctor and his/her patient should take precedence over all other considerations. Professional courtesy may lead to poor psychiatric care for physicians and their families because of embarrassment over the lack of a complete give-and-take contract.

2.   An ethical psychiatrist may refuse to provide psychiatric treatment to a person who, in the psychiatrist's opinion, cannot be diagnosed as having a mental illness amenable to psychiatric treatment.

SECTION 7

A physician shall recognize a responsibility to participate in activities contributing to an improved community.

1.   Psychiatrists should foster the cooperation of those legitmately concerned with the medical, psychological, social, and legal aspects of mental health and illness. Psychiatrists are encouraged to serve society by advising and consulting with the executive, legislative, and judiciary branches of the government. A psychiatrist should clarify whether he/she speaks as an individual or as a representative of an organization. Furthermore, psychiatrists should avoid cloaking their public statements with the authority of the profession (e.g., "Psychiatrists know that . . .").
2.   Psychiatrists may interpret and share with the public their expertise in the various psychosocial issues that may affect mental health and illness. Psychiatrists should always be mindful of their separate roles as dedicated citizens and as experts in psychological medicine.
3.   On occasion psychiatrists are asked for an opinion about an individual who is in the light of public attention, or who has disclosed information about himself/ herself through public media. It is unethical for a psychiatrist to offer a professional opinion unless he/she has conducted an examination and has been granted proper authorization for such a statement.
4.   The psychiatrist may permit his/her certification to be used for the involuntary treatment of any person only following his/her personal examination of that person. To do so, he/she must find that the person, because of mental illness, cannot form a judgment as to what is in his/her own best interests and that, without such treatment, substantial impairment is likely to occur to the person or others.

(Reprinted with the permission of the American Psychiatric Association and the American Medical Association. Copyright 1981.)

Ethical Principles of Psychologists

PREAMBLE

Psychologists respect the dignity and worth of the individual and strive for the preservation and protection of fundamental human rights. They are committed to increasing knowledge of human behavior and of people's understanding of themselves and others and to the utilization of such knowledge for the promotion of human welfare. While pursuing these objectives, they make every effort to protect the welfare of those who seek their services and of the research participants that may be the object of study. They use their skills only for purposes consistent with these values and do not knowingly permit their misuse by others. While demanding for themselves freedom of inquiry and communication, psychologists accept the responsibility this freedom requires: competence, objectivity in the application of skills, and concern for the best interests of clients, colleagues, students, research participants, and society. In the pursuit of these ideals, psychologists subscribe to principles in the following areas: 1. Responsibility, 2. Competence, 3. Moral and Legal Standards, 4. Public Statements, 5. Confidentiality, 6. Welfare of the Consumer, 7. Professional Relationships, 8. Assessment Techniques, 9. Research With Human Participants, and 10. Care and Use of Animals.

Acceptance of membership in the American Psychological Association commits the member to adherence to these principles.

Psychologists cooperate with duly constituted committees of the American Psychological Association, in particular, the Committee on Scientific and Professional Ethics and Conduct, by responding to inquiries promptly and completely. Members also respond promptly and completely to inquiries from duly constituted state association ethics committees and professional standards review committees.

Principle 1
RESPONSIBILITY

In providing services, psychologists maintain the highest standards of their profession. They accept responsibility for the consequences of their acts and make every effort to ensure that their services are used appropriately.

a. As scientists, psychologists accept responsibility for the selection of their research topics and the methods used in investigation, analysis and reporting. They plan their research in ways to minimize the possibility that their findings will be misleading. They provide thorough discussion of the limitations of their data, especially where their work touches on social policy or might be construed to the detriment of persons in specific age, sex, ethnic, socioeconomic, or social groups. In publishing reports of their work, they never suppress disconfirming data, and they acknowledge the existence of alternative hypotheses and explanations of their finding. Psychologists take credit only for work they have actually done.

222

b. Psychologists clarify in advance with all appropriate persons and agencies the expectations for sharing and utilizing research data. They avoid relationships that may limit their objectivity or create a conflict of interest. Interference with the milieu in which data are collected is kept to a mininum.

c. Psychologists have the responsibility to attempt to prevent distortion, misuse, or suppression of psychological findings by the institution or agency of which they are employees.

d. As members of governmental or other organizational bodies, psychologists remain accountable as individuals to the highest standards of their profession.

e. As teachers, psychologists recognize their primary obligation to help others acquire knowledge and skill. They maintain high standards of scholarship by presenting psychological information objectively, fully, and accurately.

f. As practitioners, psychologists know that they bear a heavy social responsibility because their recommendations and professional actions may alter the lives of others. They are alert to personal, social, organizational, financial, or political situations and pressures that might lead to misuse of their influence.

Principle 2
COMPETENCE

The maintenance of high standards of competence is a responsibility shared by all psychologists in the interest of the public and the profession as a whole. Psychologists recognize the boundaries of their competence and the limitations of their techniques. They only provide services and only use techniques for which they are qualified by training and experience. In those areas in which recognized standards do not yet exist, psychologists take whatever precautions are necessary to protect the welfare of their clients. They maintain knowledge of current scientific and and professional information related to the services they render.

a. Psychologists accurately represent their competence, education, training, and experience. They claim as evidence of educational qualifications only those degrees obtained from institutions acceptable under the Bylaws and Rules of Council of the American Psychological Association.

b. As teachers, psychologists perform their duties on the basis of careful preparation so that their instruction is accurate, current, and scholarly.

c. Psychologists recognize the need for continuing education and are open to new procedures and changes in expectations and values over time.

d. Psychologists recognize differences among people, such as those that may be associated with age, sex, socioeconomic, and ethnic backgrounds. When necessary, they obtain training, experience, or counsel to assure competent service or research relating to such persons.

e. Psychologists responsible for decisions involving individuals or policies based on test results have an understanding of psychological or educational measurement, validation problems, and test research.

f. Psychologists recognize that personal problems and conflicts may interfere with professional effectiveness. Accordingly, they refrain from undertaking any activity in which their personal problems are likely to lead to inadequate performance or harm to a client, colleague, student, or research participant. If engaged in such activity when they become aware of their personal problems, they seek competent professional assistance to determine whether they should suspend, terminate, or limit the scope of their professional and/or scientific activities.

Principle 3
MORAL AND LEGAL STANDARDS

Psychologists' moral and ethical standards of behavior are a personal matter to the same degree as they are for any other citizen, except as these may compromise the fulfillment of their professional responsibilities or reduce the public trust in psychology and psychologists. Regarding their own behavior, psychologists are sensitive to prevailing community standards and to the possible impact that conformity to or deviation from these standards may have upon the quality of their performance as psychologists. Psychologists are also aware of the possible impact of their public behavior upon the ability of colleagues to perform their professional duties.

a. As teachers, psychologists are aware of the fact that their personal values may affect the selection and presentation of instructional material. When dealing with topics that may give offense, they recognize and respect the diverse attitudes that students may have toward such materials.

b. As employees or employers, psychologists do not engage in or condone practices that are inhumane or that result in illegal or unjustifiable actions. Such practices include, but are not limited to, those based on considerations of race, handicap, age, gender, sexual preference, religion, or national origin in hiring, promotion, or training.

c. In their professional roles, psychologists avoid any action that will violate or diminish the legal and civil rights of clients or of others who may be affected by their actions.

d. As practitioners and researchers, psychologists act in accord with Association standards and guidelines related to practice and to the conduct of research with human beings and animals. In the ordinary course of events, psychologists adhere to relevant governmental laws and institutional regulation. When federal, state, provincial, organizational, or institutional laws, regulations, or practices are in conflict with Association standards and guidelines, psychologists make known their commitment to Association standards and guidelines and, wherever possible, work toward a resolution of the conflict. Both practitioners and researchers are concerned with the development of such legal and quasi-legal regulations as best serve the public interest, and they work toward changing existing regulations that are not beneficial to the public interest.

Principle 4
PUBLIC STATEMENTS

Public statements, announcements of services, advertising, and promotional activities of psychologists serve the purpose of helping the public make informed judgments and choices. Psychologists represent accurately and objectively their professional qualifications, affiliations, and functions, as well as those of the institutions or organizations with which they or the statements may be associated. In public statements providing psychological information or professional opinions or providing information about the availability of psychological products, publications, and services, psychologists base their statements on scientifically acceptable psychological findings and techniques with full recognition of the limits and uncertainties of such evidence.

a. When announcing or advertising professional services, psychologists may list the following information to describe the provider and services provided: name, highest relevant academic degree earned from a regionally accredited institution, date, type, and level of certification or licensure, diplomate status, APA membership status, address, telephone number, office hours, a brief listing of the type of psychological services offered, an appropriate presentation of fee information, foreign languages spoken, and policy with regard to third-party payments. Additional relevant or important consumer information may be included if not prohibited by other sections of these Ethical Principles.

b. In announcing or advertising the availability of psychological products, publications, or services, psychologists do not present their affiliation with any organization in a manner that falsely implies sponsorship or certification by that organization. In particular and for example, psychologists do not state APA membership or fellow status in a way to suggest that such status implies specialized professional competence or qulifications. Public statements include, but are not limited to, communication by means of periodical, book, list, directory, television, radio, or motion picture. They do not contain (i) a false, fraudulent, misleading, deceptive, or unfair statement; (ii) a misinterpretation of fact or a statement likely to mislead or deceive because in context it makes only a partial disclosure of relevant facts; (iii) a testimonial from a patient regarding the quality of a psychologists' services or products; (iv) a statement intended or likely to create false or unjustified expectations of favorable results; (v) a statement implying unusual, unique, or one-of-a-kind abilities; (vi) a statement intended or likely to appeal to a client's fears, anxieties, or emotions concerning the possible results of failure to obtain the offered services; (vii) a statement concerning the comparative desirability of offerd services; (viii) a statement of direct solicitation of individual clients.

c. Psychologists do not compensate or give anything of value to a representative of the press, radio, television, or other communication medium in anticipation of or in return for professional publicity in a news item. A paid advertisement must be identified as such, unless it is apparent from the context that it is a paid advertisement. If communicated to the public by use of radio or television, an advertisement is prerecorded and approved for broadcast by the psychologist, and a recording of the actual transmission is retained by the psychologist.

d. Announcements or advertisements of "personal growth groups," clinics, and agencies give a clear statement of purpose and a clear description of the experiences to be provided. The education, training, and experience of the staff members are appropriately specified.

e. Psychologists associated with the development or promotion of psychological devices, books, or other products offered for commercial sale make reasonable efforts to ensure that announcements and advertisements are presented in a professional, scientifically acceptable, and factually informative manner.

f. Psychologists do not participate for personal gain in commercial announcements or advertisements recommending to the public the purchase or use of proprietary or single-source products or services when that participation is based solely upon their identification as psychologists.

g. Psychologists present the science of psychology and offer their services, products, and publications fairly and accurately, avoiding misrepresentation through sensationalism, exaggeration, or superficiality. Psychologists are guided by the primary obligation to aid the public in developing informed judgments, opinions, and choices.

h. As teachers, psychologists ensure that statements in catalogs and course outlines are accurate and not misleading, particularly in terms of subject matter to be covered, bases for evaluating progress, and the nature of course experiences. Announcements, brochures, or advertisements describing workshops, seminars, or other educational programs accurately describe the audience for which the program in intended as well as eligibility requirements, educational objectives, and nature of the materials to be covered. These announcements also accurately represent the education, training, and experience of the psychologists presenting the programs and any fees involved.

i. Public announcements or advertisements soliciting research participants in which clinical services or other professional services are offered as an inducement make clear the nature of the services as well as the costs and other obligations to be accepted by participants in the research.

j. A psychologist accepts the obligation to correct others who represent the psychologist's professional qualifications, or associations with products or services, in a manner incompatible with these guidelines.

k. Individual diagnostic and therapeutic services are provided only in the context of a professional psychological relationship. When personal advice is given by means of public lectures or demonstrations, newspaper or magazine articles, radio or television programs, mail, or similar media, the psychologist utilizes the most current relevant data and exercises the highest level of professional judgment.

l. Products that are described or presented by means of public lectures or demonstrations, newspaper or magazine articles, radio or television programs, or similar media meet the same recognized standards as exist for products used in the context of a professional relationship.

Principle 5
CONFIDENTIALITY

Psychologists have a primary obligation to respect the confidentiality of information obtained from persons in the course of their work as psychologists. They reveal such information to others only with the consent of the person or the person's legal representative, except in those unusual circumstances in which not to do so would result in clear danger to the person or to others. Where appropriate, psychologists inform their clients of the legal limits of confidentiality.

a. Information obtained in clinical or consulting relationships, or evaluative data concerning children, students, employees, and others, is discussed only for professional purposes and only with persons clearly concerned with the case. Written and oral reports present only data germane to the purposes of the evaluation, and every effort is made to avoid undue invasion of privacy.

b. Psychologists who present personal information obtained during the course of professional work in writings, lectures, or other public forums either obtain adequate prior consent to do so or adequatly disguise all identifying information.

c. Psychologists make provisions for maintaining confidentiality in the storage and disposal of records.

d. When working with minors or other persons who are unable to give voluntary, informed consent, psychologists take special care to protect these persons' best interests.

Principle 6
WELFARE OF THE CONSUMER

Psychologists respect the integrity and protect the welfare of the people and groups with whom they work. When conflicts of interest arise between clients and psychologists' employing institutions, psychologists clarify the nature and direction of their loyalties and responsibilities and keep all parties informed of their commitments. Psychologists fully inform consumers as to the purpose and nature of an evaluative, treatment, educational, or training procedure, and they freely acknowledge that clients, students, or participants in research have freedom of choice with regard to participation.

a. Psychologists are continually cognizant of their own needs and of their potentially influential position vis-a-vis persons such as clients, students, and subordinates. They avoid exploiting the trust and dependency of such persons. Psychologists make every effort to avoid dual relationships that could impair their professional judgment or increase the risk of exploitation. Examples of such dual relationships include, but are not limited to, research with and treatment of employees, students, supervisees, close friends, or relatives. Sexual intimacies with clients are unethical.

b. When a psychologist agrees to provide services to a client at the request of a third party, the psychologist assumes the responsibility of clarifying the nature of the relationships to all parties concerned.

c. Where the demands of an organization require psychologists to violate these Ethical Principles, psychologists clarify the nature of the conflict between the demands and these principles. They inform all parties of psychologists' ethical responsibilities and take appropriate action.

d. Psychologists make advance financial arrangements that safeguard the best interests of and are clearly understood by their clients. They neither give nor receive any remuneration for referring clients for professional services. They contribute a portion of their services to work for which they receive little or no financial return.

e. Psychologists terminate a clinical or consulting relationship when it is reasonable clear that the consumer is not benefiting from it. They offer to help the consumer locate alternative sources of assistance.

Principle 7
PROFESSIONAL RELATIONSHIPS

Psychologists act with due regard for the needs, special competencies, and obligations of their colleagues in psychology and other professions. They respect the prerogatives and obligations of the institutions or organizations with which these other colleagues are associated.

a. Psychologists understand the areas of competence of related professions. They make full use of all the professional, technical, and administrative resources that serve the best interests of consumers. The absence of formal relationships with other professional workers does not relieve psychologists of the responsibility of securing for their clients the best possible professional service, nor does it relieve them of the obligation to exercise foresight, diligence, and tact in obtaining the complementary or alternative assistance needed by clients.

b. Psychologists know and take into account the traditions and practices of other professional groups with whom they work and cooperate fully with such groups. If a person is receiving similar services from another professional, psychologists do not offer their own services directly to such a person. If a psychologist is contacted by a person who is already receiving similar services from another professional, the psychologist carefully considers that professional relationship and proceeds with caution and sensitivity to the therapeutic issues as well as the client's welfare. The psychologist discusses these issues with the client so as to minimize the risk of confusion and conflict.

c. Psychologists who employ or supervise other professionals or professionals in training accept the obligation to facilitate the further professional development of these individuals. They provide appropriate working conditions, timely evaluations, constructive consultation, and experience opportunities.

d. Psychologists do not exploit their professional relationships with clients, supervisees, students, employees, or research participants sexually or otherwise. Psychologists do not condone or engage in sexual harassment. Sexual harassment is defined as deliberate or repeated comments, gestures, or physical contacts of a sexual nature that are unwanted by the recipient.

e. In conducting research in institutions or organizations, psychologists secure appropriate authorization to conduct such research. They are aware of their obligations to future research workers and ensure that host institutions receive adequate information about the research and proper acknowledgment of their contributions.

f. Publication credit is assigned to those who have contributed to a publication in proportion to their professional contributions. Major contributions of a professional character made by several persons to a common project are recognized by joint authorship, with the individual who made the principal contribution listed first. Minor contributions of a professional character and extensive clerical or similar nonprofessional assistance may be acknowledged in footnotes or in an introductory statement. Acknowledgment through specific citations is made for unpublished as well as published material that has directly influenced the research or writing. Psychologists who compile and edit material of others for publication publish the material in their own name appearing as chairperson or editor. All contributors are to be acknowledged and named.

g. When psychologists know of an ethical violation by another psychologist, and it seems appropriate, they informally attempt to resolve the issue by bringing the behavior to the attention of the psychologist. If the misconduct is of a minor nature and/or appears to be due to lack of sensitivity, knowledge, or experience, such an informal solution is usually appropriate. Such informal corrective efforts are made with sensitivity to any rights to confidentiality involved. If the violation does not seem amenable to an informal solution, or is of a more serious nature, psychologists bring it to the attention of the appropriate local, state, and/or national committee on professional ethics and conduct.

Principle 8
ASSESSMENT TECHNIQUES

In the development, publication, and utilization of psychological assessment techniques, psychologists make every effort to promote the welfare and best interests of the client. They guard against the misuse of assessment results. They respect the client's right to know the results, the interpretations made, and the bases for their conclusions and recommendations. Psychologists make every effort to maintain the security of tests and other assessment techniques within limits of legal mandates. They strive to ensure the appropriate use of assessment techniques by others.

a. In using assessment techniques, psychologists respect the right of clients to have full explanations of the nature and purpose of the techniques in language the clients can understand, unless an explicit exception to this right has been agreed upon in advance. When the explanations are to be provided by others, psychologists establish procedures for ensuring the adequacy of these explanations.

b. Psychologists responsible for the development and standardization of psychological tests and other assessment techniques utilize established scientific procedures and observe the relevant APA standards.

c. In reporting assessment results, psychologists indicate any reservations that exist regarding validity or reliability because of the circumstances of the assessment or the inappropriateness of the norms for the person tested. Psychologists strive to ensure that the results of assessments and their interpretations are not misused by others.

d. Psychologists recognize that assessment results may become obsolete. They make every effort to avoid and prevent the misuse of obsolete measures.

e. Psychologists offering scoring and interpretation services are able to produce appropriate evidence for the validity of the programs and procedures used in arriving at interpretations. The public offering of an automated interpretation service is considered a professional-to-professional consultation. Psychologists make every effort to avoid misuse of assessment reports.

f. Psychologists do not encourage or promote the use of psychological assessment techniques by inappropriately trained or otherwise unqualified persons through teaching, sponsorship, or supervision.

Principle 9
RESEARCH WITH HUMAN PARTICIPANTS

The decision to undertake research rests upon a considered judgment by the individual psychologist about how best to contribute to psychological science and human welfare. Having made the decision to conduct research, the psychologist considers alternative directions in which research energies and resources might be invested. On the basis of this consideration, the psychologist carries out the investigation with respect and concern for the dignity and welfare of the people who participate and with cognizance of federal and state regulations and professional standards governing the conduct of research with human participants.

a. In planning a study, the investigator has the responsibility to make a careful evaluation of its ethical acceptability. To the extent that the weighing of scientific and human values suggests a compromise of any principle, the investigator incurs a correspondingly serious obligation to seek ethical advice and to observe stringent safeguards to protect the rights of human participants.

b. Considering whether a participant in a planned study will be a "subject at risk" or a "subject at minimal risk," according to recognized standards, is of primary ethical concern to the investigator.

c. The investigator always retains the responsibility for ensuring ethical practice in research. The investigator is also responsible for the ethical treatment of research participants by collaborators, assistants, students, and employees, all of whom, however, incur similar obligations.

d. Except in minimal-risk research, the investigator establishes a clear and fair agreement with research participants, prior to their participation, that clarifies the obligations and responsibilities of each. The investigator has the obligation to honor all promises and commitments included in that agreement. The investigator informs the participants of all aspects of the research that might reasonably be expected to influence willingness to participate and explains all other aspects of the research about which the participants inquire. Failure to make full disclosure prior to obtaining informed consent requires additional safeguards to protect the welfare and dignity of the research participants. Research with children or with participants who have impairments that would limit understanding and/or communication requries special safeguarding procedures.

e. Methodological requirements of a study may make the use of concealment or deception necessary. Before conducting such a study, the investigator has a special responsibility to (i) determine whether the use of such techniques is justified by the study's prospective scientific, educational, or applied value; (ii) determine whether alternative procedures are available that do not use concealment or deception; and (iii) ensure that the participants are provided with sufficient explanation as soon as possible.

f. The investigator respects the individual's freedom to decline to participate in or to withdraw from the research at any time. The obligation to protect this freedom requires careful thought and consideration when the investigator is in a position of authority or influence over the participant. Such positions of authority include, but are not limited to, situations in which research participation is a student, client, or employee of the investigator.

g. The investigator protects the participant from physical and mental discomfort, harm, and danger that may arise from research procedures. If risks of such consequences exist, the investigator informs the participant of that fact. Research procedures likely to cause serious or lasting harm to a participant are not used unless the failure to use these procedures might expose the participant to risk of greater harm, or unless the research has great potential benefit and fully informed and voluntary consent is obtained from each participant. The participant should be informed of procedures for contacting the investigator within a reasonable time period following participation should stress, potential harm, or related questions or concerns arise.

h. After the data are collected, the investigator provides the participant with information about the nature of the study and attempts to remove any misconceptions that may have arisen. Where scientific or humane values justify delaying or withholding this information, the investigator incurs a special responsibility to monitor the research and to ensure that there are no damaging consequences for the participant.

i. Where research procedures result in undesirable consequences for the individual participant, the investigator has the responsibility to detect and remove or correct these consequences, including long-term effects.

j. Information obtained about a research participant during the course of an investigation is confidential unless otherwise agreed upon in advance. When the possibility exists that others may obtain access to such information, this possibility, together with the plans for protecting confidentiality, is explained to the participant as part of the procedure for obtaining informed consent.

Principle 10
CARE AND USE OF ANIMALS

An investigator of animal behavior strives to advance understanding of basic behavioral principles and/or to contribute to the improvement of human health and welfare. In seeking these ends, the investigator ensures the welfare of animals and treats them humanely. Laws and regulations notwithstanding, an animal's immediate protection depends upon the scientist's own conscience.

    a. The acquisition, care, use, and disposal of all animals are in compliance with current federal, state or provincial, and local laws and regulations.

    b. A psychologist trained in research methods and experienced in the care of laboratory animals closely supervises all procedures involving animals and is responsible for ensuring appropriate consideration of their comfort, health, and humane treatment.

    c. Psychologists ensure that all individuals using animals under their supervision have received explicit instruction in experimental methods and in the care, maintenance, and handling of the species being used. Responsibilities and activities of individuals participating in a research project are consistent with their respective competencies.

    d. Psychologists make every effort to minimize discomfort, illness, and pain of animals. A procedure subjecting animals to pain, stress, or privation is used only when an alternative procedure is unavailable and the goal is justified by its prospective scientific, educational, or applied value. Surgical procedures are performed under appropriate anesthesia; techniques to avoid infection and minimize pain are followed during and after surgery.

    e. When it is appropriate that the animal's life be terminated, it is done rapidly and painlessly.

This version of the Ethical Principles of Psychologists (Formerly entitled Ethical Standards of Psychologists) was adopted by the American Psychological Association's Council of Respresentatives on January 24, 1981. The revised Ethical Principles contain both substantive and grammatical changes in each of the nine ethical principles constituting the Ethical Standards of Psychologists previously adopted by the Council of Representatives in 1979, plus a new tenth principle entitled Care and Use of Animals. Inquiries concerning the Ethical Principles of Psychologists should be addressed to the Administrative Officer for Ethics, American Psychological Association, 1200 Seventeenth Street, N.W., Washington, D.C. 20036.

These revised Ethical Principles apply to psychologists, to students of psychology, and to others who do work of a psychological nature under the supervision of a psychologist. They are also intended for the guidance of nonmembers of the Association who are engaged in psychological research or practice.

Any complaints of unethical conduct filed after January 24, 1981, shall be governed by this 1981 revision. However, conduct (a) complained about after January 24, 1981, but which occurred prior to that date, and (b) not considered unethical under prior versions of the principles but considered unethical under the 1981 revision, shall not be deemed a violation of ethical principles. Any complaints pending as of January 24, 1981, shall be governed either by the 1979 or by the 1981 version of the Ethical Principles, at the sound descretion of the Committee on Scientific and Professional Ethics and Conduct. (Reprinted with the permission of the American Psychological Association. Copyright 1981.)

AMERICAN NURSES' ASSOCIATION
Code for Nurses
1976

Point 1
The nurse provides services with respect for human dignity and the uniqueness of the client unrestricted by considerations of social or economic status, personal attributes, or the nature of health problems.

Point 2
The nurse safeguards the client's right to privacy by judiciously protecting information of a confidential nature.

Point 3
The nurse acts to safeguard the client and the public when health care and safety are affected by incompetent, unethical, or illegal practice of any person.

Point 4
The nurse assumes responsibility and accountability for individual nursing judgments and actions.

Point 5
The nurse maintains competence in nursing.

Point 6
The nurse exercises informed judgment and uses individual competence and qualifications as criteria in seeking consultation, accepting responsibilities, and delegating nursing activities to others.

Point 7
The nurse participates in activities that contribute to the ongoing development of the profession's body of knowledge.

Point 8
The nurse participates in the profession's efforts to implement and improve standards of nursing.

Point 9
The nurse participates in the profession's efforts to establish and maintain conditions of employment conducive to high quality nursing care.

Point 10
The nurse participates in the profession's effort to protect the public from misinformation and misrepresentation and to maintain the integrity of nursing.

Point 11
The nurse collaborates with members of the health professions and other citizens in promoting community and national efforts to meet the health needs of the public.

International Council of Nurses
Code for Nurses
Ethical Concepts Applied to Nursing

The fundamental responsibility of the nurse is fourfold: to promote health, to prevent illness, to restore health and to alleviate suffering.

The need for nursing is universal. Inherent in nursing is respect for life, dignity and rights of man. It is unrestricted by considerations of nationality, race, creed, colour, age, sex, politics or social status.

Nurses render health services to the individual, the family and the community and coordinate their services with those of related groups.

Nurses and people

The nurse's primary responsibility is to those people who require nursing care.

The nurse, in providing care, promotes an environment in which the values, customs and spiritual beliefs of the individual are respected.

The nurse holds in confidence personal information and uses judgement in sharing this information.

Nurses and practice

The nurse carries personal responsibility for nursing practices and for maintaining competence by continual learning.

The nurse maintains the highest standards of nursing care possible within the reality of a specific situation.

The nurse uses judgement in relation to individual competence when accepting and delegation responsibilities.

The nurse when acting in a professional capacity should at all times maintain standards of personal conduct which reflect credit upon the profession.

Nurses and society

The nurse shares with other citizens the responsibility for initiating and supporting action to meet the health and social needs of the public.

Nurses and co-workers

The nurse sustains a cooperative relationship with co-workers in nursing and other fields.

The nurse takes appropriate action to safeguard the individual when his care is endangered by a co-worker or any other person.

Nurses and the profession

The nurse plays the major role in determining and implementing desirable standards of nursing parctice and nursing education.

The nurse is active in developing a core of professional knowledge.

The nurse, acting through the professional organization, participates in establishing and maintaining equitable social and economic working conditions in nursing.

(Reprinted with the permission of the International Council of Nurses. Copyright 1973.)

CODE OF ETHICS OF THE NATIONAL ASSOCIATION OF SOCIAL WORKERS

As adopted by the 1979 NASW Delegate Assembly, effective July 1, 1980.

Preamble

This code is intended to serve as a guide to the everyday conduct of members of the social work profession and as a basis for the adjudication of issues in ethics when the conduct of social workers is alleged to deviate from the standards expressed or implied in this code. It represents standards of ethical behavior for social workers in professional relationships with those served, with colleagues, with employers, with other individuals and professions, and with the community and society as a whole. It also embodies standards of ethical behavior governing individual conduct to the extent that such conduct is associated with an individual's status and identity as a social worker.

This code is based on the fundamental values of the social work profession that include the worth, dignity, and uniqueness of all presons as well as their rights and opportunities. It is also based on the nature of social work, which fosters conditions that promote these values.

In subscribing to and abiding by this code, the social worker is expected to view ethical responsibility in as inclusive a context as each situation demands and within which ethical judgement is required. The social worker is expected to take into consideration all the principles in this code that have a bearing upon any situation in which ethical judgement is to be exercised and professional intervention or conduct is planned. The course of action that the social worker chooses is expected to be consistent with the spirit as well as the letter of this code.

In itself, this code does not represent a set of rules that will prescribe all the behaviors of social workers in all the complexities of professional life. Rather, it offers general principles to guide conduct, and the judicious appraisal of conduct, in situations that have ethical implications. It provides the basis for making judgements about ethical actions before and after they occur. Frequently, the particular situation determines the ethical principles that apply and the manner of their application. In such cases, not only the particular ethical principles are taken into immediate consideration, but also the entire code and its spirit. Specific applications of ethical principles must be judged within the context in which they are being considered. Ethical behavior in a given situation must satisfy not only the judgement of the individual social worker, but also the judgement of an unbiased jury of professional peers.

This code should not be used as an instrument to deprive any social worker of the opportunity or freedom to practice with complete professional integrity; nor should any disciplinary action be taken on the basis of this code without maximum provision for safeguarding the rights of the social worker affected.

The ethical behavior of social workers results not from edict, but from a personal commitment of the individual. This code is offered to affirm the will and zeal of all social workers to be ethical and to act ethically in all that they do as social workers.

The following codified ethical principles should guide social workers in the various roles and relationships and at the various levels of responsibility in which they function professionally. These principles also serve as a basis for the adjudication by the National Association of Social Workers of issues in ethics.

In subscribing to this code, social workers are required to cooperate in its implementation and abide by any disciplinary rulings based on it. They should also take adequate measures to discourage, prevent, expose, and correct the unethical conduct of colleagues. Finally, social workers should be equally ready to defend and assist colleagues unjustly charged with unethical conduct.

The NASW Code of Ethics

I. The Social Worker's Conduct and Comportment as a Social Worker

A. Propriety -- The social worker should maintain high standards of personal conduct in the capacity of identity as social worker.
1. The private conduct of the social worker is a personal matter to the same degree as is any other person's, except when such conduct compromises the fulfillment of professional responsibilities.
2. The social worker should not participate in, condone, or be associated with dishonesty, fraud, deceit, or misrepresentation.
3. The social worker should distinguish clearly between statements and actions made as a private individual and as a representative of the social work profession or an organization or group.

B. Competence and Professional Development -- The social worker should strive to become and remain proficient in professional practice and the performance of professional functions.
1. The social worker should accept responsibility or employment only on the basis of existing competence or the intention to acquire the necessary competence.
2. The social worker should not misrepresent professional qualifications, education, experience, or affiliations.

C. Service -- The social worker should regard as primary the service obligation of the social work profession.
1. The social worker should retain ultimate responsibility for the quality and extent of the service that individual assumes, assigns, or performs.
2. The social worker should act to prevent practices that are inhumane or discriminatory against any person or group of persons.

D. Integrity -- The social worker should act in accordance with the highest standards of professional integrity and impartiality.

1. The social worker should be alert to and resist the influences and pressures that interfere with the exercise of professional discretion and impartial judgement required for the performance of professional functions.

2. The social worker should not exploit professional relationships for personal gain.

E. Scholarship and Research -- The social worker engaged in study and research would be guided by the conventions of scholarly inquiry.

1. The social worker engaged in research should consider carefully its possible consequences for human beings.

2. The social worker engaged in research should ascertain that the consent of participants in the research is voluntary and informed, without any implied deprivation or penalty for refusal to participate, and with due regard for participants' privacy and dignity.

3. The social worker engaged in research should protect participants from unwarranted physical or mental discomfort, distress, harm, danger, or deprivation.

4. The social worker who engages in the evaluation of services or cases should discuss them only for the professional purposes and only with persons directly and professionally concerned with them.

5. Information obtained about participants in research should be treated as confidential.

6. The social worker should take credit only for work actually done in connection with scholarly and research endeavors and credit contributions made by others.

II. The Social Worker's Ethical Responsibility to Clients

F. Primacy of Clients' Interests -- The social worker's primary responsibility is to clients.

1. The social worker should serve clients with devotion, loyalty, determination, and the maximum application of professional skill and competence.

2. The social worker should not exploit relationships with clients for personal advantage, or solicit the clients of one's agency for private practice.

3. The social worker should not practice, condone, facilitate or collaborate with any form of discrimination on the basis of race, color, sex, sexual orientation, age, religion, national origin, marital status, political belief, mental or physicial handicap, or any other preference or personal characteristic, condition or status.

4. The social worker should avoid relationships or commitments that conflict with the interests of clients.

5. The social worker should under no circumstances engage in sexual activities with clients.

6. The social worker should provide clients with accurate and complete information regarding the extent and nature of the services available to them.

7. The social worker should apprise clients of their risks, rights, opportunities, and obligations associated with social service to them.

8.   The social worker should seek advice and counsel of colleagues and supervisors whenever such consultation is in the best interest of clients.

9.   The social worker should terminate service to clients, and professional relationships with them, when such service and relationships are no longer required or no longer serve the clients' needs or interests.

10.   The social worker should withdraw services precipitously only under unusual circumstances, giving careful consideration to all factors in the situation and taking care to minimize possible adverse effects.

11.   The social worker who anticipates the termination or interruption of service to clients should notify clients promptly and seek the transfer, referral, or continuation of service in relation to the clients' needs and preferences.

G.   Rights and Prerogatives of Clients -- The social worker should make every effort to foster maximum self-determination on the part of clients.

1.   When the social worker must act on behalf of a client who has been adjudged legally incompetent, the social worker should safeguard the interests and rights of that client.

2.   When another individual has been legally authorized to act in behalf of a client, the social worker should deal with that person always with the client's best interest in mind.

3.   The social worker should not engage in any action that violates or diminishes the civil or legal rights of clients.

H.   Confidentiality and Privacy -- The social worker should respect the privacy of clients and hold in confidence all information obtained in the course of professional service.

1.   The social worker should share with others confidences revealed by clients, without their consent, only for compelling professional reasons.

2.   The social worker should inform clients fully about the limits of confidentiality in a given situation, the purposes for which information is obtained, and how it may be used.

3.   The social worker should afford clients reasonable access to any official social work records concerning them.

4.   When providing clients with access to records, the social worker should take due care to protect the confidences of others contained in those records.

5.   The social worker should obtain informed consent of clients before taping, recording, or permitting third party observation of their activities.

I.   Fees -- When setting fees, the social worker should ensure that they are fair, reasonable, considerate, and commensurate with the service performed and with due regard for the clients' ability to pay.

1.   The social worker should not divide a fee or accept or give anything of value for receiving or making a referral.

III.   The Social Worker's Ethical Responsibility to Colleagues

J.   Respect, Fairness, and Courtesy -- The social worker should treat colleagues with respect, courtesy, fairness, and good faith.

1.   The social worker should cooperate with colleagues to promote professional

interests and concerns.

2.   The social worker should respect confidences shared by colleagues in the course of their professional relationships and transactions.

3.   The social worker should create and maintain conditions of practice that facilitate ethical and competent professional performance by colleagues.

4.   The social worker should treat with respect, and represent accurately and fairly, the qualifications, views, and findings of colleagues and use appropriate channels to express judgements on these matters.

5.   The social worker who replaces or is replaced by a colleague in professional practice should act with consideration for the interest, character, and reputation of that colleague.

6.   The social worker should not exploit a dispute between a colleague and employers to obtain a position or otherwise advance the social worker's interest.

7.   The social worker should seek arbitration or mediation when conflicts with colleagues require resolution for compelling professional reasons.

8.   The social worker should extend to colleagues of other professions the same respect and cooperation that is extended to social work colleagues.

9.   The social worker who serves as employer, supervisor, or mentor to colleagues should make orderly and explicit arrangements regarding the conditions of their continuing professional relationship.

10.   The social worker who has the responsibility for employing and evaluating the performance of other staff members, should fulfill such responsibility in a fair, considerate, and equitable manner, on the basis of clearly enunciated criteria.

11.   The social worker who has the responsibility for evaluating the performance of employees, supervisees, or students should share evaluations with them.

K.   Dealing with Colleagues' Clients -- The social worker has the responsibility to relate to the clients of colleagues with full professional consideration.

1.   The social worker should not solicit the clients of colleagues.

2.   The social worker should not assume professional responsibility for the clients of another agency or a colleague without appropriate communication with that agency or colleague.

3.   The social worker who serves the clients of colleagues, during a temporary absence or emergency, should serve thoses clients with the same consideration as that afforded any client.

IV.   The Social Worker's Ethical Responsibility to Employers and Employing Organizations

L.   Commitments to Employing Organizations -- The social worker should adhere to commitments made to the employing organization.

1.   The social worker should work to improve the employing agency's policies and procedures, and the efficiency and effectiveness of its services.

2.   The social worker should not accept employment or arrange student field placements in an organization which is currently under public sanction by NASW for violating personnel standards, or imposing limitations on or penalties for professional actions on behalf of clients.

3.   The social worker should act to prevent and eliminate discrimination in the employing organization's work assignments and in its employment policies and practices.

4. The social worker should use with scrupulous regard, and only for the purpose for which they are intended, the resources of the employing organization.

V. The Social Worker's Ethical Responsibility to the Social Work Profession

M. Maintaining the Integrity of the Profession -- The social worker should uphold and advance the values, ethics, knowlege, and mission of the profession.
1. The social worker should protect and enhance the dignity and integrity of the profession and should be responsible and vigorous in discussion and criticism of the profession.
2. The social worker should take action through appropriate channels against unethical conduct by any other member of the profession.
3. The social worker should act to prevent the unauthorized an unqualified practice of social work.
4. The social worker should make no misrepresentation in advertising as to qualifications, competence, service, or results to be achieved.

N. Community Service -- The social worker should assist the profession in making social services available to the general public.
1. The social worker should contribute time and professional expertise to activities that promote respect for the utility, the integrity, and the competence of the social work profession.
2. The social worker should support the formulation, development, enactment and implementation of social policies of concern to the profession.

O. Development of Knowledge -- The social worker should take responsibility for identifying, developing, and fully utilizing knowledge for professional practice.
1. The social worker should base practice upon recognized knowledge relevant to social work.
2. The social worker should critically examine, and keep current with emerging knowledge relevant to social work.
3. The social worker should contribute to the knowledge base of social work and share research knowledge and practice widsom with colleagues.

VI. The Social Worker's Ethical Responsibility to Society

P. Promoting the General Welfare -- The social worker should promote the general welfare of society.
1. The social worker should act to prevent and eliminate discrimination against any person or group on the basis of race, color, sex, sexual orientation, age, religion, national origin, marital status, political belief, mental or physical handicap, or any other preference or personal characteristic, condition, or status.
2. The social worker should act to ensure that all persons have access to the resources, services, and opportunities which they require.
3. The social worker should act to expand choice and opportunity for all persons, with special regard for disadvantaged or oppressed groups and persons.

4.   The social worker should promote conditions that encourge respect for the diversity of cultures which constitute American society.

5.   The social worker should provide appropriate professional services in public emergencies.

6.   The social worker should advocate changes in policy and legislation to improve social conditions and to promote social justice.

7.   The social worker should encourage informed participation by the public in shaping social policies and institutions.

(Reprinted with the permission of the National Association of Social Workers.)

Index